FEMINIST
CRITICS
READ
EMILY
DICKINSON

FEMINIST
CRITICS
READ
EMILY
DICKINSON

EDITED WITH AN INTRODUCTION BY

Suzanne Juhasz

INDIANA UNIVERSITY PRESS • BLOOMINGTON

Copyright © 1983 by Indiana University Press

Manufactured in the United States of America

Library of Congress Cataloging in Publication Data
Main entry under title:

Feminist critics read Emily Dickinson.

Bibliography: p.
Includes index.
1. Dickinson, Emily, 1830–1886—Criticism and
interpretation—Addresses, essays, lectures.
2. Feminism and literature—Addresses, essays, lectures.
I. Juhasz, Suzanne, 1942–
PS1541.Z5F36   1983   811'.4   82-48265
ISBN 0-253-32170-0
  2 3 4 5 87 86 85 84

CONTENTS

For Alexandra, Jennifer, and Antonia Juhasz

PREFACE

In 1976, when I began research for a book on Emily Dickinson, there was almost no feminist scholarship on the poet. Reading through the vast amount of criticism about America's greatest woman writer, I often felt alone with my feminist perspective. Consequently, I was both delighted and excited when, at the Modern Language Association Meetings of 1978 and 1979, I began to hear feminist papers on Dickinson. During the same period, new feminist essays were appearing in print. This book was generated from my recognition that such work, and such colleagues, now existed. By making this collection I wanted to demonstrate the fact and significance of feminist Dickinson criticism as a body of scholarship and to make it readily available to others interested in the subject. These overlapping and contrasting studies delineate a feminist approach to Dickinson that radically alters her position in contemporary literary studies.

It has been a thoroughgoing pleasure to bring this book into being. Working with the scholars whose research and ideas are represented here has been consistently stimulating and rewarding for me as editor. They are friends and colleagues whose presence enriches my life.

SUZANNE JUHASZ 1

Introduction
Feminist Critics Read Emily Dickinson

THIS IS THE FIRST COLLECTION of critical essays on Dickinson from a feminist perspective. Of course, feminist criticism itself is still relatively new as a literary discipline, emerging in the late sixties as a recognizable and potent point of view. Still, feminist criticism comes only recently to Dickinson: perhaps because her position as a great writer was already so well established, perhaps because she is so complex and difficult a writer, probably for a combination of these reasons. Yet it seems inevitable that Dickinson, who is, after all, the greatest woman poet in the English language, be studied in the context (cultural, psychological, historical, and literary) of her womanhood. The central assumption of feminist criticism is that gender informs the nature of art, the nature of biography, and the relation between them. Dickinson is a woman poet, and this fact is integral to her identity. Feminist criticism's sensitivity to the components of female experience in general and to Dickinson's identity as a woman generates essential insights about her.

The contribution of feminist criticism to Dickinson studies is twofold. Its first function is revisionary. Traditional criticism has presented Dickinson not only partially but falsely. By splitting her identity into two mutually exclusive elements, "woman" and "poet," traditional criticism has represented two persons, not one. Further fragmentation occurs when her poetry is divorced from any serious consideration of its connection to the person who wrote it. The insights that result from visions seen in this broken mirror are necessarily suspect. If, further, the critic is either overtly or covertly sexist in attitude, that is, either accepts or ignores the unnatural position in which a patriarchal society has placed women, the resulting analysis of Dickinson's biography and poetry must consequently be skewed.

Feminist criticism begins by putting the pieces together: woman and poet, woman poet and her poetry. This is what I am calling revisionary activity. Next, feminist criticism moves from re-interpretation to new

1

kinds of interpretation, because it observes from a perspective that not only takes into account the significance of gender in life and art but sees female gender, in particular, as a positive instead of a negative factor. In Dickinson's case, this means assuming both that her actions make sense and that her actions and her poetry are related in a way that also makes sense as well as art. In Dickinson's case, this means assuming her own knowledge of, and responsibility for, what she did; trying to understand and interpret her acts according to her own terms. In Dickinson's case, finally, this means recognizing the power that Dickinson derived from creating a world in which she could be herself, from creating a self with which she could accomplish her best. Increasingly, feminist criticism seeks to understand that power in relation to Dickinson's enormous achievements.

As I have pointed out at length in my chapter on Dickinson in *Naked and Fiery Forms: Modern American Poetry by Women, A New Tradition,*[1] literary studies of Dickinson in both the nineteenth and twentieth centuries have generally made the distinction between woman and poet. In fact, there has been a thoroughgoing insistence that these categories be mutually exclusive. Works as different in approach and scope as George Whicher's "classic" study, *This Was a Poet: A Critical Biography of Emily Dickinson,*[2] and John Cody's psychoanalytic biography, *After Great Pain: The Inner Life of Emily Dickinson,*[3] arrive at remarkably similar conclusions. "Perhaps as a poet she could find the fulfillment she had missed as a woman," sighs Whicher.[4] Cody's final remarks are even more devastating.

> It was Mrs. Dickinson's failure as a sufficiently loving and admirable developmental model that set in motion the series of psychological upheavals which were unmitigated misfortunes for Emily Dickinson, *the woman*. These maturational impasses consigned her to a life of sexual bewilderment, anxiety and frustration by impairing those processes of psychic growth which would have made the roles of wife and mother possible. With reference to Emily Dickinson *the artist*, one cannot speak of misfortunes at all. For, amazing as it may seem, Mrs. Dickinson's inadequacies, the sequence of internal conflicts to which they gave rise, and the final psychotic breakdown all conspired in a unique way to make of Emily Dickinson a great and prolific poet.[5] [italics Cody's]

In summary, says Cody, "the violent disharmonies and unceasing restlessness of her inner life ... thus appear in her case to have contributed copiously to *the transformation of woman into poet*" (p. 492). This time the italics are mine.

A somewhat longer look at these two representatives of traditional Dickinson criticism helps us further to understand the difficulties raised by their approach.

Whicher's book is literally separated into units biographical and literary, having no ideological relation to one another. That is, in the biography he insists that she wrote because she was the victim of a failed love affair (he opts for Charles Wadsworth as the lover, a married man): "Only a Robert Browning could have released the Lady of Shalott, and no Robert Browning came her way" (p. 139). Her poetry is understood to be compensatory activity. But when Whicher turns to the poetry, he identifies as the forces that influenced it the Puritan tradition, American humor, and the country's current spiritual unrest. Her own life becomes curiously irrelevant to her art. It is only when he moves on to a final discussion of style that there is some attempt to explain "the transformation of woman into poet," to use Cody's trenchant phrase. In demonstrating a "development" in her love poems from verse into art, he shows her moving from the personal to the universal, the subjective to the objective, the childish to the mature, the feminine to what we can only assume is its opposite, the masculine. "She was all woman when she wrote [poem 176, which reveals] a mind overwhelmed by an emotion from which it cannot detach itself, as the consciousness of a heartbroken child has no room for anything but its sense of grief" (p. 272). He amplifies: "not until she realized that a death blow to her heart had become a life blow to her mind was she able to look upon her grief as though it were the agony of another person, a supposed person even. Only then did the mature poet in her come into being" (p. 272).

Cody's bias is psychoanalytic. He sees Dickinson's failure as a woman, her inability to assume normal female identiy, to be caused by the emotional inaccessibility of her mother and by her mother's inadequacies as a woman, which kept her from being a satisfactory role model for her daughter. This led, he argues, to a psychotic breakdown, and thence to poetry. "The point, important for American literature, is that threatening personality disintegration compelled a frantic Emily Dickinson to create poetry—for her a psychosis-deflecting activity" (p. 391). What is especially damaging about Cody's book is not really its earnest attempt to demonstrate Dickinson's "insanity" and psychotic breakdown. For, in the light of history, the labels, be they "sane" or "insane," that get affixed at one time or another to a particular set of personality characteristics and actions are rather irrelevant. Rather, it is his assumptions about "normal" female development, female (and male) gender identity, and the nature of creativity and achievement. Cody supposes that a woman acquires female identity through positive identification with her mother. If this does not come about, if she cannot admire her mother and has suspicions "that to be a female is to be secondrate" (p. 55), if she cannot find another woman to act as a role model, "she may at last be driven to pattern herself on a masculine model" (p. 55), and this will in the course of things lead to gender confusion and "deep psychological trouble . . . protracted adolescence and an almost insurmountable crisis in sexual identity" (p. 55).

Like Whicher, Cody associates creativity and achievement with the masculine. He asserts that it was Dickinson's abnormal identification with her father that "though blocking her completion as a woman, stimulated her to use her mind" (p. 103). Cody's remarks, both those quoted above and those quoted earlier, unhesitatingly stereotype the woman as wife and mother, the male as poet. Dickinson's fundamental problem, according to Cody, was that she never settled into either a "thoroughgoing and 'mature' masculine identification" (p. 171) or a female one. It was her ambivalence and confusion that gave rise to, in his opinion, her latent homosexuality, her sexual terror, and her general psychological mess. That it was more "normal" for Emily Dickinson to be a poet than a wife-and-mother, that it was also probably quite normal for her not to see Emily Norcross Dickinson as a role model, that the observation "to be a female is secondrate" in this society is indeed accurate, that for her to be a poet was not to be masculine but to be herself, that gender confusion itself in a woman like Dickinson is probably more "normal" than its alternatives, that it is quite understandable why she would not wish to "grow up" into the sex roles available to her—in Cody's Freudian context these ideas would never, and could never, arise.

Cody makes only one reference to other women writers in his book, commenting on Dickinson's passionate admiration of the Brontës, Elizabeth Barrett Browning, George Sand, and George Eliot. "One cannot escape the conclusion," he says, "that it was partly because they were admirable *women* that Emily almost worshipped them. . . . Undoubtedly they represented the kind of woman Emily deeply wanted to be, the kind she longed to have as guide, preceptor, and friend. No matter that, in reality, several of these gifted women appear to have been profoundly uncertain of their own femininity" (p. 97). Of course they were.

As others before me have pointed out, Freud's system articulates and enshrines the profoundly sexist norms of our patriarchal culture. In applying them to Dickinson, Cody, who says he admires her, wreaks havoc with the context and content of her life and art. His description of Dickinson after the prolific years of the 1860s is astonishing: "loveless, excluded, almost burned out as a poet, and reduced to the status of a queer, hypochondriacal, and depressed old maid" (p. 438).

For these writers Dickinson's "failure" as a "woman" led her to the compensatory act of poetry. But of course, since writing poetry is a masculine, not a feminine, skill, this act cut her off even further from the fulfillment of her true destiny: womanhood.

Much criticism of Dickinson, however, has perpetuated the system of fragmentation in another way: by dealing with the poetry as if it had never been written by anybody in particular, especially not this particular woman. When contexts for the poetry have been sought, Whicher's lead has been followed. Her work has been placed in assorted literary and cultural categories, such as American transcendentalism, American Puritanism, English Romanticism, and American modernism. Such contexts, while not entirely irrelevant, nevertheless lead to false and damaging assumptions, because they are seen as cultural and historical norms. As Sandra Gilbert and Susan Gubar have shown for women writing in the nineteenth century,[6] as Margaret Homans has shown for women poets writing in the nineteenth century,[7] and as Joanne Feit Diehl has shown for Emily Dickinson writing in the context of nineteenth-century Romanticism,[8] a woman's relationship to any masculine tradition *begins* by being that of outsider, not insider. We are only just beginning to understand the complexities and confusions caused by this dislocation.

Other critics, heirs to the textual close-sightedness of New Criticism, have talked about the poems alone, one by one or in groups, but always independent of their creator. This approach, while it can lead to serious and well-documented appreciation of her craft, as represented most admirably by Charles Anderson's *Emily Dickinson's Poetry: Stairway of Surprise,*[9] is particularly misleading for discussing the work of women writers. Poetry is always a product of a person, and when the very situations permitting that person to author it are extraordinary rather than ordinary, the formal and thematic norms that organize a given poem or body of poems cannot themselves be taken for granted. Attention to the relationship between biography and art is a requisite of feminist criticism. To disregard it further strengthens those divisions continually created by traditional criticism, so that nothing about the woman writer can be seen whole.

Although thus far I have been talking about "traditional" Dickinson criticism, it is enlightening to look at very recent contributions to the field to see how, in the midst of our post-modernist sophistication, the old categories and assumptions continue to prevail in works that are not feminist. Studies as diverse and new as Sharon Cameron's *Lyric Time: Dickinson and the Limits of Genre*[10] and David Porter's *Dickinson: The Modern Idiom*[11] can serve to exemplify my point.

Cameron ambitiously discusses "the problematics of temporality"—in the English lyric at large and in Dickinson's poems particularly. Her book brings to bear upon the problem, and upon Dickinson, the collected wisdom of an amazing number of theoreticians, both philosophical and literary: Aristotle, Freud, Kant, Bergson, Derrida, Poulet, and many others. For all its intelligence, *Lyric Time* exemplifies those kinds of Dickinson criticism which, as they construct contexts and analyses for the poems, completely disregard the fact of gender. This is the "sin" of omission, and, although it seems the least culpable of them all, what tends to emerge here are abstracted ideas, universal forms, but no one we could with any confidence call "Dickinson."

Here is an example of how a typical analytic sequence works in *Lyric Time*. After a careful discussion of poem 510, "It was not Death, for I stood up," Cameron writes, " 'It was not Death' insists on the problematic features of the doubleness of names and insists, also, that it is this doubleness that has the power to liberate us. For dialectical knowledge in which experience is put in touch with its antithesis involves the mind's ability to construct, through memory, a connection between that which is not present at a given moment in time and that which is. Such knowledge frees the mind of the constraints of the moment by making it conscious of those elements of its own experience that, if they were not hidden, would transform it" (p. 51). This is followed by a series of quotations, one after the other in rapid succession, from Fredric Jameson (*Marxism and Form: Twentieth-Century Dialectical Theories of Literature*), Herbert Marcuse ("A Note on Dialectic"), Hegel, and Freud ("The Antithetical Sense of Primal Words"). Such persistent movement to the thought of others repeatedly abstracts and generalizes the themes and implications of Dickinson's poems.

Although close attention is paid to the structures of language and meaning in each poem scrutinized, these discussions only underline Dickinson's generic function in the book. She represents the problem of time in the lyric, and her peculiarities as a writer are useful primarily as they *exaggerate* general tendencies and issues. Not only does this lead to the loss of a specific Dickinson whose art is an extension and manifestation of her specific biographical, psychological, cultural situation, but, even more unfortunately, it leads to the conclusion that many poems are "failures," displaying, for example, what Cameron calls "narrative breakdown."

> The disjunction between the two parts of "I got so I could take his name" is revelatory of narrative breakdown, not of controlled narrative transformation. The speaker is not in possession of her story, or rather she is in possession of two stories, the bringing together of which points to a fundamental ambivalence and an attendant obfuscation of meaning. As a consequence of the ambivalence, meaning becomes symptomatic, breaks out into gesture where it cannot be fully comprehended and where it often expresses feelings that seem antithetical to the earlier intention of its speaker or author—it is difficult to distinguish adequately between the two in such instances, since both are victims of the same confusion. [pp. 60-61]

Here Dickinson's art seems put to the service of the book's organizing theories about time and the lyric rather than vice versa, and the poem suffers accordingly.

David Porter, on the other hand, expresses in his introduction his especial concern with discovering and preserving Dickinson's *"otherness"* (p. 1). But Dickinson's "fugitive identity" turns out to be defined essentially "by what she did not do" (p. 5). She did not, it appears, connect her language to reality; neither did she establish a conceptual agenda for her work, so that it is cut off from history as well as experience. Because of these absences she becomes, in Porter's view, forerunner to a particularly disturbing strain of radical modernism: "the menacing ascendance of consciousness and the disappearance of an artistic goal"; it is "the onset of Babel in American poetry" (p. 6).

Whereas Cameron asserts Dickinson's generality, Porter stresses her specialness. Likewise, while Cameron seems oblivious to her femaleness and to feminism in general, Porter desires to deal with her identity as a woman and with her relation to the women as well as the men who have followed her. Nevertheless, Porter, who sees Dickinson's female life as a "wreck" (strangely subverting Adrienne Rich's meaning as he uses the title of her poem) and who sees Dickinson's poetry as brilliant but irrevocably limited by its absences, never comprehends how her life and art support one another to create plenty where he would find lack. Moreover, his basic definitions of the social function of the poet and of reality itself ignore the real experience of women in our culture, in both their personal and their artistic lives.

Each of the categories that organize his study—the function of her poems and her function as poet—have primary albeit overlooked connections with her gender. For example, her poetry, according to Porter, can be characterized by "the profound and consequential turning of language from its representational function to its self-regarding and willful condition as literature, separate from experience and of an autogenous energy that worked deliberately to create its own corporeality" (p. 135). This separation between language and "reality" was occasioned, he explains, by her famous "withdrawal from the world."

> The autogenerative concentration on language both reflects and was caused by Emily Dickinson's withdrawal from the world. She withdrew in all the physical ways with which we are familiar, and we must at long last consider what the effect was on her poems. Most crucially, her language became idiosyncratic, disengaged from outside authority, and thus in its own way inimitably disordered. The lack of architecture is a consequence of the linguistic reflexiveness, and both are part of the

> harsh artistic freedom that opens up when reality and language undergo
> a separation. . . . When she disengaged her idiom from the complicated
> texture of social existence, she made it self-conscious, private, and mo-
> mentary in its grasp. [pp. 114-115]

Finally, he claims, "when language breeds, removed from exterior referents, it becomes almost pure locution, and meaning cannot be established" (p. 121).

Such an analysis calls into question Porter's unexplored definition of
reality itself. The assumption that the social world is the only place
wherein reality resides gives no experiential status to the events that Dickinson's poems so obviously are about: psychological, emotional, mental
acts. Porter is insistent about this: "Dickinson has no subject, least of all
reality" (p. 129). This myopia ignores both the significance of the mental
world and the reason why Dickinson might have been drawn to it. Feminist critics have repeatedly pointed to the conflict that a woman wanting
to be a poet must necessarily experience between the social role of woman
and the work of poet. We have relabelled the "retreat" a strategy: a move
into a space where she could "select, apportion, focus, examine, explore,
satiate herself exactly as she wished and needed to do, such that poetry
could result. In the outer world, this manner of control would have been
impossible. It gave her, as well, the possibility for complete and thorough
experience, for risk, intensity, range, and depth, that as a woman she could
never have achieved in the world at large."[12]

The second major tenet of Porter's critique is that Dickinson's poetry,
because it is in his opinion unaccountable to the outside world and with
limited bearing on actual experience in that world, is "thus without sufficient architectural design to create a technical wholeness fully responsive
to such a provisional world" (p. 138). Porter contrasts her disorderly and
fragmentary compositional habits with the "conscious selection and revision, development, coherence of viewpoint, designed body of completed
work" which we associate with "more conventional poets, including those
of the highest rank" (p. 82). Dickinson, on the other hand, demonstrates
"the lack of an advancing, coherent, and complicated intention" (p. 83).
He connects this lack of architectural design with the following "facts"
about Dickinson: 1) her lack of dates and destruction of worksheets ("She
could not have thought of herself as a personage, a figure in history" [p.
138]); 2) her lack of an *ars poetica*, which makes her "unlike every other
major American poet" [p. 140]; 3) the lack in her poetry of politics, indeed, history itself ("There is . . . no social role for herself" [p. 146]); 4)
"that lifelong indecision that made her impotent to face the contingency
of the world and live in it" (p. 151). All of this poetic inadequacy leads to
the proposition that the Dickinson idiom "cannot be a model for a body

of work or a body of knowledge . . . it achieves no experiential breadth and holds no dialogue with history" (pp. 292-95). At the same time, however, Porter asserts, as he has in his pages about Dickinson as a woman poet, that the Dickinson idiom can serve "particularly for the women poets whose lives it discovers" (p. 292). The connection between her inability to see herself as a person in history, or to write as one, which consequently makes her different from every other major American poet, and the fact that her style is so suited to the exploration of the hidden lives of women is never made. But surely, Porter's list of "absences" describes what would have been the daily situation for a woman trying to write, with a minimal tradition of women poets behind her, who saw very little connection between her own experience and that of her male predecessors, a woman whose normative life as a female was especially defined by its private nature and its exclusion from the concerns of "history," a woman who would of necessity, as Sandra Gilbert and Susan Gubar have shown so thoroughly and compellingly in "Towards a Feminist Poetics,"[13] have written the truth of female experience in exactly this "fragmentary" and "time-free" way.

I have taken so long to discuss Porter's book because I found reading it such a disquieting experience. Here is a scholar who does excellent work on the texts of the poems, who acknowledges the need to treat Dickinson as a woman poet, yet who succeeds, although he repeatedly expresses his admiration for her (just as Cody does), in devaluing her achievement on grounds both literary and moral that completely disregard the nature of female experience.

Both Cameron and Porter, for all their cogent moments of scholarship, present a Dickinson in whom we cannot really believe, and this is largely due to their inability to connect with seriousness or sophistication the woman and the poet. Especially, neither brings an understanding of female experience to her or his observations about human experience as it is articulated in, or responsible for, Dickinson's lyrics.

On the other hand, other recent studies that lack a specifically feminist analysis, such as Robert Weisbuch's *Emily Dickinson's Poetry*,[14] are sensitive enough to the particular nature of her psychological stances and supportive enough of the conclusions to which they lead her to provide both genuine insight into her work and little in the way of misleading or false interpretation. Weisbuch's book is not feminist, but neither is it sexist, either implicitly or explicitly. That is something.

When feminist criticism does turn to Dickinson, its first act is to observe and declare the necessary conjunction between woman and poet. The first of these essays, Elsa Green's "Emily Dickinson was a Poetess," published in *College English* in 1972,[15] sets out the issue with absolute clarity: "Unless Emily Dickinson's poems are approached as a woman's art based on female human experience, readers are free to avoid challenges to the clichés which have long served otherwise intelligent and thoughtful people as the truth about women" (p. 70). Subsequent articles, such as Barbara Williams's "A Room of Her Own: Emily Dickinson as Woman Artist" (1978),[16] my own " 'A Privilege So Awful': The Poetry of Emily Dickinson" (1976),[17] and Adrienne Rich's "Vesuvius at Home: The Power of Emily Dickinson" (1976),[18] present the same central premise: that Dickinson was a woman poet; that this identity brought her power. Rich's essay can serve to exemplify this first and crucial revision of traditional Dickinson criticism.

"Given her vocation," writes Rich, "she was neither eccentric nor quaint; she was determined to survive, to use her powers, to practice necessary economics" (p. 101). When "woman" and "poet" are not viewed as mutually exclusive terms, there occurs a total shift in the perspective from which the events of Dickinson's life and the acts of her poetry are viewed. The famous puzzle stops being one, because it starts making sense.

In her final paragraph, Rich makes even clearer the source of these perspectives themselves.

> To say "yes" to her powers was not simply a major act of nonconformity in the nineteenth century; even in our time it has been assumed that Emily Dickinson, not patriarchal society, was "the problem." The more we come to recognize the unwritten and written laws and taboos underpinning patriarchy, the less problematical, surely, will seem the methods she chose. [p. 121]

From a feminist perspective, Dickinson's life was neither a flight, nor a cop-out, nor a sacrifice, nor a substitution, but a strategy, a creation, for enabling her to become the person she was. "It was a life deliberately organized on her terms. The terms she had been handed by society—Calvinist Protestantism, Romanticism, the nineteenth century corsetting of women's bodies, choices, and sexuality—could spell insanity to a woman of genius," asserts Rich (p. 102).

Rich sees the power as well as the "sense" in Dickinson's life: she looks at that quality in Dickinson's art, as well, poems not only wonderful but centrally important for the world's knowledge of human experience. Rich calls them the work of a "mind engaged in a lifetime's musing on essential problems of language, identity, separation, relationship, the integrity of the self; a mind capable of describing psychological states more accurately than any poet except Shakespeare" (p. 107); she calls Dickinson's art "the poetry of extreme states, the poetry of danger," which "can allow its readers to go further in our own awareness, take risks we might not have dared; it says, at least: 'Someone has been here before' " (p. 120).

These introductory essays are, as I have been suggesting, of crucial significance, because, as they radically alter the position from which the looking is taking place, they view a situation that needs be neither deplored nor rearranged. An identity created by combining woman and poet into woman poet makes sense on its own terms and possesses the power of its own terms. From this central viewpoint more recent feminist Dickinson criticism has expanded its knowledge of what it is seeing: Dickinson's life and art in its literary, cultural, historical, psychological, and aesthetic milieus.

Three books that have contributed importantly to our new knowledge of Dickinson are Karl Keller's *The Only Kangaroo among the Beauty: Emily Dickinson and America*,[19] Sandra Gilbert and Susan Gubar's *The Madwoman in the Attic: The Woman Writer and the Nineteenth-Century Literary Imagination*, and Margaret Homans's *Women Writers and Poetic Identity: Dorothy Wordsworth, Emily Brontë, and Emily Dickinson*. Keller studies Dickinson in the context of "America": that is, he juxtaposes her with major American literary figures who precede, accompany, and follow her, as well as with the literary women, in both America and England, who were her contemporaries. He is seeking to understand identity from a perspective that is literary, historical, and cultural as well as feminist. Gilbert and Gubar write a revisionary life for Dickinson from, primarily, the context that her own poems provide. They use her own images and her own poetic "plots" to explain the person she became. Homans uses language—Dickinson's understanding of its functions and her manipulations of it—as a way to understand how Dickinson was able to become a successful woman poet when others of her female predecessors, like Dorothy Wordsworth and Emily Brontë, were thwarted and frustrated by their sense of their female identity. These studies reveal a Dickinson whose life and art were inextricably associated, and who used language as a force for creating not only the self but the world she would inhabit.

Keller's work, of the three, the only one entirely devoted to Dickinson, is at once the most ambitious and the most modest. This is because its method results from his belief that Dickinson's "silences and slips" are a part, essential but not debilitating, of who Dickinson was.

> Saving a life like Emily Dickinson's from that hall of tortures called biography while saying something accurate and moving perhaps means leaving her silences and her slips alone—not the unknowns, but the white spaces where we have little or no ability to look with *our* eyes . . .
> There *is* a life in her poems, but it is a life she fragments for us, and

that is what one has—not pieces of a figure but sides, each one imagined or real as she understood it or as we do. The sides outline a figure without making it whole or fully satisfying. What went on in her life and mind moment by moment is unfathomable. . . .[20]

Keller's technique—"playing her off against some American writers with whom we know she had some rather definite intellectual relations or with whom we may reasonably imagine she shares some rather definite intellectual characteristics" (p. 4)—helps us to know her without the pretense that one will know her whole, to "see how far the illuminations go, then to enjoy the different color each of the affinities takes. Silly even to feel that the confines of American history and culture delineated her as they defined her. Instead, they reveal how wide a world her circumference took in" (p. 4).

The context with which Keller is especially concerned is American Puritanism:

> . . . for we should have known all along, as this study tries to show, that she was a post-Puritan woman standing up, that she bent Puritan conventions to meet her own needs, that she used Puritan teleology as ground to dance on, that the Puritan-projected American future could not faze her, that she found the ambiguous universe a tease, that certain language structures were for her a measure of security, that she was vulnerable to criticism, that she was deliberately myopic about society's forms, that she went wild, that she found poetry fun and funny. [p. 7]

Keller's informality and humor, as well as his solid scholarship, make his book not merely enlightening but a joy to read: it helps to reveal Dickinson, finally, as entirely human. But what about Dickinson as a woman? How does feminism inform Keller's portrait?

In ways both direct and indirect. Addressing issues immediately concerned with gender, Keller is always insistent upon the importance of hers. "Her being a woman is an issue to us precisely because it was an issue to her," he writes (p. 35). In chapters on her relation to Anne Bradstreet, or the activist feminists of her day, or Harriet Beecher Stowe, or the English women writers whom she so greatly admired—the Brontës, George Eliot, Elizabeth Barrett Browning—Keller shows how her conscious concern with her own gender made a use of her Puritan heritage (which encouraged individual salvation and turning inward to create a private life) that was radical, liberating, and authoritative. What other women, before her time and during it, were able to do gave her both positive (in the case of Bradstreet and the English writers) and negative (in the case of Stowe and the New England bluestockings) examples that aided her in using privacy as a power station' (Weisbuch's apt phrase).

She appears to have sensed the inseparability of privacy and culture. For one thing, she had no institution—such as holy orders or prison or academia—to provide her with the detachment necessary for critical perspective, revaluation, or changes of course. She had to do it on her own. In that private space she had distance to see with and play with. This privacy was a natural advantage in a community that was culturally rich enough to be able to afford it. She was smart enough, too, to take advantage of it to build a world of her own. [p. 241]

In other chapters, in which he defines her in contrast to male writers such as Edwards, Hawthorne, Emerson, and Whitman, Keller isolates qualities that are not labelled as "feminine" but do make sense as the way a woman writing in her situation would proceed. Her a-historicalism, for example. "For her, experience was never historical. Though she might often have wished it otherwise, Now preempted almost everything else" (p. 106). Or the difference between her privacy and pure egotism. "Her solipsism is not strong enough to impose a will on the world to make it yield, narcissistically, a pattern of herself" (p. 118). Also, her "*anti*philosophical" stance.

> . . . Emily Dickinson was the first really *anti*philosophical poet in American literature. A poetry of experience categorically denies the possibility of a poetry of comment, of ratiocination; a poetry of sensation goes even further in closing off its universe to the *merely* felt, the profoundly thought. If Emily Dickinson's epigrams *seem* profound, it is their seeming so that makes us aware that their wit is, like that of her poems, viscerally wrung from the strictures of daily experience. . . . Swinging thus between improvisation and aphorism, between her confused experience and the hopefully sure universal, between metaphor and idea, she proceeds with the illusion that the making of meaning gives life quality. [pp. 180, 181]

Finally, I think that the most provocative aspect of the book is the way in which it ultimately reverses the most fundamentally sexist assumptions of American literary history: that it is defined by Emerson, Whitman, and the rest of the boys, so that Dickinson is viewed as either 1) a complete anomaly, or 2) just like the rest of them, only we hadn't noticed it before. Suddenly, who Dickinson was and why gives us a perspective on the others.

> The usual indigenous poet, even when as much of an anomaly as Emily Dickinson was in many ways, participates in the given and the ongoing and helps make the course of things. . . . But Emily Dickinson must be thought of as indigenous in still another sense: she is now strong enough as a writer in our literary history to transform our view of the

culture itself. She makes *it* indigenous to *her.* We may understand much of it somewhat differently because of her. [p. 334]

" 'A Woman White': Emily Dickinson's Yarn of Pearl" is the final chapter in Gilbert and Gubar's ground-breaking work on nineteenth-century women writers. Like Keller, Gilbert and Gubar are interested in the multifariousness of Dickinson's roles; they are especially interested in their function as *roles.* For they contend that Dickinson's "posing" was "essential to her poetic self-achievement."[21] Whereas the woman novelist constructs a narrative voice in which she can place her assertive, thus "non-feminine" self, the subject of the lyric poet is herself. Thus Dickinson, they argue, turns her life into a verse-drama. "This writer and her pro-tagonist(s) become for all practical purposes one—one 'supposed person' achieving the authority of self-creation by enacting many highly literary selves and lives" (p. 585). "For Dickinson, indeed," they conclude, "art is not so much *poesis*—making—as it is *mimesis*—enactment, and this is because she believes that even consciousness is not so much reflective as it is theatrical" (p. 586).

The first role Gilbert and Gubar study in all of its complications is the "Daisy": Dickinson as child. This brings them rapidly to discussions of her attitudes toward self, art, men, love, and patriarchal society. They in-sist that her refusal to turn into an adult woman, as that role was defined by her society, was her path to creating the possibility in her own powerful self, but that it took its toll, as well, upon her psychic and actual mobility.

> Rather early in her life as artist, Dickinson must have half-consciously perceived that she could avoid the necessity of renouncing her art by renouncing, instead, that concept of womanliness which required self-abnegating renunciation. Or, to put it another way, she must have de-cided that to begin with she could try to solve the problem of being a woman by refusing to admit that she was a woman. . . . On the other hand . . . the child mask (or pose or costume) eventually threatened to become a crippling self, a self that in the crisis of her gothic life fiction locked her into her father's house in the way that a little girl is con-fined to a nursery. [pp. 590, 591]

The role that most epitomizes the complexity of Dickinson's undertak-ing, with its strengths and terrors, her most dramatic pose in both life and poetry, was the woman in white.

> That Dickinson's white dress implies not a single supposed person but a series of characters suggests, however, not just the artful complexity of her strategy for escaping Requirements but also the dangers implicit in that strategy. Impersonating simultaneously a "little maid" in white,

a fierce virgin in white, a nun in white, a bride in white, a madwoman in white, a dead woman in white, and a ghost in white, Dickinson seems to have split herself into a series of incubae, haunting not just her father's house but her own mind. . . . The ambiguities and discontinuities implicit in her white dress became, therefore, as much signs of her own psychic fragmentation as of her society's multiple (and conflicting) demands upon women. As such, they objectified the enigma of the poet's true personality—for if she was both Daisy and Empress, child and ghost, who was she "really"? [pp. 621-22]

Finally, the authors describe yet another role which they see as truly integrating, that of the spinner/spider, who may well represent sexual decay in patriarchal myth, but who represents as well the witch, the sorceress, "a crucial if 'neglected' emblem of art, and of the artist as the most triumphant secret self" (p. 633). Examining the imagery in Dickinson's spider poems, Gilbert and Gubar observe how "all these poems seem to say that, as Dickinson defines it, female art must almost necessarily be secret art; mental pirouettes silently performed in the attic of Nobodaddy's house, the growth of an obscure underwater jewel, or, especially, a spider's unobtrusively woven yarn of pearl" (p. 634).

Gilbert and Gubar's own work is much like the spinning they describe, casting back and forth between the images projected by both the poems and the life to provide ways of seeing Dickinson's complexities, tensions, achievements. What they do not acknowledge is how these complexities and tensions are manifested in the poetry, itself, in its language and forms. They do not "read" the poems; instead they search them for the images that, to use their own metaphor, are lodged like so many pearls in these oysters, and use the garnered images to understand the biography. Nevertheless, their concept of the theatrical element in Dickinson's life provides both vivid emblems for its history and an important assessment of the creative, as opposed to reactive, processes in Dickinson's life.

A study that does treat, with sensitivity and sophistication, Dickinson's language and its role in her creation of herself as woman poet is Margaret Homans's chapter on Dickinson in *Women Writers and Poetic Identity*. Homans's approach uses both feminist and linguistic scholarship to discuss how woman's traditional identification with "otherness," in society and in language, is the central problem with which she must deal in becoming a poet.

In her discussion of the masculine tradition, Homans explains how language itself embodies and enacts patriarchal assumptions.

Language's operation is to identify otherness as self, to appropriate objects and transform them into subject. Adamic language, theoretically ideal because its words are synonymous with their meanings, is also the type of appropriative language, since Adam understood language to mean control over the beasts he named, and he named the woman as well.[22]

Dickinson uses her understanding of otherness, or femaleness, to question traditional language structures and to attempt reversals of them that will allow her to create a poetic identity.

Homans shows how it is Dickinson's identification with Eve, who can learn other languages besides Adam's—for example, that of Satan, who lies—that enables her to understand the figurativeness of language. "She understands and makes use of a general dislocation between words and their referents" (p. 193). Dickinson is also able to challenge hierarchy in language, that hierarchy which is at the heart of male supremacy. For, argues Homans, "the desire to be at the center generates hierarchical thinking, but even the potentially neutral concept of opposition also turns into hierarchy, because it is impossible ever to be entirely disinterested and one element must be primary and the other secondary" (p. 36).

In the following paragraph Homans summarizes her position.

> This recognition of the fictionality of nature's traditional sexual iden-
> tification is part of Dickinson's larger discovery about language's fictive-
> ness. Her resistance to appropriating nature is one model for improving
> the status of the woman writer in relation to the tradition; another lies
> in her challenge to the assumption that opposition is necessary for lan-
> guage to have meaning. Her undoing of rhetorical dualism becomes a
> model for a revised pattern of relations between the sexes, in her recog-
> nition that the opposition of the sexes is as figurative as any other kind
> of opposition, not a literal necessity. The traditional determinisms that
> have maintained this opposition need no longer operate, just as the
> tradition of Mother Nature, once it is recognized as a tradition and
> therefore figurative, not actual, ceases to be confining. A tradition of
> masculine dominance may be at the root of dualistic language, and her
> feminine identity, particularly her sense of inheritance from Eve, may
> be the origin of her readiness to object to that structure of language. She
> disrupts traditional relations between the sexes by means of the kind of
> undoing of hierarchical language that she employs in poems about the
> idea of opposition itself. Dickinson brings to those poems in which the
> poet's identity is explicitly feminine her knowledge that her best power
> lies in the manipulation of language to reverse its ordinary meanings.
> She uses that linguistic power first to reverse the ordinary direction of
> power between a feminine self and a masculine other, and then, as in
> the poems where she undoes antithetical language, uses it to discard
> the idea of dominance altogether. [p. 201]

Homans presents these arguments by means of careful and subtle readings of Dickinson's poems. Her work is of especial value because it takes

the central feminist positions—the necessity of the conjunction between woman and poet and the recognition of the power that Dickinson achieved by this conjunction—and expands their application from the realm of biography into the perhaps more exciting, more provocative, and more various world of the poetry itself.

Definitions of power are clarified and enlarged as feminist critics explore the literary and biographical implications of gender. While none of these three studies ignores or minimizes the difficulties and, indeed, suffering, that also defines Dickinson's life as an artist, they do examine, in more and more kinds of detail, the nature of her achievement. For Keller, the source of her power lies in her appropriation of existing structures—beliefs, tradition, institutions—which she then manipulates to construct a world and a self on her own terms. Gilbert and Gubar stress the artifice, and artfulness, of her creativity: especially, the enactment of roles that can mediate between life and art to establish the possibility of living both. Homans points to disruption and reversal as central to Dickinson's power: the altering of patriarchal structures—hierarchies and dualism in language and relationships—to form new ones that suit her. All show Dickinson, of necessity, responding to the repressions that surround and threaten to control her, change her into something other than she is or might be. Her power—of appropriation, of role-playing, of disrupting and reversing—is not an evasion but an active and radical engagement with those forces.

The essays in this collection, accepting, now, the conjunction of woman and poet as given, accepting as well the premise that Dickinson's actions make sense, are dedicated to the continued exploration and definition of Dickinson's power.

Image and language are their subjects. Biography is viewed, by Sandra Gilbert, Karl Keller, and Barbara Mossberg, as defined by those images that Dickinson constructs for herself, of herself. Gilbert looks at the deliberateness of Dickinson's creation of herself as "the myth of Amherst." Mossberg focuses upon that difficult and pervasive persona of Dickinson's, the little girl. Keller, speaking as the male critic in reaction to Dickinson, discusses how she presents herself to, and does not present herself to, the male, the critic.

Joanne Dobson is concerned with archetypal images, particularly the archetype of the masculine as Dickinson encounters it within her own psyche and projects it into the external world. Image in Adalaide Morris's essay, on the other hand, is more poetic than biographical. She looks at imagery, vocabulary, and position in Dickinson's love poems to see what they reveal about Dickinson's understanding of love between female and male, female and female.

Language is the dominant subject in Margaret Homans's essay, which is also concerned primarily with Dickinson's love poems. The love poems become a focus around which many of these essays turn, especially conducive, as they are, to the study of sex roles, of femaleness and maleness, of power and the lack of it. Homans examines the close correlation between language and social structures to show how Dickinson's use of metaphoric and metonymic language reveals a critique of duality and hierarchy in human relations, such as love, and an attempt to create different patterns where hierarchies are superseded in death.

The last two essays are devoted to Dickinson's language as its forms reveal her sense of herself as a poet. Cristanne Miller studies Dickinson's grammatical and syntactical deviations as they embody a larger program for continuous disruption, necessary that the woman poet may create for herself. Joanne Feit Diehl studies Dickinson's language as weapon and defense, articulating her independence from and control over the external world.

Always at issue is power. Keller defines it this way: "Making a world in which one could be oneself. That's power."[23] Showing the relation between such power and the structures (strictures) of the existing world, he gives this definition of suttee, which feminist theorists like Mary Daly have seen as emblematic of patriarchy's mutilation of the female.

> *Suortù*: a woman defying her fate. Was that Emily Dickinson? I think she was really a headier version of that. I think she thought it was her fate to defy. A woman defying her fate is what a man would expect of a woman. A woman accepting her fate to defy means accepting one's nature, one's humanity, one's gender, one's difference, one's ability, onself.

Defying and making go together to create this power, one an act in response, the other an act in creation. A look at the vocabulary these feminist critics use helps us to a better understanding of the process of power that Dickinson developed.

These words occur and reoccur: *critique, strategy, subversion, appropriation, deviation, renunciation, transformation, control, possibility.* I have placed them in an order that seems to outline the process itself by which response turns into creation. When the words combine in a sentence, as in this one from Joanne Feit Diehl's essay, the idea of process is underlined.

> Adopting qualities associated with the Christian deity, and transforming these into a linguistic process that she describes as both more human and equable than the Christian, Dickinson creates an alternative power potentially subversive of any external authority based upon the sovereignty of a male-identified divinity or predicated upon the supremacy of those within the religious fold.[24]

These new essays, with their overlapping themes, show Dickinson first understanding her situation (*critique*) and then enacting in various ways (*strategy*) her attempts at solution. *Subversion, appropriation, deviation* are all kinds of *sabotage*, working upon the system, working within the system, using its own elements to turn them on purpose to her purposes. *Renunciation* is really a particular form of appropriation upon which Dickinson relied. The giving up of something valued may look like self-denial and is a firmly rooted patriarchal expectation for women (suttee being one of its extremest forms), but as a way of saying "no" it can also be, and was for Dickinson, an act of autonomy. It cleared a space. A space wherein *transformation* might occur. But a space within the patriarchy. For transformation is the kind of magic that turns what is there at hand into something else. Something suddenly new, a creation. Transformation is a more practical, and more political, kind of magic than, say, fantasy. It is Dickinson's stock in trade.

Transformation leads both to *control* and to *possibility*. Control, an enactment of power, requires the presence of an other, be it society, nature, person, or aspect of self. Control reminds us of the existing presence of the world. *Possibility* is beyond. It is the direction in which Dickinson always heads, and it is a space she sometimes creates for herself, after a transformation has taken place. Control and possibility are aspects of her power.

If we are fully to understand Dickinson's power, we must realize not only what she did but how she did it. I am referring now not to the locutions of biography and poems, the steps taken, but to a component of her power common to both her life and her art: style. We are concerned equally with Dickinson's lifestyle and her language style. Sandra Gilbert, commenting in her essay on the "curiously theatrical language evoked by Dickinson's odd combinations of speech and silence, frankness and mystery," concludes: "For if the mysteries of this poet's life are often riddles of absence or silence, then the mysteries of her art are marvels of transformation, 'conversions of the mind' (#593) in which we see a great performer turning defeat into triumph like a magician changing water into wine."[25] Adalaide Morris makes the following comment on the imagery of her love poems: "The linked imagery of intensity, explosiveness, suppression, and mutilation suggests the extravagance of Dickinson's commitments."[26] Words like *theatrical* and *extravagance* point to the largeness of Dickinson. She may call and even keep herself "small," for reasons resolutely political if not always pleasing, but her style gives her away and is a part of that power which attracts us so. She makes claims for herself, with gestures displaying her bravado, wit, fierceness, and flamboyance. She is not only good; she is grand. Her very extravagance makes room for us in her undertaking, even though she wrote poems she did not publish, because it invites, demands, an audience.

The critical procedure of the nine writers collected here is characterized by its response to such a subject. Feminist criticism does not differ from traditional criticism in avoiding the knowledge or techniques of the scholarly disciplines. Attempting to understand the interrelationships between biography and art, essential to its enterprise, the study of a woman poet, it uses whatever information history, psychology, sociology, linguistics, and literary scholarship have to offer. What seems to differ most radically is the matter of perspective, and perspective is created not only by the critic's pre-existing beliefs—that, for example, gender must be seen, analyzed as it informs biography and art—but by the space it gives to the subject's own view of herself. The perspective of feminist criticism contains the premise that the poet is who she says she is, who she shows herself to be. This is why, I think, the focus or emphasis on image and language which dominates this volume occurs. Traditional criticism has trouble believing Dickinson. It rearranges her poems and reexplains her life. It is true that Dickinson, of all woman poets, often dissembles, through ironies or downright lies. But this "slantyness" is one large part of what she in fact does say, does show. We need not believe her lies to believe *her*. The ability to see Emily Dickinson in terms of *her* own perspective requires a degree of sophistication, surely. But it is a head start, and a new start, on approaching, approximating, her truth.

As I write, only one full-length book on Dickinson with a feminist perspective has been published: Keller's. Two are in press: Joanne Feit Diehl's *Dickinson and the Romantic Imagination* and Barbara Clarke Mossberg's *Emily Dickinson: When a Writer Is a Daughter*. My own exploration of mental space in Dickinson and what happens there is nearing completion. Feminist criticism of Dickinson, as I said earlier, is relatively recent. The essays in this volume are an example of what is now being accomplished. We are hardly finished with Dickinson. No one, no one school of criticism or one critic, could ever be. She is, after all, so large. And as demanding as she is rewarding. I see this book as representative of the beginning of feminist concern with Dickinson. I find its provocations exciting, both in their own right and as they raise issues for work that is to come.

NOTES

1. Suzanne Juhasz, *Naked and Fiery Forms: Modern American Poetry by Women, A New Tradition* (New York: Harper and Row, 1976), pp. 7-32.
2. George Whicher, *This Was A Poet: A Critical Biography of Emily Dickinson* (Ann Arbor: University of Michigan Press, 1938).
3. John Cody, *After Great Pain: The Inner Life of Emily Dickinson* (Cambridge, Massachusetts: The Belknap Press of Harvard University Press, 1971).
4. Whicher, p. 113.

5. Cody, p. 404.

6. Sandra Gilbert and Susan Gubar, *The Madwoman in the Attic: The Woman Writer and the Nineteenth-Century Literary Imagination* (New Haven and London: Yale University Press, 1979).

7. Margaret Homans, *Women Writers and Poetic Identity: Dorothy Wordsworth, Emily Brontë, and Emily Dickinson* (Princeton, New Jersey: Princeton University Press, 1980).

8. Joanne Feit Diehl, *Dickinson and the Romantic Imagination* (Princeton University Press, 1981).

9. Charles Anderson, *Emily Dickinson's Poetry: Stairway of Surprise* (New York: Holt, Rinehart and Winston, 1960).

10. Sharon Cameron, *Lyric Time: Dickinson and the Limits of Genre* (Baltimore and London: Johns Hopkins University Press, 1979).

11. David Porter, *Dickinson: The Modern Idiom* (Cambridge, Mass. and London: Harvard University Press, 1981).

12. Suzanne Juhasz, " 'The Undiscovered Continent': Emily Dickinson and the Space of the Mind," *The Missouri Review* 3, No. 1 (Fall 1979): 87.

13. *The Madwoman in the Attic.*

14. Robert Weisbuch, *Emily Dickinson's Poetry* (Chicago and London: University of Chicago Press, 1975).

15. Elsa Greene, "Emily Dickinson Was a Poetess," *College English* 34 (October 1972): 63-70.

16. Cheryl Brown and Karen Olson, eds., *Feminist Criticism: Essays on Theory, Poetry, and Prose* (Metuchen, New Jersey, and London: The Scarecrow Press, 1978), pp. 69-91.

17. *Naked and Fiery Forms*, pp. 7-32.

18. Sandra Gilbert and Susan Gubar, eds., *Shakespeare's Sisters: Feminist Essays on Women Poets* (Bloomington and London: Indiana University Press, 1979), pp. 99-121.

19. Karl Keller, *The Only Kangaroo Among the Beauty: Emily Dickinson and America* (Baltimore and London: Johns Hopkins University Press, 1979).

20. Keller, p. 2.

21. Gilbert and Gubar, p. 584.

22. Homans, p. 37.

23. "Notes on Sleeping with Emily Dickinson," p. 68.

24. " 'Ransom in a Voice': Language as Defense in Dickinson's Poetry," p. 157.

25. "The Wayward Nun beneath the Hill: Emily Dickinson and the Mysteries of Womanhood," p. 27.

26. " 'The Love of Thee – A Prism Be': Men and Women in the Love Poems of Emily Dickinson," p. 101.

SANDRA M. GILBERT **II**

The Wayward Nun
beneath the Hill

Emily Dickinson and the Mysteries of Womanhood

YOUNG MABEL LOOMIS TODD had been living for two months in Amherst, Massachusetts, where her husband, David, had just been appointed Director of the Amherst College Observatory, when on November 6, 1881, she wrote her parents an enthusiastic letter about one of the town's most fascinating citizens:

> I must tell you about the *character* of Amherst. It is a lady whom the people call the *Myth*. She is a sister of Mr. Dickinson, & seems to be the climax of all the family oddity. She has not been outside of her own house in fifteen years, except once to see a new church, when she crept out at night, & viewed it by moonlight. No one who calls upon her mother & sister ever see her, but she allows little children once in a great while, & one at a time, to come in, when she gives them cake or candy, or some nicety, for she is very fond of little ones. But more often she lets down the sweetmeat by a string, out of a window, to them. She dresses wholly in white, & her mind is said to be perfectly wonderful. She writes finely, but no one *ever* sees her. Her sister, who was at Mrs. Dickinson's party, invited me to come & sing to her mother sometime. . . . People tell me the *myth* will hear every note—she will be near, but unseen. . . . Isn't that like a book? So interesting.[1]

By now that letter has become almost as famous as the Mythic Miss Dickinson herself, largely because it sems to have contributed to a process of mystification and fictionalization that surrounded one of America's greatest writers with what Thomas Wentworth Higginson once called a "fiery mist."[2]

Higginson himself also, of course, contributed to this process that transformed a reclusive poet-cook into a New England Nun of Love-and-Art.[3] More than a decade before Mabel Todd recorded the rumours she had heard about "the rare mysterious Emily,"[4] he visited his self-styled

"Scholar" in her Amherst home, and though his notes on the meeting are not as gothic as the stories Mrs. Todd reported to her parents, they add both fire and mist to the mythic portrait, with their description of how there was "a step like a pattering child's in entry" and "a little plain woman . . . in a very plain & exquisitely clean white pique . . . came to me with two day lilies, which she put in a sort of childlike way into my hand & said, 'These are my introduction' in a soft frightened breathless childlike voice. . . ."[5] Interestingly enough, moreover, even the "little plain woman's" most prosaic remarks seemed to enhance the evolving Myth with just the dash of paradox needed to give a glimmer of irony to the dramatic halo around her: "She makes all the bread," Higginson observed, "for her father only likes hers & says, '& people must have puddings,' this *very* dreamily, as if they were comets—so she makes them."[6]

After her death, in fact, a number of Dickinson's admirers like to dwell on that ineffable glimmer of irony. "Even though her mind might be occupied with 'all mysteries and all knowledge,' including meteors and comets, her hands were often busy in most humble household ways," wrote her cousin Helen Knight Wyman in a 1905 article for the *Boston Cooking School Magazine* on "Emily Dickinson as Cook and Poetess."[7] She "wrote indefatigably, as some women cook or knit," added R. P. Blackmur in 1937.[8] As the Myth grew and glowed, drama, domesticity, and Dickinson seem to have become inseparable. It is no wonder, then—given this unlikely, often absurdly literary image of an obsessively childlike, gothic yet domestic spinster—that recent readers of Dickinson's verse have struggled to deconstruct the "Myth of Amherst" and discover instead the aesthetic technician, the intellectual, and the visionary, whose lineaments would seem to have been blurred or obliterated in the "fiery mist" generated not by the poet herself but by her friends and admirers.

I want to argue here, however, that though their fictionalizations may sometimes have been crude or melodramatic, Mabel Loomis Todd, Thomas Wentworth Higginson, and many others were not in fact projecting their own fantasies onto the comparatively neutral (if enigmatic) figure of Emily Dickinson. Rather, as I will suggest, all these observers were responding to a process of self-mythologizing that led Dickinson herself to use all the materials of daily reality, and most especially the details of domesticity, as if they were not facts but metaphors, in order to recreate herself-and-her-life as a single, emblematic text, and often, indeed, as a sort of religious text—the ironic hagiography, say, of a New England Nun. More specifically, I want to suggest that Dickinson structured this life/text around a series of "mysteries" that were distinctively female, deliberately exploring and exploiting the characteristics, even the constraints, of nineteenth-century womanhood so as to transform and transcend them.

Finally, I want to argue that such a provisional and analytic acceptance of the Dickinson Myth may serve the reality of Dickinson's art better than the contemptuous rejection of legend that has lately become fashionable. For by deciphering rather than deconstructing the intricate text of this poet's life, we may come closer to understanding the methods and materials of her actual, literary texts. Throughout this essay, therefore, I will try to "read" biographical mysteries, and I will use the word "mystery" in almost all the current as well as a few of the archaic senses given by the *OED*. These include "a religious truth known only from divine revelation"; "a mystical presence"; a "religious . . . rite, especially a sacramental rite of the Christian religion"; "an incident in the life of [Christ] regarded . . . as having a mystical significance"; "a hidden or secret thing . . . a riddle or enigma"; "a 'secret' or highly technical operation in a trade or art"; a secret rite; a "miracle-play"; "a service, occupation; office, ministry"; "a handicraft, craft, art, trade, profession, or calling"; and finally "a kind of plum cake." All these senses of "mystery"—even, or perhaps especially, the plum cake—have some application to both the Myth and the mythmaking of Emily Dickinson.

For like her Romantic precursor John Keats, one of the poets to whom she turned most often for sustenance, Dickinson understood that a "life of any worth is a continual allegory."[9] Thus she ambitiously undertook to live (and to create) "a life like the scriptures, figurative—which [some] people can no more make out than they can the hebrew Bible." Such a life, as Keats observed, need not be theatrical; one might be both public and melodramatic without achieving true significance. "Lord Byron cuts a figure—but he is not figurative—," Keats commented wryly, and Dickinson would have seen such a remark as offering her permission to dramatize the private "trivia" of domesticity, rather than public turmoil, permission even to conflate puddings and comets. For again, like Keats, she would have perceived the essential reciprocity of the life/text and the literary text. About Shakespeare, for instance, Keats famously observed that he "led a life of Allegory: his works are the comments on it."[10] But as I hope to show, the same striking statement can be made about the mysteries Dickinson enacted and allegorized.

Dickinson's impulse to enact mysteries can be traced back almost to her childhood. Two episodes from her year at Mount Holyoke, for instance, seem to have signalled what was on the way. The first is one that Mabel Todd claimed to have heard about from the poet's sister Vinnie. The seventeen-year-old Emily, wrote Mrs. Todd, "was never floored. When the Euclid examination came and she had never studied it, she went to the blackboard and gave such a glib exposition of imaginary figures that the dazed teacher passed her with the highest mark."[11] The second episode is more famous and has been widely discussed, even by biographers and critics who dislike the "Myth of Amherst." Throughout Dickinson's time at Mount Holyoke, the school was in the throes of an evangelical revival eagerly encouraged by Mary Lyon, the school's founder and principal. According to Clara Newman Turner, there was an occasion when "Miss Lyon . . . asked all those who wanted to be Christians to rise. The wording of the request was not such as Emily could honestly accede to and she remained seated—the only one who did not rise."[12]

In these two episodes, we can discern the seeds of personal and religious mysteries that Dickinson was to develop and dramatize throughout both her life/text and her literary texts. Moreover, these two episodes suggest that we can reduce the major Dickinsonian mysteries to two categories: mystery as puzzle (secret, riddle, enigma, or blackboard battle with imaginary figures), and mystery as miracle (mystic transformation, inexplicable sacrament, or private parallel to traditional Christian professions of faith). If we bear these two categories in mind as we meditate on Dickinson's "life as Allegory," we find that, on the one hand, at the center of this poet's self-mythologizing mystery-as-puzzle we confront a kind of absence or blank, the enigmatic wound that many biographers have treated as if it were the subject of a romantic detective novel called "The Mystery of the Missing Lover." At the center of the Dickinson mystery-as-miracle, on the other hand, we encounter a presence or power, the "white heat" (365) of Dickinson's art, whose story we might label "The Mystery of the Muse." Yet these two mysteries—we might also call them the mysteries of Life and Art—are of course connected. For, even more than most other writers, Emily Dickinson the poet mysteriously transformed the pain associated with the puzzle at the center of her life into the miracle of her art; through that transformation, indeed, she became the "Myth of Amherst."

To speak of puzzles and miracles, however—or even to speak of all the finely distinguished definitions of "mystery" that the *OED* offers—is still to speak in generalities. When one becomes more specific, however, the puzzle of Dickinson's life is, at least on the surface, vulgarly and easily defined: who *was* "he"? Were there several of "him"? And was it because of "him" (or "them") that this brilliant woman more or less completely withdrew from the world? When she declared, at the age of thirty-eight, that "I do not cross my Father's ground to any House or town,"[13] was she secretly anticipating "his" return? By now, a century and a half since Emily Dickinson was born, it seems fairly certain that we will never know "his" (or "their") identity. But that the "Myth of Amherst" spent part of her poetic lifetime nurturing romantic feelings about someone, whether real or imaginary, is quite certain: we know, for instance, from her so-called Master letters and from the later letters to Judge Lord, that this puzzling poet was a dazzling writer of love letters, better than Charlotte Brontë and at least as good as John Keats. In addition, she produced a series of elegant and often sensual verses memorializing romance, real or imaginary—poems that range from the suave and courtly "The Daisy follows soft the Sun –" (106) to the subtly voluptuous "Wild Nights – Wild Nights!" (249)

It is clear, too, that Dickinson's relationship with her real or imaginary lover (or lovers) gave her "great pain" that must have had something to do with her renunciation of him and/or the world. Her heartbroken and heartbreaking "Master" letters suggest this, and impassioned poems like "Why make it doubt – it hurts it so –" (462) and "My life closed twice before its close –" (1732) would be hard to understand otherwise. Poem 462, for instance, is obviously tormented and almost certainly autobiographical:

> Why make it doubt – it hurts it so –
> So sick – to guess –
> So strong – to know –
> So brave – upon its little Bed
> To tell the very last They said
> Unto Itself – and smile – And shake –
> For that dear – distant – dangerous – Sake –
> But – the Instead – the Pinching fear
> That Something – it did do – or dare –
> Offend the Vision – and it flee –
> And They no more remember me –
> Nor ever turn to tell me why –
> Oh, Master, This is Misery –

Mysteriously, the poet/speaker transforms herself here into an "it"—a mere lump of suffering flesh—but the identity of the Master whose favor she begs is more mysterious. Still, even the stumblings and hesitations, the advances and retreats in this work authenticate the pain it expresses. Gasping and elliptical, it seems like a speech spun out of delirium; reading it, we become witnesses to a crisis in love's fever, watchers by the sickbed of romance.

It is difficult, though, to ignore the curiously theatrical language evoked by Dickinson's odd combination of speech and silence, frankness and mystery. In the sentence before last I used the words *seems, fever, romance*. These words do, of course, refer to states of being that are somehow "true," but their truth is more likely the truth of art, of metaphor, than the truth of "reality." As we watch this puzzling enactment of "a woman's life," we may begin to feel rather like a dazed audience watching a brilliant schoolgirl solve entirely imaginary problems in geometry. Significantly, indeed, the more vivid the mystery-as-puzzle of Dickinson's life becomes, the more it melts into the mystery-as-miracle of Dickinson's art. For if the mysteries of this poet's life are often riddles of absence or silence, then the mysteries of her art are marvels of transformation, "conversions of the mind" (593) in which we see a great performer turning defeat into triumph like a magician changing water into wine.

Dickinson wrote a number of verses that not only enact but also describe and analyze such marvelous transformations. In these works, her Master/lover has stopped being an ordinary man—if he ever was one—and becomes a miraculous and sacramental being, on at least one occasion a god in the garden of love, and, more frequently, a muse in the heaven of invention. In poem 322, "There came a day at Summer's Full / Entirely for me," for example, the speaker's lover is a "Sealed Church" with whom she is "Permitted to commune" on this one transfigured occasion. When the two part, she declares that "Each bound the Other's Crucifix – / We gave no other Bond –." But that, she adds, is "Sufficient troth, that we shall rise – / Deposed – at length, the Grave – / To that new Marriage, / Justified – through Calvaries of Love –." Most striking here is Dickinson's deft fusion of the language of love with the vocabulary of Christianity, a poetic gesture that goes back at least to the medieval romance—for instance to the "Cave of Love" inhabited by Tristan and Isolde—but that this self-mythologizing New England nun makes distinctively her own. For as she transforms her real or imaginary lover/Master into a suffering god of love and herself into his "Empress of Calvary," Dickinson performs a complementary conversion. Defining herself and her lover as "Sealed churches" and their erotic communion as a sacrament, she converts the Christianity she had begun to reject as a seventeen-year-old Mount Holyoke student into a complex theology of secular love.

In "I have a King, who does not speak –" (103) and "My Life had stood – a Loaded Gun –" (754) she performs equally skillful but slightly different acts of poetic prestidigitation, converting the mysterious figure she romanticizes from a lover into a male muse. Significantly, moreover, though the male muse in both these poems is given an impressive title—in one he is a King, in the other a Master—he is strangely passive and silent in both works; indeed, it is his passivity and silence that apparently empower the poet's triumphant speech. The enigmatic "King who does not speak," for instance, enables Dickinson, like a modern priestess of Delphi, to "peep" at night, "thro' a dream" into "parlors shut by day."

> And if I do – [she declares] when morning comes –
> It is as if a hundred drums
> Did round my pillow roll,

> And shouts fill all my Childish sky,
> And Bells keep saying "Victory"
> From steeples in my soul!

Similarly, when the poet imagines herself as a "Loaded Gun" she arranges for her owner and Master to carry her into "Sovereign Woods" where "everytime I speak for Him – / The Mountains straight reply –"

> And do I smile [she adds ironically], such cordial light
> Upon the Valley glow –
> It is as a Vesuvian face
> Had let its pleasure through –

Plainly, no matter what Dickinson meant by the famous riddle that ends this mysterious work,[14] the central mystery-as-miracle the poem records is the woman writer's appropriation of her Master/owner's power. Though he has identified her, seized her, carried her away, it is finally she who, in a kind of prototypical role reversal, guards him with her deadly energy. "None stir the second time–" / she boasts, "On whom I lay a yellow Eye – / Or an emphatic Thumb."

The mysteries of Dickinson's art accomplished some transformations of experience, however, that were even more remarkable than those recorded in "I have a King" and "My Life had stood." There, the poet had made the Master/lover who evidently humbled her into a figure who paradoxically strengthened her. But in other poems, she converted "great pain" itself—the humiliating vicissitudes of romance, for instance, along with all the other terrors of her life—into an extraordinary source of energy. "A *Wounded* Deer – leaps highest," she insists quite early in her poetic career (165, written in 1860), and in the same poem she also points out the power of "The *Smitten* Rock that gushes! / The *trampled* Steel that springs!"— eerie transformations of anguish into energy. A year or two later (1861), in poem 281, one of her many mortuary poems, she exclaims that the sight of death is "so appalling – it exhilarates – / So over Horror, it half Captivates –." Brooding by someone's deathbed, she remarks that here "Terror's free – / Gay, Ghastly, Holiday"—an even eerier transformation of agony into energy. In a number of poems about volcanoes, moreover, she speculates

> If the stillness is Volcanic
> In the human face
> When upon a pain Titanic
> Features keep their place –

and wonders

> If at length the smouldering anguish
> Will not overcome –

> And the palpitating Vineyard
> In the dust be thrown?
>
> [175]

Finally, in a poem that is both searingly sincere and a triumph of irony, Dickinson describes the way she herself has been transformed through the sufferings of love into a paradoxical being, an *Empress* of *Calvary*, a Queen of Pain.

> Title divine – is mine!
> The Wife – without the Sign!
> Acute Degree – conferred on me –
> Empress of Calvary!
>
> [1072]

Surely this poem's central image is almost the apotheosis of anguish converted into energy, what Dickinson elsewhere called the "ecstasy of death." Transforming the puzzles of life into the paradoxes of art, the poet/speaker is on a kind of "gay, ghastly, Holiday," reminding us that she is the same woman who once told Thomas Wentworth Higginson that "I had a terror . . . I could tell to none – and so I sing, as the Boy does by the Burying Ground – because I am afraid –."[15]

It is significant, however, that the "gay, ghastly, Holiday" into which Dickinson so often converts her "great pain" is *not* a weekend in "Domingo" or a passage to India. On the contrary, though she characterizes herself as an Empress of Calvary, this poet is always scrupulously careful to explain that she "never saw a moor . . . never saw the sea" (1052). Her muse-like "King who does not speak" maintains his inspiring silence in a *parlor*, after all, and even the Master who owns the "Loaded Gun" of her art sleeps on an "Eider-Duck's / Deep Pillow" that sounds as homely as any bedding nineteenth-century New England had to offer. Dickinson loved exotic place-names—admiring, for instance, the "mail from Tunis" that the hummingbird brought to the bushes on her father's ground (1463)—but nevertheless the news of those distances came to her at home, in her parlor, her kitchen, her garden. For her,

> Eden is that old-fashioned House
> We dwell in every day
> Without suspecting our abode
> Until we drive away.
>
> [1657]

Moreover, as Adrienne Rich has reminded us in one of the best recent essays on Emily Dickinson's cloistered art,[16] Dickinson felt that although

> Volcanoes be in Sicily
> And South America

I judge from my Geography –
Volcanoes nearer here
A Lava step at any time
Am I inclined to climb –
A Crater I may contemplate
Vesuvius at Home.

[1705]

For as a mistress of the mysteries of transformation, Dickinson was not just an extravagant miracle-worker, an Empress of Calvary; she was a magician of the ordinary, and hers was a Myth of *Amherst*, a Myth, that is, of the daily and the domestic, a Myth of what could be seen "New Englandly."[17] In this commitment to dailiness, moreover, even more than in her conversions of an unidentified figure into a muse and agony into energy, she defines and enacts distinctive mysteries of womanhood that have great importance not only for her own art but also for the female poetic tradition of which she is a grandmother.

Many male poets, of course, have also performed miracles of literary transformation. Some, for instance, have metamorphosed beloved women into muses (one thinks of Keats's "La Belle Dame sans Merci"). Others have transformed agony into energy (Donne's Holy Sonnets). Still others have even converted the ordinary into the emblematic, the secular or domestic into the sacred (Wordsworth, Stevens, George Herbert). What is notable about Dickinson, however, is (first) that in poems and letters she performs all these kinds of transformations, sometimes simultaneously, and (second) that the images into which she transforms ideas and events are so often uniquely "female"; that is, they are associated with women's literature and women depicted in literature, or else they are associated with woman's life and woman's place. Specifically, the womanly mysteries-as-miracles of Emily Dickinson's life/text fall into five major groups: the mystery of romance (a woman's literary genre); the mystery of renunciation (a woman's duty); the mystery of domesticity (a woman's sphere); the mystery of nature (figuratively speaking, a woman's analog or likeness); and the mystery of *woman's* nature.

As we have already seen, the first two of these groups include poems in which Dickinson describes and discusses her transformations of her mysterious master into an empowering muse as well as her conversion of agony into energy—both metamorphoses accomplished with the aid of imagery drawn from "female gothic" novels like *Jane Eyre* and *Wuthering Heights* or with the help of ideas drawn from the works of a woman artist of renunciation like George Eliot. With astonishing frequency, however, this poet's transformative processes are facilitated not just by literary models but by anti-literary female activities. More often than not, indeed, she negotiates the difficult passage from life to art through the transformation of objects and images drawn from her "ordinary" daily domestic experience. In fact, she uses such objects not only as key symbols in an elaborate mythology of the household, but also as props in her poetry's parallel mysteries of romance and renunciation.

No doubt the most striking and ubiquitous of Dickinson's domestic symbols is her white dress. As I have argued elsewhere, that extraordinary costume is in one sense a kind of ghostly blank, an empty page on which in invisible ink this theatrical poet quite consciously wrote a letter to the world that never wrote to her.[18] But to begin with, of course, Dickinson's radiantly symbolic garment was "just" a dress, an "ordinary" "everyday" item of clothing not unlike the morning dresses many Victorian young ladies wore. At the Dickinson Homestead in Amherst, indeed, it is still possible to see a white cotton dress said to have been the poet's. Enshrouded in a very prosaic and very modern plastic bag, its carefully protected tucks and ruffles remind the viewer that such a costume would have had to be maintained—laundered, ironed, mended—with intense dedication. And Dickinson was as conscious of that requirement as her descendants are, not only conscious that her white dress made special demands on her life but conscious that the idea of her dress made special demands on her art. In a fairly early poem she confessed this most dramatically.

A solemn thing – it was – I said –
A woman – white – to be –
And wear – if God should count me fit –
Her blameless mystery –

A hallowed thing – to drop a life
Into the purple well –
Too plummetless – that it return –
Eternity – until –

I pondered how the bliss would look –
And would it feel as big –
When I could take it in my hand –
As hovering – seen – through fog –

And then – the size of this "small" life –
The Sages – call it small –
Swelled – like Horizons – in my vest –
And I sneered – softly – "small"!

[271]

Though it is in some ways obscure—what exactly is "the purple well," for instance?—this poem is particularly clear about one point: Dickinson's white dress is the emblem of a "blameless *mystery*," a kind of miraculous transformation that rejoices and empowers her. Dropping her life into that puzzling purple well, she renounces triviality and ordinariness in order to "wear"—that is, to *enact*—solemnity, dedication, vocation. In return, she will receive an indefinable bliss associated with the transformative power of "Eternity." But—and this is just as important—even as she dedicates her self and her life to becoming "a woman – white," she realizes the intrinsic significance of that self and life. "The Sages – call it small –": to conventionally "wise" men her female works and days may seem tiny, trivial; but as she meditates upon her own transformative powers, she feels this apparently "small" life swell "like Horizons – in my vest –" and, sneering "softly – 'small'!", she utters the arrogance to which, as an artist of the ordinary, she has a right.

If the mysteries of romance and renunciation that Dickinson enacted in life and recorded in her poetry both parallel and complement the mystery of domesticity she also explored, all three quasi-religious concerns are particularly well served by her transformation of an ordinary white dress into the solemn habit of a New England nun. Apparently (or so she often hints) some event connected with the secret drama of her relationship with a muse-like Master (or a masterful Muse) affected her so deeply that it forced the very idea of whiteness across the shadow line that usually separates the metaphorical from the literal. Most people, after all, are capable of imagining themselves in what Dickinson calls "uniforms of snow." Even most poets, however, don't make the passage from the mental pretense implied in the metaphorical to the physical pretense of a theatrical enactment. Yet this is the extraordinary passage that Dickinson did make. What she also called her "white election" (528), therefore, suggests not only that she transformed her life into art more readily than most other writers but also that, more than most, she used her "small" life itself as an instrument of her great art: even the most ordinary materials of her life, that is, became a set of encoded gestures meant both to supply imagery for, *and* to supplement, the encoded statements of her verse.

In one of her most famous self-explanations, Dickinson once assured Higginson that "When I state myself, as the Representative of the Verse – it does not mean me – but a supposed person."[19] The remark may seem a reasonable confession to those who have grown accustomed to New Critical theories about the "extinction" of personality in poetry, but if one meditates long enough on the central mysteries of this artist's "life of Allegory," it is impossible not to conclude that even in making such an apparently straightforward remark she was performing one of her most cunning acts of transformation. For after all, the point her white dress most definitively makes is that she herself, the "real" Emily Dickinson, was as much a "supposed person" as the so-called "Representative of the Verse." Clad in her white costume, she was, in literal fact, the "Myth of Amherst," and this precisely because she was the mystery—both the puzzle and the miracle—of Amherst.

Into what sort of extraordinary "supposed person" did this transfiguration of a white dress convert her, however? As I have suggested elsewhere, Dickinson as a "woman – white" was a relative of Wilkie Collins's notorious *Woman in White,* of many a gothic ghost and pallid nun, of Elizabeth Barrett Browning's Aurora Leigh (who wears a "clean white morning gown"), of the redeemed spirits in the Biblical book of *Revelation* (who go in shining white raiment), and of Hawthorne's "Snow Maiden" (who wears, of course, a "uniform of snow").[20] In addition, as Mabel Todd noticed, she is related to Charles Dickens's Miss Havisham (who flaunts a tattered, decades-old wedding dress to assert, as Dickinson also did, that she is "the Wife without the Sign").[21] Like Hawthorne's Hester Prynne, moreover, the "Myth of Amherst" uses an item of apparel to signify both tribulation and redemption, while like Melville's Moby Dick she embodies the contradictory mystery of her identity in a color that is no color, a color that is an absence of color. At the same time, however, the line that probably tells us most about the allegorical (rather than allusive) "meaning" of her white dress is the one that promises the least: "Big my secret but it's *bandaged.*"

Appearing in poem 1737, which seems devoted to some of the more painful (and melodramatic) aspects of Dickinson's romance, this sentence tells us simply that the speaker's secret is a bandaged *wound,* but we cannot doubt that the mysterious hurt is bandaged in white—bandaged, that is, in this poet's central metaphor for aesthetic redemption born of pain, bandaged in myth born of mystery—and therefore, as she also tells us, "It will never get away." Earlier in the poem, however, though Dickinson does not actually tell us her "secret" she gives us a useful clue about its function in her life. The work begins by describing the constancy of anguish that sustains this wounding hidden love.

> Rearrange a "Wife's" affection!
> When they dislocate my Brain!
> Amputate my freckled Bosom!
> Make me bearded like a man!
>
> Blush, my spirit, in thy Fastness –
> Blush, my unacknowledged clay –
> Seven years of troth have taught thee
> More than Wifehood ever may!
>
> Love that never leaped its socket –

Trust entrenched in narrow pain –
Constancy thro' fire – awarded –
Anguish – bare of anodyne!

[1737]

In particular, however, the poet insists that her secret incurable "anguish" is a

Burden – borne so far triumphant–
None suspect me of the crown,
For I wear the "Thorns" till *Sunset* –
Then – my Diadem put on.

[1737]

A crown of thorns converted into a glittering diadem: without presuming to speculate about the "facts" Dickinson may or may not be describing through this secularized crucifixion imagery, it is possible to see that her fictionalizing of those "facts" tells us something crucial about the transformative energy her white dress represents. For as the garment of a mythic or supposed person who is the Empress of Calvary, that dress is once again a paradoxical image of agony transformed into energy; in itself, in fact, it is a paradoxical, even an oxymoronic, costume—as oxymoronic as the "fiery mist" with which Higginson complained that she surrounded herself. Through this artful bandage, this cloth that both shrouds and staunches, conceals and reveals, the mysterious poet of transformation converts absence into presence, silence into speech, in the same way that Christ, through *his* mysteries, converted thorns into jewels, bread and wine into flesh and blood, death into life.

At first, of course, it may seem that in her dependency on Christian imagery, as in her allusions to male-created female characters from Hester Prynne to Miss Havisham, Dickinson was enacting and examining traditional masculine mysteries rather than distinctively feminine ones. Not only is her Christianity notably heterodox, however; the real white dress on which she founded her drama of supposition was significantly different from the white garments she would have encountered in most male-authored sources. For the white dresses imagined by the nineteenth-century male writers who seem to have been most interesting to Dickinson are invariably exotic or supernatural. Wilkie Collins's woman in white is a madwoman attired in the uniform of her derangement. Hawthorne's snow maiden is an eerily romantic being dressed for a fairy tale. Dickens's Miss Havisham wears a gown designed for a most unusual occasion—a wedding that has been indefinitely postponed. Even Melville's metaphysical whale is a freak of nature who represents the freakishness of Nature. Only a female-created character, Elizabeth Barrett Browning's

Aurora Leigh, wears an *ordinary* dress—a "clean white morning gown" transformed by art into an extraordinary costume.[22]

But of course, like Aurora, another "supposed person" whose life as a woman was inseparable from her defiantly female poetry, Emily Dickinson wore such a dress,[23] an ordinary dress made extraordinary by neither circumference nor circumstance but only by the white heat of her creative energy. And indeed, she tells us in one of her most direct poems, this transformation of the ordinary into the extraordinary is a bewitching female art she actually learned from Elizabeth Barrett Browning.

> I think I was enchanted
> When first a sombre Girl –
> I read that Foreign Lady –
> The Dark – felt beautiful –

she begins, describing her first encounter with Barrett Browning's "witch-craft." Then she goes on to list a series of witty transformations through which the common became the uncommon, the daily the divine.

> The Bees – became as Butterflies –
> The Butterflies – as Swans –
> Approached – and spurned the narrow grass –
> And just the meanest Tunes

> That Nature murmured to herself
> To keep herself in Cheer –
> I took for Giants – practising
> Titanic Opera –

> The Days – to Mighty Metres stept –
> The Homeliest – adorned
> As if unto a Jubilee
> 'Twere suddenly confirmed – . . .

> [593]

It is not insignificant, surely, that these metamorphoses, like so many others Dickinson explores in her life/text, not only depend upon the patriarchal Christian mysteries of transformation, they parody and subvert them. For ultimately, Dickinson's symbolic use of her white dress in life and art is only one example of what is not only a striking mythology of domesticity but also an extraordinary theology of the ordinary, the homely, the domestic, a theology that constitutes a uniquely female version of the philosophy Thomas Carlyle called "natural supernaturalism."[24] Like many of her male contemporaries, including Carlyle himself, this woman who had even as a schoolgirl rejected Christianity grew up doubting traditional Christian pieties. But where Carlyle substituted a belief in the grandest sacraments of nature for his lost faith in the established Church, Dickinson celebrated mysteries that such Victorian sages would have thought "smaller"—the sacraments of the household, the hearth, the garden. And where in his famous *Sartor Resartus (The Tailor Retailored)* Carlyle saw all the natural world as the metaphorical clothing of a mysterious God's cosmic energy, Dickinson in both life and art transformed her own clothing into a metaphor for the energy that moved her own, female mysteries. Thus, although she never yielded to Miss Lyon's evangelical fervor, although she was never born again as a "hopeful" Christian, this skeptical poet was converted, and by a woman teacher, to a religion that parodied and paralled patriarchal Christianity.

An alternate version of the last stanza of Dickinson's tribute to Barrett Browning (593) tells us that when she first "read that Foreign Lady"

> The Days – to Mighty Metres stept –
> The Homeliest – adorned
> As if unto a *Sacrament*
> 'Twere suddenly confirmed –

and then the poet goes on to explain her own transformation further:

> I could not have defined the change –
> Conversion of the Mind
> Like Sanctifying in the Soul –
> Is witnessed – not explained –

Learning from Barrett Browning how to see the sacramental radiance of the ordinary world around her—the "small" world of the household and the garden—this onetime dissenter seems to have been born again as a "wayward nun" dedicated to celebrations that her Father and her minister might find mysterious indeed. " 'Twas a Divine Insanity –" she goes on to say, describing her introduction to Barrett Browning, and adds that she means to keep herself "mad" (since such madness is of course "divinest sense"):

> The Danger to be Sane
> Should I again experience –
> 'Tis Antidote to turn –
>
> To Tomes of solid Witchcraft –
> Magicians be asleep –
> But Magic – hath an Element
> Like Deity – to keep –

Converted to this new religion, she finds that the life that the "Sages" called "small" really has "swelled like Horizons" in her breast, and her days transformed by "Magic," are stepping to "Mighty Metres."

In fact, I would argue that once she had learned the female mysteries of "solid Witchcraft" from Elizabeth Barrett Browning's powerful example, Emily Dickinson became a "wayward nun" (722) who regularly spoke—in life as well as in art—through an elaborate code of domestic objects, a language of flowers and glasses of wine, of pieces of cake and bread and pudding—and of a white dress, a point her Amherst neighbors intuited quite early. If we return to Mabel Todd's description of the "Myth of Amherst," moreover, we can see, now, that Mrs. Todd's observations emphasize not only the mystery and magic but even the *textuality* of the behavior that characterized Dickinson's "life of Allegory." Indeed, beginning with two observations that subtly contradict each other ("She dresses wholly in white, . . . but no one *ever* sees her") the fascinated Mrs. Todd goes on to report gestures that sound more like those of a goddess or a priestess than those of a New England spinster. "Her sister . . . invited me to come & sing . . . & if the performance pleases her, a servant will enter with wine for me, or a flower . . . but just probably the token of approval will not come then, but a few days after, some dainty present will appear for me at twilight. People tell me that the *myth* will hear every note—she will be near, but unseen. . . . *Isn't that like a book?*" [italics mine]. That the "myth" will be near but unseen recalls the schoolgirl working her magic on imaginary figures, transforming an ordinary blackboard into a setting for epic prestidigitation. But the code of wine and flowers or wine and cake suggests the rituals of a strange yet oddly familiar religion. Put together, moreover, these puzzles and miracles that haunted even the more prosaic souls of Amherst are indeed "like a book." In fact, they are part of the book of poems that a supposed person named Emily Dickinson actually wrote.

It should not be surprising, of course, that a woman poet transformed the minutiae of her life into the mysteries of her art. That is, after all, what countless male poets do, though with very different material. More to the point, celebrations of domesticity streamed from the pens of almost all the female novelists and poets who were Dickinson's contemporaries, as Nina Baym shows in her study of nineteenth-century American "Woman's Fiction."[25] Even more than most of these writers, moreover—many of whom were tough, independent professionals and some of whom seem to have propagandized for domesticity without transforming its details into significant metaphors or myths—Dickinson was actually immersed in the transformative mysteries of the household. As one of her relatives explained a few years after her death,

> Emily Dickinson was a past mistress in the art of cookery and housekeeping. She made the desserts for the household dinners; delicious

confections and bread, and when engaged in these duties had her table and pastry board under a window that faced the lawn, whereon she ever had pencil and paper to jot down any pretty thought that came to her, and from which she evolved verses, later.[26]

In fact, a number of Dickinson's poems were written on the backs of recipes, for the mysteries of the kitchen, the view from the kitchen window, and the mysteries of art seem to have been almost inseparable for this writer who confined herself absolutely to the intricate interior of the "Homestead" that was ostensibly her "Father's" but which, through both striking and subtle metamorphoses, she made her own.

I should immediately note, however, that I am not arguing here for a return to the image of Emily Dickinson best represented by John Crowe Ransom's 1956 description of her as "a little home-keeping person" whose life was "a humdrum affair of little distinction."[27] Such a vision of the "Myth of Amherst," or of any other woman poet, implies that the very substance of most female lives is so trivial, so "humdrum," that it could not possibly inspire or energize great art. On the contrary, I am suggesting that for Dickinson the private life of the household was as charged with potential meaning as the public life of politics and philosophy. Or perhaps it was charged with potentially greater meaning. For this ironic "little home-keeping person" placed herself quite consciously in a great tradition of women writers who have scorned patriarchal male definitions of what is important in history and what is not important.

Near the beginning of that tradition, we hear Jane Austen's Catherine Morland speaking in *Northanger Abbey*:

> ... history, real solemn history, I cannot be interested in. ... I read it a little as a duty; but it tells me nothing that does not either vex or weary me. The quarrels of popes and kings, with wars or pestilences in every page; the men all so good for-nothing, and hardly any women at all, it is very tiresome. ... [ch. 14]

At the modern end of the tradition, we hear the voice of Virginia Woolf:

> When one has read no history for a time the sad-coloured volumes are really surprising. That so much energy should have been wasted in the effort to believe in something spectral fills one with pity. Wars and Ministries and legislation—unexampled prosperity and unbridled corruption tumbling the nation headlong to decay—what a strange delusion it all is!—invented presumably by gentlemen in tall hats ... who wished to dignify mankind. Our point of view they ignore entirely: we have never felt the pressure of a single law; our passions and despairs have nothing to do with trade; our virtues and vices flourish under all Governments impartially.[28]

And in between we hear the characteristically compressed comment of Emily Dickinson: " 'George Washington was the Father of his Country' – 'George Who?' That sums all Politics to me –"[29]

Like Austen, who claimed that hers was an art of the miniature, an art that engraved domestic details on a "little bit (two Inches wide) of Ivory,"[30] Dickinson created out of what the "Sages" might call "small" details a mystery-play that questioned the very concept of size. Like Woolf, whose Mrs. Dalloway and Mrs. Ramsay transform the "hum-drum" acts of party-giving, stew-making, knitting, and sewing into rich aesthetic rituals, Dickinson invented a religion of domesticity, a mystery cult in which she herself was a kind of blasphemously female "Word made Flesh" (1651) and the servings of cake and wine she sent to chosen friends were sacramental offerings.[31] But even more than Austen or Woolf the self-consciously female "Myth of Amherst" had a vision of what Muriel Rukeyser has called a "world split open"—a world transformed through the transformation of vision itself.[32] In this, interestingly, she was a prototypical modernist-surrealist as well as a prototypical modern woman poet who followed her great mother Elizabeth Barrett Browning in creating a new way of seeing for all the poetic daughters who have come after her. Another anecdote recounted by one of Dickinson's bemused relatives will help illustrate the kind of distinctively female, proto-modernist surrealism that marked this writer's transformed and trans-formative vision of domestic details. The poet's "little nephew [Ned]," wrote her cousin Clara Newman Turner in 1900,

> boylike had a way of leaving anything superfluous to his immediate needs at Grandma's. After one of these little "Sins of Omission," over came his high-top rubber boots, standing erect and spotless on a silver tray, their tops running over with Emily's flowers. At another time the little overcoat was returned with each velvet pocket pinned down, and a card with "Come in" on one, and "Knock" on the other. The "Come in" proved to be raisins; the "Knock," cracked nuts.[33]

Besides telling us, again, about Dickinson's wit and charm, this story tells us something about her ability to see, "New Englandly," of course, through the ordinariness of things to the seeds of the extraordinary, the roots of difference concealed behind appearance. For if boots can hold flowers and pockets can hide raisins, then it is no wonder that the flesh may be a word and words may be "esoteric sips / Of the communion Wine" (1452)—sacramental signals of mysterious power and energy. It is no wonder, either, that such power is not to be found by questing through distances but instead is lodged "at home," in an ordinary bedroom; no wonder that the priestess of this power once took her niece up to that room and, mimicking locking herself in, "thumb and forefinger closed on an imaginary key," said "with a quick turn of her wrist, 'It's just a turn – and freedom, Matty!' "[34] Going *in* to the ordinary, *in* to the seed, *in* to the flower in the boot, *in* to the flesh in the word and the word in the wine was the central maneuver of all Dickinson's mysteries of transformation, a point that should go far in explaining not only the sometimes puzzling imagery of her life/text but also her sometimes puzzling dislocations of language.

Such dislocations, after all, are really other kinds of transformations, and they come about because as she enters and splits open the common-place Dickinson also necessarily cracks open ordinary usages, revising and reinventing the vocabulary she has inherited from a society that does not share her piercing visions. "They shut me up in Prose," Dickinson tells us punningly in poem 613,

> As when a little Girl
> They put me in the Closet –
> Because they liked me "still" –

But "Still!" she boasts, "Could themself have peeped—"

> And seen my Brain – go round –
> They might as wise have lodged a Bird
> For Treason – in the Pound –
>
> Himself has but to will
> And easy as a Star
> Abolish his Captivity –
> And laugh – No more have I –

To this wayward nun, as to all winged things, walls and fences pose no problems: she frets not at the convent walls of language because she knows she can leap over them any time she pleases, or perhaps, more accurately, she can transform them into windows whenever she wants. A number of phrases from the poems quoted in these pages exemplify such linguistic metamorphoses: "hovering seen through fog," "the Instead – the Pinching fear," even "They shut me up in Prose." All these trans-formations of vocabulary abolish the "Captivity" implicit in ordinary usage, and—importantly—they do this by expanding, rather than annihilating, meaning.[35]

Ultimately, moreover, such expansions of meaning, together with the transformations of vision that energized them, must have led Dickinson from an exploration and enactment of the mysteries of domesticity to related celebrations of the mysteries of nature and of woman's nature. This priestess of the daily, after all, continually meditated upon the

extraordinary possibilities implicit in the ordinary flowerings of the natural world. In her "real" life as the "Myth of Amherst," she created a
conservatory and a herbarium; in the supposed life of her poetry, she saw
through surfaces to the "white foot" (392) of the lily, to the "mystic
green" (24) where "Nicodemus' Mystery / Receives its annual reply"
(140), to the time of "Ecstasy–and Dell" (392) and to the time when
"the Landscape listens" (258). In one of her most astonishing visions of
transformation, too, she recorded the moment when "the Eggs fly off in
Music / From the Maple Keep" (956). For hers was a world of processes
in which everything was always turning into everything else, a world in
which her own, and Nature's, "cocoon" continually tightened, and colors
"teased," and, awakening into metamorphosis, she struggled to take "the
clue Divine" (1099).

That this vision of nature-in-process, together with her transformative
visions of domesticity, eventually brought Dickinson back to a complementary vision of the mystical powers in woman's nature seems inevitable.
It is in the female human body, after all, that the primary transformations
of human nature happen: egg and sperm into embryo, embryo into baby,
blood into milk. (And it is the female bird who produces and nurtures
those musical eggs.) As anthropologists observe, moreover, and as a poet
of domesticity like Dickinson knew perfectly well, it is women who perform the primary transformations of culture: raw into cooked, clay into
pot, reed into basket, fiber into thread, thread into cloth, cloth into dress,
lawless baby into law-abiding child.[36] And it is because of such natural and
cultural transformations, Erich Neumann tells us, that the Great Mother
was worshipped throughout the matriarchal ages he postulates.[37]

Though Dickinson may not have consciously worshipped such a goddess, some glimmering consciousness of that deity's powers must always
have been with her, presiding over *all* the mysteries she served. Two poems
tell us this, the poem from which I take my title and one other. Both are
quite clearly matriarchal prayers, but they emphasize different aspects of
Dickinson's distinctively female answer to traditional Christianity. In the
first, she tells us quite frankly both who she worships and who she is:

> Sweet Mountains – Ye tell Me no lie –
> Never deny Me – Never fly –
> Those same unvarying Eyes
> Turn on Me – when I fail – or feign,
> Or take the Royal names in vain –
> Their far – slow – Violet Gaze –
>
> My Strong Madonnas – Cherish still –
> The Wayward Nun – beneath the Hill –
> Whose service – is to You –

> Her latest Worship – When the Day
> Fades from the Firmament away –
> To lift Her Brows on you –

[722]

In the second, interestingly enough, Dickinson tells us what she will not tell us—as if to remind us that her mysteries are both miracles and puzzles:

> Only a Shrine, but Mine –
> I made the Taper shine –
> Madonna dim, to whom all Feet may come,
> Regard a Nun –
>
> Thou knowest every Woe –
> Needless to tell thee – so –
> But can'st thou do
> The Grace next to it – heal?
> That looks a harder skill to us –
> Still – just as easy, if it be thy Will
> To thee – Grant me –
> Thou knowest, though, so Why tell thee?

[918]

With this last poem, of course, we come full circle back to where we began; we confront once more the mystery of absence, the gap that haunts Dickinson's own account of her life, as well as everybody else's story of it. Now, however, we may be able to see how richly and powerfully this wayward nun transformed that apparent emptiness into a fullness, how the hollow rubber boot bloomed with flowers and the flowers had white feet and the silent eggs suddenly began to sing. Now, too, it may be clear that most of the OED's senses of the word "mystery" have some application to this artist's "life of Allegory." Certainly her fivefold transformations—of romance, renunciation, domesticity, nature, and woman's nature—tell us truths about her own religion while hinting at paradoxical enigmas and riddles; certainly, too, her poetic "witchcraft" involves both esoteric and ordinary arts—the secrets of the poet as well as the skills of the housewife. As she mythologizes her self, moreover, she even transforms her own life into a kind of "miracle-play," a mysterious existence in which, as the Empress of Calvary, she enacts mysteries that parallel those that marked the life of Christ. And didn't she, finally, speak to her communicants both literally and figuratively through "a kind of plum cake"? Sending her famous black cake to her friend Nellie Sweetser in 1883, she wrote "Your sweet beneficence of Bulbs I return as Flowers, with a bit of the swarthy Cake baked only in Domingo."[38] But of course by "Domingo" she meant her own kitchen, where her mysteries of culinary and literary transformation took place side by side.

NOTES

1. Jay Leyda, *The Years and Hours of Emily Dickinson*, 2 vols. (New Haven: Yale University Press, 1960), vol. 2, p. 357.

2. See T. W. Higginson to ED, in *The Letters of Emily Dickinson*, 3 vols., ed. Thomas H. Johnson (Cambridge: Harvard University Press, 1958), vol. 2, p. 461: "I have the greatest desire to see you, always feeling that perhaps if I could once take you by the hand I might be something to you; but till then you only enshroud yourself in this fiery mist & I cannot reach you, but only rejoice in the rare sparkles of light."

3. For a newspaper story about a real "New England Nun" whose career would have been known to Dickinson, see Leyda, vol. 1, p. 148. For a fictionalized account of a "New England Nun" that mythologizes female domesticity in a way partly (though not wholly) comparable to Dickinson's own, see Mary E. Wilkins Freeman, "A New England Nun," in *A New England Nun and Other Stories* (New York: Harper & Row, 1891).

4. Leyda, vol. 2, p. 376.

5. Ibid., p. 151.

6. Ibid.

7. *The Boston Cooking-School Magazine*, June–July 1906.

8. Quoted by James Reeves in an *Introduction to the Selected Poems of Emily Dickinson* reprinted in *Emily Dickinson: A Collection of Critical Essays*, ed. Richard B. Sewall (Englewood Cliffs, N.J.: Prentice-Hall, 1963), p. 119.

9. John Keats, to George and Georgiana Keats, Friday, Feb. 18, 1819.

10. Ibid.

11. Leyda, vol. 1, p. 131.

12. Ibid., p. 135.

13. *Letters*, vol. 2, p. 460.

14. "Though I than He – may longer live / He longer must – than I – / For I have but the power to kill / Without – the power to die –"

15. *Letters*, vol. 2, p. 404.

16. Adrienne Rich, "Vesuvius at Home: The Power of Emily Dickinson," in *Shakespeare's Sisters: Feminist Essays on Women Poets*, ed. Sandra M. Gilbert and Susan Gubar (Bloomington: Indiana University Press, 1979).

17. See poem 285: ". . . Without the Snow's Tableau/Winter, were lie – to me – / Because I see – New Englandly. . . ."

18. See Sandra M. Gilbert and Susan Gubar, *The Madwoman in the Attic: The Woman Writer and the Nineteenth-Century Literary Imagination* (New Haven: Yale University Press, 1979), pp. 613-21.

19. *Letters*, vol. 2, p. 412.

20. See Gilbert and Gubar, *The Madwoman*, pp. 613-21.

21. For Mabel Todd on Dickinson's similarity to "Miss Haversham" [sic], see Leyda, vol. 2, p. 377.

22. See Elizabeth Barrett Browning, *Aurora Leigh*, in *The Poetical Works of Elizabeth Barrett Browning* (New York: Crowell, 1891), pp. 21, 28, 149.

23. Nancy Rexford, costume curator at the Northampton Historical Society, has assured me that the white Dickinson dress at the Amherst Homestead is a comparatively "ordinary" cotton day dress—what we would now, perhaps, call a "house dress" or at least a dress designed for casual wear—fashioned in the style of the 70s or 80s, the period when Dickinson would have worn it regularly. She also notes, however, that it was not at that time at all "ordinary" for such a garment to be made in *white* unless it was a child's dress or a summer costume designed for wearing at the seaside (which Dickinson's plainly was not).

24. See Carlyle, *Sartor Resartus*, book 2, chapter 8, "Natural Supernaturalism." Carlyle's picture, incidentally, was one of three portraits that hung on ED's bedroom wall. The other two were of Eliot and Barrett Browning.

25. Nina Baym, *Woman's Fiction* (Ithaca: Cornell University Press, 1978).

26. Leyda, vol. 2, p. 482.

27. "Emily Dickinson: A Poet Restored," in *Emily Dickinson*, ed. Sewall, p. 89.

28. Virginia Woolf, "Modes and Manners of the Nineteenth Century," in *Books and Portraits* (London: The Hogarth Press, 1977), p. 23.

29. To Mrs. J. G. Holland, 1884; *Letters*, vol. 3, p. 849.

30. *Jane Austen's Letters to Her Sister Cassandra and Others*, ed. R. W. Chapman, 2d ed. (London: Oxford University Press, 1952), pp. 468-69.

31. For a related, but differently designed, discussion of "A Word made Flesh" and its implications for Dickinson's own sense of herself as somehow divine, see Margaret Homans, *Women Writers and Poetic Identity* (Princeton: Princeton University Press, 1980), pp. 212-14.

32. See Muriel Rukeyser, "Käthe Kollwitz" ("What would happen if one woman told the truth about her life? / The world would split open") in Rukeyser, *The Speed of Darkness* (New York: Random House, 1968).

33. Leyda, vol. 2, p. 481.

34. Ibid., p. 483.

35. Homans, analyzing this phenomenon, argues differently (but to the same end) that Dickinson deliberately exploits language's potential for ambiguity, duplicity, and fictiveness (*Women Writers and Poetic Identity*, pp. 165-214 passim).

36. See, for instance, Sherry Ortner, "Is Female to Male as Nature Is to Culture?" in *Woman, Culture, and Society*, ed. Michelle Zimbalist Rosaldo and Louise Lamphère (Stanford: Stanford University Press, 1974).

37. Erich Neumann, *The Great Mother* (Princeton: Princeton University Press, 1955).

38. *Letters*, vol. 3, p. 783.

BARBARA ANTONINA
CLARKE MOSSBERG **III**

Emily Dickinson's Nursery Rhymes

EMILY DICKINSON MAY NOT have written for the "nursery," but she wrote about the nursery, and in fact she dwelt in the nursery in both symbolic and literal ways throughout her creative life. She was a *career child*. "How to grow up I don't know," she wrote. "I wish we always were children."[1] When she is grown, she has one prayer: that she be a child.[2] She never ceased to be preoccupied about her parents, even after they died. She stayed at home all her life, nursing her girlish habits, dress, and obsessions. And in her letters and poetry, she stayed at home as well.[3] Maintaining the child's point of view, she ambled through a stern Puritan-Calvinist intellectual and social Victoriana, a sly goose girl whose presence transformed the terrain into the land of Mother Goose, no less arbitrary or hard, but one in which the child's voice and experience could be heard. Why did an adult Emily Dickinson prefer this terrain? Being a "madwoman in the attic"[4] is one thing. But a little girl in the nursery? What is she up to, with her spools, and dolls? If we turn to children's literature, it becomes clearer why working within this genre is so useful and indeed necessary for Dickinson's psychology as a poet.

Children's literature differs from adult literature only in perspective, a function of the child's smaller size, lesser ability to do and comprehend, and constant growth. As Bruno Bettelheim has pointed out about fairy tales,[5] children's literature addresses children's psychological and physical realities and in the process enables children to cope with them. The major issues of literature—freedom, conflict, self-reliance, and growth—have great import to children, who naturally identify with characters coping with adversity, struggling to gain independence, triumphing over larger and more powerful forces, and feeling love and ambivalence. In this sense all literature is children's literature, but the latter stresses the child's sense of being small and inferior in the universe, lacking physical, mental, and social power, being dependent, and feeling—and fighting against being—

45

insignificant, impotent, different, alien, confined, and lonely. Universal fears acquire greater emphasis when they are a function of children's dependence and physical and emotional needs. Thus in children's literature we see as dominant themes the fears of abandonment, rejection, and persecution. The theme of security is manifested most often in plots about the loss and gain of parental love or the making of a marital match that will insure one's social, financial, and emotional security (such as Snow White or Cinderella). Fantasies of nurture, being loved "most of all," acquiring the most wealth or land (it has to be the "most"), or achieving special distinction or even divine notice, derive from children's earliest needs. Dreams of acquiring or exercising independence and autonomy derive from a later childhood stage, when "locomotive" skills are being developed.[6] Psychologists tell us this is a time of great ambivalence on both children's and parents' parts, and hence the glee we see in nursery rhymes:

> I skipped over water
> I danced over sea
> And all the birds in the air
> Couldn't catch me
>
> [from "I had a little nut tree"]

Here the image of freedom without ambivalence, a world without limit or law, is consoling to those whose world is bound by physical inabilities and a chorus of No's.

In general, fantasies in children's literature center around self-esteem: the child wants to be powerful and valued, to possess the ability to overcome larger forces through mental faculties—by using wit, magic, or language (often the same thing); to achieve because he or she is smaller and considered useless, or has what are considered to be liabilities. In "Jack and the Beanstalk," for example, Jack is considered gullible and dull and a useless fool by his mother. When he manages to acquire so-called "magic seeds," instead of money, he is sent to bed without dinner. But sure enough, his seeds are magical. They produce a beanstalk so large it grows to the sky. The first aspect of this fantasy, then, is vindication: child knows best. The second aspect centers around his ability and desire to climb the stalk, exercising and in fact establishing his autonomy, leaving the house of his mother to enter a larger world. Leaving aside the Freudian implications of a "stalk" growing during the night, and the boy climbing it to encounter and overcome the giant ogre, with the aid of the ogre's wife who prefers him to her husband, the story addresses any sense of inadequacy by having the fantasy rest on his small size, which is essential to success. The happy ending is not that Jack escape the ogre, or gains the giant's wealth, and thus can live happily ever after with a princess. No: he has proven that his mother was wrong to have underestimated him.

Now she will esteem him. Much of children's literature deals with children or unfavored creatures (rodents, insects) outsmarting adults or larger creatures who are revealed as fools, to children's delight and consolation. Always, the children or small creatures are able to outwit grown-ups and giants because of unique abilities that are integrally tied up with their small size.

Looking at Emily Dickinson's poetry in this light, we can see the same kind of patterns, linked to her chronicles of a little girl, an Alice of Amherst. Her creation and obsessive use of the little girl persona appears to be a brilliant but inevitable metaphor for her experience as a woman poet in her culture, reflecting and resolving her "small size"—the lack of society's esteem for and encouragement of her mental abilities. Of course we could say that this image interferes with the reader's perception of Dickinson's mature poetic gifts. A childish image has been imposed on Dickinson, perhaps because in evoking the little girl persona she calls into play past cultural stereotypes about women. She appears so "female" in her themes and images and style, so little and conscribed, somehow, on the page, in her worldly experience, in her world vision, or in our picture of her—that little face, peering somberly out of the grayness. This image has in fact been cherished by those who use it as a rationale to "protect" her (usually from feminist or psychological critics),[7] or to put her metaphorically on the children's shelf, ways to avoid taking seriously what she says about her experience and conflicts as a female poet in her culture. Seeing her as a child could be a way to neutralize her, neuter her, keep her well-behaved, as if against her will—to shut her up.

Certainly Dickinson herself conceptualized being treated like a child as a form of punishment or reprisal:

> They shut me up in Prose –
> As when a little Girl
> They put me in the Closet –
> Because they liked me "still" –

However, she mocks the effort of a society which still attempts to control, if not negate, her adult liberating self-expression:

> Still! Could themself have peeped –
> And seen my Brain – go round –
> They might as wise have lodged a Bird
> For Treason – in the Pound –

[613]

Dickinson equates the little girl's punishment and repression (symbolized by the closet) with the "prose" she is expected to live and write as an adult woman. In her letters, Dickinson dissociates herself from her family by virtue of her poetic sensibility; she tells her correspondents that her father disdains poetry in favor of the Bible, "real life," and "Prose."[8] She and Susan Gilbert are the "only poets" in a world where everyone else is "prose."[9] "Prose," then, is Dickinson's term for society's valuing, and repressive enforcement, of conformity; poetry is that which is free from the limiting rules and restrictions of conventional behavior—conceptually the same rules she breaks when she speaks her mind. "Poetry" is not only what she says, and the way she says it, but the fact that she says it at all: virtuous women are supposed to be "still," like children. Therefore Dickinson has ambivalence about being considered a little girl.

But Dickinson's sense that society equates an accomplished female poet with an unruly little girl provides a rationale for pursuing the logic and meaning of her cultivation of the image of the child even at the risk of being dismissed as a little girl herself. If she qualifies as a Mother Goose, wryly commenting on and chronicling childhood, she is also the wolf in "grandmother's" clothing, using the nursery as headquarters for her potshots at a patriarchal Yankee culture; it is a war, waged by an adult and poetically mature Dickinson, a "Brief Campaign of Sting and Sweet" (159). That is, an adult uses the child persona to affect a certain kind of subversiveness—a safe vantage from which to criticize and fend off an encroaching absurd world in which she as a female, even an adult female, has no power or important role. Feigning the child's innocence allows to her indulge in various heresies with impunity. This is especially evident in the poems where she confronts and attacks institutional religion, using a pose of childish inquiry as a shield. In "What is Paradise" (215) Dickinson simply wants to know: do they wear new shoes there; will she be scolded for being tired or cross; will she get lost? The innocently curious child does not know better. Can she help it if she cannot imagine *not* feeling tired or cross? This is an indictment of her "childish" life on earth. Similarly, in poem 413 she disparages heaven with a perversity that is startlingly accurate for its childlikeness: "I don't like Paradise." Such a candid conclusion could only be expressed by the innocent child without the adult's wisdom, pragmatism, fear—or knowledge of when to be quiet:

> I never felt at Home – Below –
> And in the Handsome Skies
> I shall not feel at Home – I know –
> I don't like Paradise –
>
> Because it's Sunday – all the time –
> And Recess – never comes –
> And Eden'll be so lonesome
> Bright Wednesday Afternoons –

> If God could make a visit –
> Or ever took a Nap –
> So not to see us – but they say
> Himself – a Telescope
>
> Perennial beholds us –
> Myself would run away
> From Him – and Holy Ghost – and All –
> But there's the "Judgment Day!"

The voice of the child in this poem has several implications. The persona's whole life has been experienced as the alienated schoolchild; she cannot imagine that she will be any more "at home" in a place which will only make permanent her sense of loneliness. On earth, time is punctuated by "thou shalt nots." Heaven must also be a stifling twenty-four-hour-a-day Sunday school. Thus the sulky child enters the schoolroom in the sky knowing it all, with the sulky pronouncement that she does not "like" it. Since there is no "recess," her only hope is that God might "make a visit" or at least take a nap to give her some respite from her enforced good behavior. But the eye trained on her never blinks. She squats under the gaze of a telescope which views her faults up close and magnifies them. How like the child to want to "run away" from the whole works, and how like the subversive woman, to make the depressing assumption that heaven holds no more freedom than on earth, and thus provide a rationale for not wanting to go there, and therefore to not want to behave on earth in a manner that will get her there.

The child's viewpoint here is cheekily humorous, serving to deflect any reprisals for such unorthodox but "perfectly natural" thoughts. Such subversive innocence is typical in Dickinson's poems about God ("Is Heaven a Physician? / They say that He can heal – / But Medicine Posthumous / Is unavailable – . . ." [1270]). God is often presented as a Jack and Beanstalk ogre, or worse, a demystified Wizard of Oz who is never there when she needs him or comes to call (564). He is harmless, the recipient of casual disrespect, a "docile Gentleman" (1487), "our Old Neighbor" (623); similarly, Eden is "that old-fashioned House" (1657), and Paradise is "that old mansion." She herself is the family little angel, unjustly kept out of heaven—as if she wanted to go there:

> Why – do they shut Me out of Heaven?
> Did I sing – too loud?
> But – I can say a little "Minor"
> Timid as a Bird!
>
> Wouldn't the Angels try me –
> Just – once – more –

Just – see – if I troubled them –
But don't – shut the door!

Oh, if I – were the Gentleman
In the "White Robe," –
And they – were the little Hand – that knocked –
Could – I – forbid?

[248]

Here and in other poems we see the whine of the disobedient child who
has been punished: Pleeeeeease—I'll never do it again—Give me another
chance. It is significant that the child immediately assumes that her being
"shut out" is a consequence of her failure to "shut up" or at least to be
"still." The first thought that occurs to her is "Did I sing – too loud?" Has
she been too bold, too aggressive, too unladylike—in the use of her *voice*?

Dickinson's persona's apparent eagerness to please by offering to adopt
those traits of timidity and restraint to which women and little girls must
adhere is similar to her response to her brother Austin when he also re-
proved her for being "too loud" in her use of her literary voice. Austin
became annoyed when Dickinson exulted in her ability to make metaphors, flaunting even in a self-parodic way her mastery of language. In her
reply to him, Dickinson demonstrated that she knew the terms by which
he was to be obliged: "I'll be a little ninny, a little pussy catty, a little Red
Riding Hood."[10] But offering to be "little" infers that such behavior is not
natural to *her*; letting him know that any form of obedience she enacts to
please him is only a skillful and cooperative pose in a subtle way to rebel
from those standards which demand her compliances. What is important
about "Why – do they shut Me out of Heaven?" is Dickinson's assumption that timidity and being "little" are requisites for women to go to
heaven. The word "minor" along with the diminutive "little" is significant, for besides the allusion to singing, it is a play with the concept of
"major," in the sense of importance. Dickinson offers to stifle her voice, to
speak in Prose. It is appropriate that she should point our attention to her
"little" hand, emphasizing the childish position in which she has been put.
In showing us her persona as pathetically pleading for mercy, she implies
that only a brute could ignore her. But God is such a brute:

Of Course – I prayed –
And did God Care?
He cared as much as on the Air
A Bird – had stamped her foot –
And cried "Give Me" –

[376]

The image of the bird stamping her foot upon the air suggests the childish tantrum, all the more pathetic because it is so ineffective.

But in fact, the persona's frustrated behavior reveals her more as a bratty younger sister who seeks to gain importance for herself by tattling, than as an object for pity. God is exposed in the poetry as a parent who cannot cope; humanity is a child whose needs constantly defeat him. He is reduced to a "jealous playmate" who is no fun (1719); it is as a pouting, petty, selfish child that he makes people die. Sometimes God permits an "industrious angel" to play in the afternoon (231), but heaven is more often either completely inaccessible or an oppressive schoolroom in the sky (193) where the persona is an errant pupil to whom the cause of her earthly anguish is being explained or one who fears a lordly headmaster will punish her for being "homesick" or "cross." These latter feeling are particularly ludicrous to apply to heaven, for if she is homesick it implies that she is being held in heaven against her will, which of course contradicts the very definition of heaven and paradise. The notion of being "cross" in heaven implies that the persona is so incorrigibly recalcitrant that even paradise cannot please her. Interestingly enough, a variant for her term "homesick" is "hungry"; even in heaven she is not nurtured. Dickinson's "Father" in heaven is an archetypal Yankee in this regard. Calling God a "thrifty Deity" (724), Dickinson shows him being "so economical" that he is cruel:

> His Table's spread too high for Us –
> Unless We dine on tiptoe –
> Crumbs – fit such little mouths –
> Cherries – suit Robins –
>
> [690]

Again, we see the tragicomic image of powerlessness—a table at which children cannot eat and food that is inappropriate for children. Children are dependent upon a Parent who is either sadistic or completely incompetent.

Dickinson's viewpoint makes the Bible itself a kind of children's literature, where humanity is a guilty child in the universe to an omnipotent Father. The Garden of Eden is a story of separation from a parental God; it is a parable of what psychologists call "separation anxiety," wherein the child's becoming an autonomous person results in the sense of having to forfeit the security and warmth of the parents' love and protection. Certainly Dickinson presents herself as ambivalent about her own autonomy as a poet; she relates her writing of poetry to Eve's disobedience in the garden, Eve's wicked hunger for knowledge and power and glory. Her exile, in a sense, is a weaning from paradise—a child's punishment, as in "Why do they shut Me out of Heaven?" (248). In scores of poems Dickinson shows herself being cut off from nurture or banished (as in poems 1657, 1119, and 256) for some unnamed transgression that we infer has to do with her poetic aspirations (as in "Did I sing – too loud?"). In her letters as well as her poetry, Dickinson makes her identification with Eve explicit, asking "and why am I not Eve?" and calling herself "Mrs. Adam."[11] In an early Valentine poem, she writes,

> Put down the apple, Adam,
> And come away from me,
> So shalt thou have a *pippin*
> From off my father's tree!
>
> [3]

To lure Adam, she dispenses her *father's* property, a notion she expands in "Over the Fence" (251), where she is a childish Eve confronting forbidden fruit.

> Over the fence –
> Strawberries – grow –
> Over the fence –
> I could climb – if I tried, I know –
> Berries are nice!
>
> But – if I stained my Apron –
> God would certainly scold!
> Oh, dear, – I guess if He were a Boy –
> He'd – climb – if He could!

Although the backdrop and tone of the poem are light, and Dickinson indulges in some poetic foot-shuffling ("Oh, dear," "I guess," "I know"), the issues the poem presents are serious and reflect Dickinson's deepest concerns. She describes a moral dilemma wherein she is torn between her desire for berries, or whatever illicit "forbidden fruit" they represent to her, and her sense that going "over the fence" is a disobedience to God. What is especially interesting about this poem is that the issue at stake is not her object of desire, but the "fence" itself. Is the little girl to forswear the Strawberry Symbolic, or what is required to obtain the berries (going over the fence)—or what is required to get these berries if one is a *girl*? It ensues that the real obstacle is not the fence itself; that, the speaker tells us, she is perfectly capable of climbing. The real "fence" is that she is not supposed to "climb"—a particularly significant choice of words when it is applied to women's proper behavior. Presumably, if the berries grew on her side of the fence there would be no problem.

As Dickinson wants the reader to understand it, then, she is separated from berries not by an innate inability on her part, but by arbitrary restrictions on female social behavior. That these restrictions are imposed only on her sex is made explicitly clear in the fact that boys can climb with impunity while girls have a built-in Apron which prevents them from climbing fences—not that it gets in the way but that it records tell-tale "stains." It is the wearing of the Apron, then that serves to keep the berries from the little girl—that, and the need for Aprons to be kept clean. We could say that the little girl should simply take off her apron to avoid detection, but the point seems to be that the Apron is a symbol of feminity and cannot be discarded.

The poem can be read as an allegory of Christian disobedience, with its sexual metaphors implied by apron, berries, stains, and climbing fences. The little girl is certain she will be scolded if she does get that forbidden fruit. However, she herself does not consider going "over the fence" to be inherently immoral; any second thoughts revolve around the inevitability of getting caught and stained—literally or metaphorically. She knows that if God were to judge her as a boy, like himself, he would wink at her transgression. God has a double standard for boys and girls. Therefore the poem can also be read, slight though it may appear, as a classic feminist argument against the injunctions against a woman's success. She has equal ability to climb fences, but her only recourse seems to be to posit a dig at the "Father," a doubt that he *could* climb the fence. Only ability, not fear of reprisal, could prevent him; going over the fence is a natural desire for "boys" and for girls. It is the injunction that girls must be "clean" that makes the concept of sin a relative one that favors boys getting all the berries. As long as there are standards for Aprons, girls cannot be adventurous and free. They might as well be shut up in the closet.

Of course, the little girl is not afraid of God's scolding, a form of punishment that rangs somewhere along with sending society to bed without its dinner. Such an image is a further inroad on God's prestige. God is often judged, and found lacking, from a child's standard. Dickinson sees what happened to Moses as a case of God letting him see Canaan "As Boy – should deal with lesser Boy / To prove ability" (597). Here is God, a macho figure flexing the spiritual biceps, beating the divine chest, a playground bully, full of childish cruelty, who literally *lords* it over the less powerful. Dickinson is explicitly critical of such behavior; in the poem about Moses she says, "It always felt to me – a wrong" how he is treated by God. She would not have treated him so, if she were God. We have seen this technique before, when Dickinson imagines herself in God's position only to show how she would do a better job, as a child. It is particularly ironic that God is found lacking by a child's standards.

Similarly, Dickinson thinks Noah was not "credited" (403). And in poem 1545 Dickinson reduces men to boys interacting with God; if the Bible were written, not by "faded men" but by a "warbling Teller" (such as herself?),

> All the Boys would come –
> Orpheus' Sermon captivated –
> It did not condemn –

She often criticizes the way religion is presented as too harsh and punitive. How can an "antique volume" persuade? As for herself, she identifies with John of Revelations, or the small David, the "troubadour" (1545), the one who can overcome and outwit an evil giant with her weapon—her use of language:

> I took my Power in my Hand –
> And went against the World –
> 'Twas not so much as David – had –
> But – I – was twice as bold –
>
> I aimed my Pebble – by Myself
> Was all the one that fell –
> Was it Goliath – was too large –
> Or was myself – too small?

[540]

Emily Dickinson is aware that in writing her poetry she is fighting "the world," but if she "falls" in this poem, in many others she "triumphs" —"triumph" is a key word for her—and wears the "crown," enjoys the "power and glory," wins immortality, is a royal or divine bride, and merits the Son's status at God's side. She has no problem with re-enacting the Bible in New England, using a wryly villainous and naive typology. What we must remember is that Dickinson addresses God in the terminology and ideology provided by the church, whether she is a "mouse" pleading to "Papa above" (61) for protection from a cat, or any angry little girl dealing with a "disappointing" Father who does not recognize her true abilities; identifying with the "Son" allows her to rationalize her poor treatment and neglect, for it is only a temporary martyrdom, a sign of her election and favor. But if she once asks of Jesus, "It's your little 'John'! / Don't you know – me?" (497), implying that she is the one who has been given the "revelations" to dispense, she also shows herself rejecting any obedient approach to the savior because it does not seem appropriate to the *child*. "I prayed at first, a little girl / Because they told me to," she says (576), but when she imagines God looking at her

> . . . Childish eye
> Fixed full, and steady on his own
> In Childish honesty –

she stops. She does not want to impose on him as a lowly child. It is ironic that her rejection of institutionalized religion and her refusal to become "born again" is cast in terms of religion's failure to persuade her as a child.

In nursery rhymes and other children's poetry and stories, the word "little" is used the way oregano is used in Italian cooking—it defines the genre. Thus we see little Johnny who wants to play, little pony, little Miss Muffet, little hen, little Johnny Green, little Tommy Stout, little Jack Horner, little Tom Tinker, little Boy Blue, little dog who laughed to see such a sport, little Tommy Tucker, and so on; a variant for little is "poor" or "simple" (as in poor Robin, Simple Simon). The poetry addresses the child's physical self-image. Similarly, Dickinson uses the word "little" in 226 poems and frequently uses the words "slight," "low," and "small." Emily Dickinson's dwelling on her small size does not reflect her physical or psychological reality, so much as her conscious *choice* to be "little," to play along with society's view of her insignificance and turn it to her own advantage. She stresses her "little" existence on earth:

> I was a Phoebe – nothing more –
> A Phoebe – nothing less –
> The little note the others dropt
> I fitted into place –
>
> I dwelt too low that any seek –
> Too shy, that any blame –
> A Phoebe makes a little print
> Upon the Floors of Fame –

[1009]

*   *   *   *   *

> I was the slightest in the House –
> I took the smallest Room –
> At night, my little Lamp, and Book –
> And one Geranium –
>
> So stationed I could catch the Mint
> That never ceased to fall –
> And just my Basket –
> Let me think – I'm sure
> That this was all –
>
> I never spoke – unless addressed –
> And then, 'twas brief and low –
> I could not bear to live – aloud –
> The Racket shamed me so –

And if it had not been so far –
And any one I knew
Were going – I had often thought
How noteless – I could die –

[486]

Even in her letters, Dickinson seems obsessed with her small image, perpetuating it. To Thomas Wentworth Higginson, whom she had never met, she described herself as "small like the wren."[12] Why should she do this when she was so offended at her brother's asking her for a "simpler style" in her letters? We remember that she was stung, and retorted that thereafter she would not only "be as simple as you please, the simplest sort of simple" in her literary style, but she would be "a little ninny, a little pussy catty, a little Red Riding Hood." Here she is bitter and ironic about his failure to recognize or encourage her poetic abilities, and her use of "little" and her adoption of a childish persona are a rebuke chastising what she interprets as a male insistence that she not overstep herself in her literary ambitions. Her response to Higginson, seen in this light, perhaps can make sense if we understand that she is presenting herself as an appealing female so that he will help her as a poet; she does not want to antagonize him as she did her brother, for Higginson is "perfectly powerful" to help her in her career. The little-girl persona thus is an integral part of Dickinson's aesthetic strategy. In "I was a Phoebe – nothing more," she is giving a "poor little me" routine, yes, but she is also slyly showing her "difference" from the rest of society and her ability to make do with her appointed "size." She can use the "little note" that others drop. Her voice, her words, her poetry are a function of her birdlike small size, a size which enables her to take advantage of a literary feast to which she has not been invited. She is literally keeping a low profile in her quest for immortality lest she "disturb the universe"—or at least her brother or "Father."

This may be why in "I was the slightest in the House" we see her ultra-modest lifestyle (the smallest room, her little lamp, only one geranium, speaking "brief and low") as a way of being "timid," "minor," or "still," and a way of catching the "Mint/That never ceased to fall." It is by being small or affecting a small size that she wins the wealth or poetic laurel wreath. Emily Dickinson's muse makes her live as Cinderella, low in the ashes, but it is in order to attract the pity of the fairy godmother muse. Her poems of a puritan-style adversity, in which she uses the child or other lowly and apparently ill-favored creatures as points of comparison to stress just how "low" and "small" her lot is, are disguised arrogance (just because Cinderella lives so "low" does not mean she is not the most beautiful, and her sorrow is that her beauty is unrecognized because she is forced to "cover up" her superiority). In "It would have starved a Gnat/

To live so small as I" (612), we can see how her being treated as "small" is her evidence of "election." Similarly:

> God gave a Loaf to every Bird –
> But just a Crumb – to Me –
> I dare not eat it – tho' I starve –
> My poignant luxury –
>
> To own it – touch it –
> Prove the feat – that made the Pellet mine –
> Tooo happy – for my Sparrow's chance –
> For Ampler Coveting –
>
> It might be Famine – all around –
> I could not miss an Ear –
> Such Plenty smiles upon my Board –
> My Garner shows so fair –
>
> I wonder how the Rich – may feel –
> An Indiaman – an Earl –
> I deem that I – with but a Crumb –
> Am Sovereign of them all –

[791]

This could be read as an extremely sarcastic poem, revengeful in intent, especially in the ecstasy she shows about deserving the "Pellet," the symbol of her deprivation and persecution. But in her "Cinderella complex" she defines herself as superior *because* of the neglect and injustice she experiences; in fact, being singled out for special attention reassures her. In a typical fairy-tale happy ending, she is "Sovereign of them all."

Nature and animals figure in children's literature, frequently as allies or protagonists, and metaphors for children. The creatures most often represented are those which are low on the animal hierarchy in terms of power, trainability, and domestic use to adults—such as insects, mice, and birds. Then the fantasy is compounded when they are revealed actually to possess the *most* intelligence in their dealings with an adversary world; they can take care of themselves—and usually others as well. Dickinson's snake, spider, and cocoon each are related images of her poetic identity. Her identification with birds has a similar significance. They are small ("like the wren" or phoebe). But they also "sing," a word of hallowed import to Dickinson, for singing is the unrestrained use of the voice, her metaphor for her poetry. Birds also fly and thus symbolize freedom, her escape from confinement. They also subsist on little food (in Dickinson's vision) and love. In other words, birds are survivors; they know a "lonesome glee"

(774) and they triumph (1265, for example). In "They shut me up in Prose" (613) Dickinson compares herself to a bird who has "but to will"

> And easy as a Star
> Abolish his Captivity –
> And laugh – No more have I –

Small size is the key to freedom. Appropriately, then, Dickinson expresses her determination to write poetry through the self-image of the irrepressible bird: "I shall keep singing!/With my Redbreast – /And my rhymes –" (250).

But in terms of power, Dickinson can also describe herself as smaller than the smallest creature, as one who inspires no *deus ex machina* to save her at the last minute:

> It would have starved a Gnat –
> To live so small as I –
> And yet I was a living Child –
> With Food's necessity
>
> Upon me – like a Claw
> I could not more remove
> Than I could coax a Leech away –
> Or make a Dragon – move –
>
> Nor like the Gnat – had I –
> The privilege to fly
> And seek a Dinner for myself –
> How mightier He – than I –
>
> Nor like Himself – the Art
> Upon the Window Pane
> To gad my little Being out –
> And not begin – again –

[612]

In images designed to emphasize the absurdity of her predicament, Dickinson presents herself at the mercy of a sinister lone Claw, presumably attached to some crablike or feathered or hairy beast. The effort to remove the claw or leech by "coaxing" seems particularly ludicrous, if not tragic, because it seems so futile, just as the effort to persuade an intractable dragon to go away stresses our sense of the childlike smallness and innocence of the persona, convincing us of her inability to deal with the larger, monstrous forces in her life. (And yet, was not "coaxing" often women's only recourse in dealing with a physically and politically more powerful male?)

Dickinson contrasts the nightmare quality of this child's predicament with the actual needs of a "living child" who is too weak even to cast her life away like a gnat. Her "hunger" here seems to be a consequence of powerlessness. She cannot command food, nor can she coax or merit reprieve from those responsible for her needs. Thus the tiny gnat is mightier than she, because at least he can escape the house, find his own dinner, or kill himself upon the pane. Whereas she, a "child," has neither the "privilege" nor the ability to provide for herself.

Dickinson's use of hunger as a metaphor for powerlessness is another means by which we can identify her childlike persona. Vivian Pollak has linked her metaphoric starvation to her attempt to ward off a "full" woman's body—her emaciated figure is the "stunted" child's.[13] But not letting herself grow is not only a way to metaphorically stave off a feminine fate. Hunger itself is at the center of her creative consciousness, constituting Dickinson's dominant metaphor for herself as the powerless, unloved, and angry child. The poems show that hunger and anger are analogous states for the dependent child, particularly when the hunger is a result of parental withholding. Thus we see "I had been hungry, all the years" (579) or " 'I want' – it pleaded – All its life –" (731). Like Hansel and Gretel, she is left to provide for herself:

> Deprived of other Banquet,
> I entertained Myself –
> At first – a scant nutrition –
> An insufficient Loaf –
>
> [773]

But gradually her own "food" attains "so esteemed a size" that it "almost suffices." She is able to leave a "berry" for "charity," like the robin who also experiences "famine." It is because she is so small, perhaps, that she is able to subsist on so little.

Emily Dickinson's poems about food, or more properly, starving, clarify the meaning of her little-girl person for her aesthetics. The necessity of eating is perceived by Dickinson as essentially tragic, for it makes the dependent child vulnerable to unreliable, non-existent, or punitive parents. Her poems about hunger say that she has not been nurtured in the way she needs; they are a means to criticize those responsible for nurturing her. But they are also fairy tales, which often begin with the statement (as in "Hansel and Gretel") that the parents, for whatever reason, can no longer feed their children. Thus the childen are "sent out into the world" to feed themselves or find their own fortune. Being evicted from home forces children to rely on their own wits, and leads to their growth and happy ending. Dickinson's hunger has the same function in her "weaning" poems: she is forced to "entertain" herself or to feed herself—with her own words. Thus hunger is actually necessary for her poetic growth and happy ending as an immortal poet.

But hunger is a more complex image in Dickinson's aesthetics, for Dickinson uses it as a means to characterize her relationship with her parents. In the power politics of mealtime, the child can triumph in one perverse way: by saying "no," clamping the lips, turning the cheek. It is the child's only real way of asserting an independence and individuality or controlling his or her own experience. If Dickinson does not feel she has much authority or power in her culture, she at least can say "no" to the demands her culture makes upon her and women in general. Thus we see Dickinson winning a freedom of sorts for herself by not joining sewing societies, music groups, or church groups, by not becoming "born again," by not getting married, by not leaving home. Saying "no" to a conventional life as a woman necessarily keeps Dickinson in a kind of childhood; childhood in this sense is not only a metaphor for confinement and repression, but also a place of retreat from the world's limiting expectations for women. "No" is for Dickinson "the wildest word we consign to Language" because it makes for possibility. Dickinson's child persona is in large measure a crucial aspect of her systematic refusals to become bound in a conventional woman's life.

Thus in her hunger poems, Dickinson says "no" to food—not just to maternal forms of nurture, which food ofen represents, but to anything that is available for her to take. The food she is not given, and in fact refuses to eat, is what distinguishes her from the rest of humanity: her Cinderella complex—the idea that the small, weak, powerless, neglected, persecuted will inherit the earth. This is why Dickinson takes care to establish that she takes the smallest room, lives smaller than a gnat, reads by a little lamp: it is not only a feint of modesty required of little girls and poetesses, but a sign of her superiority. It is a strewing of ashes on her face before the footman comes with the slipper to reveal her as the rightful Queen.

That Dickinson's hunger or small stature is deliberately cultivated or assumed by her as an aesthetic strategy is apparent in her hunger poems. Hunger is intrinsic to her sense of self-esteem, as we see in "I had been hungry, all the Years" (579) and "It was given to me by the Gods" (454). In both poems, the persona boasts of her "difference," established when she is starved. She refuses to eat ever after, viewing her hunger as a cherished sign of her election. Eating makes her sick in poem 579 because it makes her "common"; in poem 454, her deprivation is established "when I was a little girl . . . new – and small." While Dickinson does not specify what "it" is, "it" distinguishes her from the crowd and takes the visible shape of deprivation or poverty:

> I kept it in my Hand –
> I never put it down –
> I did not dare to eat – or sleep –
> For fear it would be gone –
> I heard such words as "Rich" –
> When hurrying to school –
> From lips at Corners of the Streets –
> And wrestled with a smile.
> Rich! 'Twas Myself – was rich –
> To take the name of Gold –
> And Gold to own – in solid Bars –
> The Difference – made me bold –

> [454]

But her wealth, her "Difference," is invisible. What can this mean, other than that she defines her wealth by her ability to write poetry—an ability which she will hint at but never explicitly acknowledge? How else is this self-defined "little" woman "bold"?

The hungry child in her poems is not a helpless or passive as "It would have starved a Gnat" (612) implies. Although the poems seem to portray Dickinson as a victim of deprivation, it becomes increasingly evident that as the child, the persona takes an active, even aggressive role in her own deprivation, maintaining her starvation deliberately and defiantly. Thus in "I had been hungry, all the years" (579), she prefers hunger and hunger's alienation to eating; to hope for "wealth," to enter the "window," to swallow the "bread," is to become part of a social or religious structure, and Dickinson refuses to relinquish that which distinguishes her from the rest of society. This is why in the poem quoted above she keeps her unnamed deprivation in her "Hand" and "never put it down," "did not dare to eat – or sleep – /For fear it would be gone." Her deprivation is her wealth.

In the following poem, she introduces a rationale for cultivating hunger as a child:

> I play at Riches – to appease
> The Clamoring for Gold –
> It kept me from a Thief, I think
> For often, overbold

> With Want, and Opportunity –
> I could have done a Sin
> And been Myself that easy Thing
> An independent Man –

> But often as my lot displays
> Too hungry to be borne

I deem Myself what I would be –
And novel Comforting

My Poverty and I derive –
We question if the Man –
Who own – Esteem the Opulence –
As We – Who never Can –

Should ever these exploring Hands
Chance Sovereign on a Mine –
Or in the long – unever term
To win, become their turn –

How fitter they will be – for Want –
Enlightening so well –
I know not which, Desire, or Grant –
Be wholly beautiful –

[801]

The source of Dickinson's "hunger" is revealed as her identity as a de-pendent woman in her culture, a "lot . . . /Too hungry to be borne." But her estrangement from the nurture to which independent men are entitled proves to be invaluable. Were Emily Dickinson not to feel dissatisfaction with her "lot" as a female, she would not be motivated to turn to language to console or free herself, to become what she "would be" if she had the opportunity. If she had "Riches," in other words, she would not need to "play at" them. And the word "playing" here signifies the child's sensi-bility. Thus Dickinson's sense of being a little girl in her culture, in terms of her dependence and her lack of autonomy and opportunity, paradoxi-cally enables her to keep herself "hungry" enough to want to "play." The "mine" Dickinson explores with her metaphorically exploring hands (holding the pen) is her identity as the little girl. This identity is cru-cial to her role as a poet, not only because it motivates the poetry, but because it improves her art: she is "fitter . . . for Want."

The necessity of hunger or even abstinence is a major theme in the poetry.[14] In poem 1282, Dickinson says that her abstinence makes her "like God," who does not need to eat to create. Thus what was originally construed as deprivation—her female identity—becomes a productive hun-ger, and finally a means of omnipotence. She needs hunger, not food, to create.

The concept of hunger is the link between Dickinson's little-girl per-sona and omnipotence: she feeds herself words as a poet to quell her hun-ger for power and glory, and in the process, gains the power and the glory.[15] In other words, the little-girl identity itself constitutes an ab-

stinence of traditional female or male fulfillments which is requisite for
going to heaven and becoming omnipotent. Emerson, in "The American
Scholar" and in his call for "The Poet," which Dickinson read and I think
took to heart, promised nothing less than this if a poet would only "shun
the company of men," and address the near, the familiar, the low: then
the poet would become "land-lord! air-lord! sea-lord!"[16] Compare Emerson's promise with the story of the little nut tree in the nursery rhyme:

> I had a little nut tree
> Nothing would it bear
> But a silver nutmeg
> And a golden pear
> The king of Spain's daughter
> Came to visit me
> And all because of my little nut tree
> I skipped over land
> I danced over the sea
> And all the birds in the air
> Couldn't catch me

Like the owner of this tree, Dickinson's little-girl poet persona is *conventionally* inadequate, but possesses unique, superior "gifts" which are
immortal. Hunger, and a small size, and a power to fast, enable her to
become "Like God," a powerful *creator*. How fitting that the ultimate
"transcendant" fantasy in children's literature, omnipotence, is also the
poet's. Thus in Emily Dickinson the motifs of "children's literature"
constitute her own aesthetics, for power and the ability to make words
and to create are identical in the child's as well as in the poet's mind.

In fact, children's literature can be characterized by a primary focus on
language itself, specifically in the context of power. For those who know
how to use it, language is literally magic. In fairy tales, words open doors
and summon divine help ("Open, Sesame," "Rumpelstiltskin"). In nursery rhymes, ladies jump seventeen times as high as the moon, owls and
eels and warming pans go on visits, women live in pumpkin shells: words
make it possible. Nursery rhymes are a particularly important form of
literature for children, for they are anarchic and rebellious, allowing laws
of logic to be transcended, order upset. In this way, nursery rhymes celebrate our cognitive abilities at the same time as they suggest the absurdity
of the world we all accept as "sensible." There is, then, what I would term
a subversive innocence in such wordplay, a linguistic freedom to mess up
the world, to accomplish the impossible, to make black white, to create
where nothing existed before, to take *liberties*, in all senses of the word:
this is a heady form of power indeed. Language makes anything possible,

which may be why children love word games, rhymes, and any literature that focuses on words themselves. Possibility is very important to those for whom so much in their own lives is impossible, and especially to Emily Dickinson, who defined herself as dwelling in "Possibility" (657), not "prose." In her letters, she exulted in her ability to use metaphors so that she could go anywhere, be anything. Although her brother advised her to calm down, and she gave her "I'll be a little ninny" reply, in her poetry she still maintains the child's sense of power and delight in her use of language, and like the child, she calls attention to her word feats (as in poem 326, "I cannot dance upon my Toes," where she commends herself on her "easy" grace with her "operatic" style).

Does all of this mean that Emily Dickinson was a children's writer? In spite of its difficulty, her poetry does appear in commercially successful editions for children, often illustrated, and is routinely included in anthologies of children's literature. I would suggest that her work appeals to the "child" in all of us—the child who wants to rebel, who delights in an anthropomorphized world, who loves to see word "play." Her work was written during the great age of nineteenth-century classics: *Peter Pan*, the story of a little boy who does not want to grow up; *Alice in Wonderland*, a little girl manipulated but undaunted by an absurd adult world; *Huckleberry Finn*, an "uncivilized" boy whose repudiation of adult society is an indictment of that society. In this company belongs Emily Dickinson, a Mother Goose whose poetry functions in the way that children's literature does for children, enabling them to cope with their psychological needs and realities; but it also is an implicit criticism of her society. We could say that the little girl is a metaphor for the restrictions she felt in dealing with a patriarchy that wanted its women "still." But the persona also allows her the freedom to express herself as a unique, autonomous, independent, powerful sensibility. Her children's literature is not for the "child" that she is, but is the attempt on the part of an adult to create and keep from growing up a little girl whose voice is indispensable to "Possibility." Dickinson put it in these terms: "The ravenousness of fondness is best disclosed by children. . . . Is there not a sweet wolf within us that demands its food?" As a poet, she used the voice of a hungry little Red Riding Hood, but this little girl controls the wolf. Dickinson's wolf within is a positive force, hungry, growling, full of teeth, *infantile*, demanding its "food." And this wolf is indeed "sweet," sweet as a *baby*, nursing on Dickinson's immortal words, the words which have somehow always been used by "Mother Gooses" for such occasions: nursery rhymes.

NOTES

1. *The Letters of Emily Dickinson*, 3 vols., ed. Thomas H. Johnson and Theodora Ward (Cambridge: The Belknap Press of Harvard University Press, 1958), vol. I, p. 241. Subsequent references will state *L.* followed by volume and page number.

2. *L.* I, p. 211. Dickinson claimed to be nostalgic for her childhood (*L.* I, pp. 14, 206) and in countless letters throughout her life defined herself to her correspondents in terms of her wistfulness for her childhood.

3. For a more extensive analysis of the daughter sensibility discussed here, see the author's *Emily Dickinson: When a Writer Is a Daughter* (Bloomington: Indiana University Press, 1982), and Sandra M. Gilbert and Susan Gubar, *The Madwoman in the Attic* (New Haven: Yale University Press, 1979).

4. Ibid.

5. Bruno Bettelheim, *The Uses of Enchantment* (New York: Knopf, 1976).

6. This term is used by Erik Erikson, a developmental psychologist, to characterize the third stage of psychosexual development in which children are able to move around by themselves (usually around two years) and simultaneously discover their sexual identity. See *Childhood and Society* (New York: W. W. Norton, 1963).

7. Dickinson's image of girlish vulnerability tends to inspire a loyal protective response in her critics. Thus she is called an "innocent, confiding child" in order to argue against her letters being published (out of decency's sake) (Millicent Todd Bingham, *Ancestor's Brocades* [New York: Harper, 1945], pp. 166-167). Similarly, William Robert Sherwood defines his purpose as "to defend Emily Dickinson's integrity—and hence her sanity" (*Circumstance and Circumference, Stages in the Life and Art of Emily Dickinson* [New York: Columbia University Press, 1968], p. 138). Ruth Miller is indignant when another critic, Clark Griffith, writes of Dickinson as "neurotic, erotic, laconic, and scared"—these are not appropriate words for Emily Dickinson (*The Poetry of Emily Dickinson* [Middletown, Conn.: Wesleyan University Press, 1968], p. 87). The epithets that have been applied to Dickinson have become legendary: among them, "girl," "myth," "creature," "poetess," "Miss Dickinson," and, of course, simply "Emily," an issue which has been dealt with eloquently in feminist criticism.

8. *L.* I, p. 161.

9. *L.* I, p. 144.

10. *L.* I, p. 117. Similarly, she tells Austin, "I shall never write any more grand letters to you, but all the *little* things, and the things called *trifles*. . . ." (*L.* I, p. 240).

11. *L.* I, p. 24. Dickinson's identification with Eve has been dealt with specifically by Gilbert and Gubar in *The Madwoman in the Attic* and by Margaret Homans in *Women Writers and Poetic Identity* (Princeton: Princeton University Press, 1981), among other studies.

12. *L.* II, p. 404.

13. Vivian Pollack, "Thirst and Starvation in Emily Dickinson's Poetry," *American Literature* 51 (March 1979): 33-49. Pollack's important essay explores the psychosocial significance of Dickinson's hunger, although arguing

that the loss of life-hunger and the ability to endure it is a kind of "death of the self."

14. See also Richard Wilbur, "Sumptuous Destitution," in *Emily Dickinson: Three Views* (Amherst, Mass., 1960); David Luisi, "Some Aspects of Emily Dickinson's Food and Liquor Poems," *English Studies* 51 (February 1971): 32-40; John Cody, *After Great Pain: The Inner Life of Emily Dickinson* (Cambridge: The Belknap Press of Harvard University Press, 1971). Cody provides an extensive psychoanalytical study of Dickinson's orality.

15. Dickinson has scores of poems and letters on this theme, including poems 455, 528, 349 ("I had the Glory – that will do"). In L. II, p. 460, she describes her yearning for power and glory as a "little girl."

16. Ralph Waldo Emerson, "The Poet," in *Essays, Second Series*, 1844.

KARL KELLER **IV**

Notes on Sleeping with Emily Dickinson

SLEEPING WITH EMILY DICKINSON, you discover a woman who loves words more than she loves *you.*

Emily Dickinson's "Wild Nights – Wild Nights!" are just in her head. They are just words in her head. And so the subjunctive:

> *Were* I with thee
> Wild Nights should be
> Our luxury!
>
> [249]

Her subjunctives give her away a great deal. They are a way she camps: discourse that plays with fantasy, that masks a masquerade, that is truthful about her desires but coyly honest that they are mere desires, elaborate pretense that is a convincing act, a lonely but attractive charade, her clowning. The wild nights do exist—*in the poetry.*

The poems on sleeping with someone are instructions, I believe, on how to "take" her. When she writes about wild nights, she is not only describing her ecstasy but also instructing us how to react to her, what to expect, what to get. She thus couples with the critic. She thus holds.

Imaginative penetration is the work of the Dickinson critic. But I think she intended interpenetration. The distinction is critical. Her distinction in this distinction is poetical.

"If anybody/Can the extasy define," Emily Dickinson says about sleeping with a man, it is to her "Half a transport – half a trouble." That's true of sleeping with her, too: "Half a transport – half a trouble." I think she was kidding. She would know the critic is not.

A man trying to write well about Emily Dickinson is an honest case of intellectual drag. The gender doesn't change, the role does. You must come off looking right, you are self-conscious, you dissemble. It is show biz.

Nothing funnier than a man telling how Emily Dickinson influenced him. "When I was a boy, I read Emily Dickinson and she . . ." The rest will trail off into the maudlin or the quaint or will be mildly fortifying. Quite different from seeing in her a sister-spirit, one who experienced what one does or oneself experiencing what she did, the experience crossing the miles and years and genders, creating out of her (knowing oneself) a precursor, or maybe a forerunner making a world in which one could be oneself. That's power.

Criticism, during the whole of Emily Dickinson's lifetime, was a male genre. Poetry also has gender. A woman—and Emily Dickinson is the best instance in American literature—can take liberties with the things of poetry-making. She is free to play, to tease, to violate, to not care, for she is an underdog, an outsider, an excrescence, an irrelevance, an erratic. The critic (male) will scan it for its adherence to regularity, its deviance from the expecter, its eccentricity, its freakishness. If Emily Dickinson "meant" to be the erratic, the freak, the myth, the "Kangaroo among the beauty," then the (male) scansion becomes the irrelevance. How summarily she then turns men into what they had made her! But only—of course—by equivocation; gender distinctions are accomplished only by equivocation. Emily Dickinson, more than most writing women I know before the mid-twentieth century, convinces one that the female is more than a gender, more in fact a separate species. Her anatomy determined her poetics. To know her, a man must perhaps study her nature more than that which nurtured her. Because of that, he can only cross over to her intellectually. He can only *imagine* her species and its aesthetics. She has her own side of the bed.

> We are always saved
> by judgment of good men

wrote Sappho, who, however, had never heard of such men as T. W. Higginson, Josiah Holland, Samuel Bowles, Thomas Niles, and others who knew Emily Dickinson's poetry and said, lying, that they wanted her. "Two . . . came to my Father's House, this winter—and asked me for my mind," she reported, ". . . [but] they would use it for the World." On the contrary, it was *women* who saved Emily Dickinson: Sue Dickinson, Lavinia Dickinson, Helen Jackson, Mabel Loomis Todd, Martha Bianchi. Women needing women, loving women, giving us women. It is an anomalous rescue, a touching one.

Aaron Copland set twelve poems of Emily Dickinson's to music. But sopranos must sing them, never a man.

Emily Dickinson's anticipation of a male readership (her critics, not her cult) nears anxiety. She performs; they analyze. When they perform the poetry, they near anxiety. She then becomes *their* critic.

I'm not sure language always has gender, but it has audience. Emily Dickinson was thoroughly conscious of her audience, but her great disaster was that she chose the wrong one—male critics: Higginson, Bowles, Holland, Newton, Niles, et al. She wanted into the marketplace, such as it was. It is one of her uglier desperations. Her language is so often shaped by what she hoped her audience would be that it can indeed be read by that audience now, an audience of male critics. Underneath all that is, however, somebody else.

Emily Dickinson had the advantage (seldom one for a woman in the 1860s and 1870s) of giving what *she* wanted to give. How simple an advantage!

This woman can tease a man. But though she goes far towards the really crazy, she never loses her inhibitions, for then there would be no imagination necessary, no lure. She pulls a man in.

How was Emily Dickinson to come close to the men she knew or wanted to know? *Poetry was not the way.* She tried it and no one responded. So why should she presume to get close to some of the rest of us? She may leave space for the male critic to come to her, but *he* must make the moves. She may move *for* him but seldom *toward* him.

"I was born bad and I never have recovered. Mine is a disgusting sex," said Alice James. She just said it straight out and she meant it. Emily Dickinson was always saying something like that, too, though not always meaning it. She could say it but it could be with irony that she could say it. Irony gave her two audiences: those who think she means what she says and those who take it facetiously. There is a family of those who are in on her, and there are those who aren't. Is there gender to this split? Are there those genders who get her code, her voice, her pose, and those genders who don't?

Surely she believed her own maxim: "Women talk; men are silent."

Emily Dickinson's is a raised voice. All poetry is hyperbole, of course, but Emily Dickinson deliberately raises her voice: it is what a woman must/ can do to get the attention of men.

A case of a man doing Emily Dickinson wrong is William Luce's script for "The Belle of Amherst." At one point Julie Harris says, plainly and plaintively (though still shouting), noting the teen-age dating in old Amherst: "I know what people say, 'Poor Emily—the only kangaroo among the beauties.' " What she *really* said (it is in a letter to T. W. Higginson in

1862) had to do with her pride in being an eccentric woman: "[I am] Myself the only Kangaroo among the Beauty." She was shouting.

Suortù: a woman defying her fate. Was that Emily Dickinson? I think she was really a heady version of that. I think she thought it was her fate to defy. A woman defying her fate is what a man would expect of a woman. A woman accepting her fate to defy means accepting one's nature, one's humanity, one's gender, one's difference, one's ability, oneself.

Imagining her audience to be male gave Emily Dickinson opportunity to play the deviant. Perhaps she could have played that among women, too, but she would not have had to be as brisk, as nasty, as coy, as teasing, as sure. These postures were created by the men in her mind.

There may have been men in her mind but, except for God, there are hardly any men to speak of in her poetry. Much of her poetry is poetry in which she wishes there were, or she fantasizes about there being, or she documents the absence of. But there are not really very many men. Yet a man can put himself there as reader quite easily. She created the space for someone to understand her, enclose her, love her—quite like all the white space around one of her poems. *She* created that white space, I think we have to believe. She lets one in lovingly.

God was Emily Dickinson's only real male test-case. And I think she knew she had the potency to drive him out, to displace him, to be sufficient. This cannot have been a satisfying position for her, however, unsure as she sometimes was that here was really anybody there to oppose her. She parleyed with this one man in her life. She made an uneasy alliance. She knew that only through a kind of treachery had he delivered up the world into her hands. She sought and found him but her own dark shadow was always larger than his white face. How did she take it: to be greater than the one man you would love? I guess God eventually learned to cling to her, being for her everywhere. He was probably delivered up into her hands. Any other man must be aware of putting himself in the same spot, the same advantage.

Emily Dickinson cannot find a center in (male-made) society, in (male-made) institutions, in her (male-made) home, and not even in the (male-made) universe. Only (perhaps, and then tentatively/tenuously) in herself—and even that isn't reliable. God is, for her, not at the center, not a hold on things, not a focus. Only herself—and she bests Emerson's betterment of the self by showing/doubting its inconsistency. It is not so much that as a woman she is free to be herself as that she is free to doubt herself. But at what a price!

Louise Bogan cutely speaks of Emily Dickinson as a cat trying to speak

English. This is almost right. Better: she is a voice trying to hide the fact that she is a real cat. In many ways she is trying to hide the fact that she is a woman. But a *man* can know she is a woman, simply because she may be trying to hide the fact. A man (Proust, Emerson, and Hemingway, for different reasons, are distinct exceptions) would not think it necessary to artfully dissemble and to make the dissembling an art. On a man the genitals do show. A woman may use poetry for stuffing. This is not dishonest, just marketing-necessity. In a man this art would be a hoot. In a woman it is camp.

George Whicher speaks of Emily Dickinson as having eyes that did not focus in the same direction. This may be accurate ophthalmology but it is only a man's trite guess about the diversity in her art. She is shifty, not schizy.

Three large concepts encompass Emily Dickinson: Necessity, Desire, and Expectation. The first two were her own concern; men enter into her life only in the third one. The conformity to (or nodding toward) expectations does not necessarily produce male factors in the poetry but produces factors that men can know fairly well: forms and structures, the communicable vocabulary, common ideas, a philosophy. The erratic in her is something else: that is the female area of her freedom. But is it chauvinist to say so?

Does Emily Dickinson cower before her critics? Is there a lot of sycophancy? I think so. And it is not much fun to watch. She rises above such a (perhaps) necessary act when she falls apart, when she is experimenting, when she is unfinished. The poetry in that state is very much her own. I'm not sure she knew a man could get off on *that* in her.

Why there is so little elegance in Emily Dickinson may perplex a person—perplex a *man*, certainly, since that was, in Emily Dickinson's environment, one of the marks of obeisance a man expected of a woman. Maybe one of the qualities one expects of her now, too. But she will not go there, or not very often, conscious, I believe, of the expectation. Instead, she is deliberately (not carelessly) indecorous. Her determined genre is indecorum; her temptation the indecent. It is not womanly of her to seek this kind of speech, but it is certainly anti-manly—who are forced then to accept her, if they accept her at all, outside the stereotype. The crudeness therefore succeeds, like porn, as art. Elegance is a submission to a set of manners. Emily Dickinson's reference to them is for her quite enough; she did not need always to live them, certainly not when she sat down to make some world of her own in her poetry.

The power of the Tease. I don't think Emily Dickinson knew she had it, or at least didn't know it was a mode of writing, of reaching, of staying, of having without being had. Where in all of literature could she have found it? I think she came by it inadvertently. It was simply natural to her to draw people to what she said but leave them unsure of precisely what she had said. She was always a little cryptic, a little elliptical with people, in manner and in talk, for it gave them room between the brief moments of her awe and her desolation. Her roles—that is, her ploys and playfulness— tease because she makes them very attractive, but they are usually too brief to really *know*: she does not let herself be known well. The brief flirtation lets you know she is there; it doesn't let you know *who* is there. But the teasing is by no means dishonest, it is a defense. You place yourself in a scene (someone else's mind, someone else's life) on your own terms; you delight someone with your terms, by your terms, on your terms, even for your terms; but no one takes over or dares by presumptuousness lay claim or even enter in—unless they are *better*. The tease has to be good enough to make sure they aren't/don't/can't. Emily Dickinson made sure by ellipsis, dodge, a vague daring, an evident superiority of language and idea, staying virtually unknown behind the flash. The lure is alluring and also a little cruel. The tease—spidery—attracts, overwhelms, and then abandons. She wins you and then will not have you even when she needs you. You are on your own, happy victim, with the lovely web, the poem. The lovely web will not fall of your weight, you will try to figure out the intricacy of it, and you will wonder where she went—or did she, dear critic/victim/ lover, become the web itself? It's what you have of her, for she has really gone on to flirt elsewhere. The tease won; *you* won. She staged all that. Such a woman!

"The difficulty is my inability to assume the receptive attitude," Alice James wrote to her brother William, "that cardinal virtue in women, the absence of which has always made me so uncharming to & uncharmed by the male sex." No lack of "the receptive attitude," however, in Emily Dickinson. She leaves herself open to men in her poetry, makes herself vulnerable to them, makes a place for them. That no one came to the party—not *really*—was not her fault. A man may come to it now, though, because that space remains there in her poetry. That space, I believe, is always there.

Hard for a man to see, I think, what is erotic about Emily Dickinson's poetry. Having slept with her once, I found it more masturbatory than anything else. Her art, I think, became a kind of orgasm withheld, though lusting still after the concealed and tantalizing, after the incomprehensible, after fantasy. She plays, but she does not climax with you. You thereby become a satisfied voyeur of unfulfilled desire, uncompleted desire.

But who is to say a life of masturbation is not a life? It is private, individual, democratic, undiscussable. A man can never penetrate that in a woman. And no one can know what it is in Emily Dickinson. The critic is totally lost at that. Anyway, wrote Margaret Fuller, "it is a vulgar error that love, *a* love, to Woman is her whole existence."

And so, as I have already said, sleeping with Emily Dickinson, you discover a woman who loves words more than she loves *you.*

"Night's possibility!" Night was often sexual to Emily Dickinson. She could/would sleep with someone.

> Because, Sir, love is sweet!
> . . . . .
> [I] nearer steal to Thee!
> Enamored. . . .
>
> [106]

Sleeping with someone—a lover-fantasy! anyone! the reader-critic!—she wants "The peace – the flight – the Amethyst." This is, to her, "Night's possibility." This may be what she gets out of the affair. It is not what one can give her.

There's some sex-talk in Emily Dickinson's lines of verse:

> A transport one cannot contain
> May yet, a transport be –

But there are also a lot of genuinely-meant inhibitions, too:

> Though God forbid it lift the lid –
> Unto it's Extasy!
>
> [184]

That is why you have to worry whether her invitation to bed with her is a tease or not. She may not really want what you have to give. You may take more than she meant to give. That is not real love.

> I let him lead me – Home.
> . . . . .
> He strove – and I strove – too –
> We didn't do it – tho'!
>
> [190]

"No Man moved Me," she exclaims boastfully at the beginning of one poem (520). When a man "made as He would eat me up" and "followed [her] – close behind," she "started [:was startled?]" and he "bowing – with a Mighty look – . . . withdrew." She frightens off that which she desires. She attracts and then scares off. She teases, we attack, she withdraws, we withdraw. It is all very perplexing.

There are few bodies in Emily Dickinson's lovers in her poems. They are usually "Fleshless Lovers" who

> met –
> A Heaven in a Gaze –
> A Heaven of Heavens – the Privilege
> Of one another's Eyes –
>
> [625]

Critical work with her is also usually remote, guess-work, unsure. "Watch me, if you want," she says, "but don't touch."

In Emily Dickinson's love poems, people don't sleep together very much. The critic cannot have that for metaphor very often, therefore. But there are other aspects of them that he can have: strong desire, strong memory, advice on luring and teasing, advice on selectivity, the invitation:

> How bountiful the Dream –
> What Plenty – it would be –
> Had all my Life but been Mistake
> Just rectified – in Thee
>
> [646]

Female bonding is missing in Emily Dickinson's poems because there is a female narrator but no (or very seldom a) female subject. There is a woman speaking (and generally speaking to men, I believe) but no woman loving a woman. "I tell you these things about myself only to legitimize my voice," Grace Strasser-Medina says for apologia in Joan Didion's novel *A Book of Common Prayer*. "We are uneasy about a story until we know who is telling it." It is her voice that is legitimate, not any relationships. *We* supply the relationships. But only on her terms. She may need us, she may not necessarily want us. But Didion has said since then to all this, "The narrator has got to be telling the story for a reason." I cannot find what that reason might have been. I cannot find what *social* reason Emily Dickinson had for writing. Where is the Common Prayer? That is the central difficulty in someone coupling critically with her. And maybe that is *her* central victory.

So what it all comes to is that you sleep with Emily Dickinson, to be sure, but only on her terms, only in her way. You lie there in awe of someone who, on her side of the bed, fantasizes (about all the world; about *you*) so well. Awe is what a male critic learns from her to have towards her if he loves her aright.

"Awe" has got to be about the vaguest word in Emily Dickinson's language.

> populate with awe my solitude –
>
> [1677]

We cannot know what she meant by it, if she meant anything at all. She says it when she needs a blank, a space, a perplexity, an upward glance, a sublime shrug, an "ahhhhhhhh!" But she sleeps with Awe, a lover:

> Ample make this Bed –
> Make this Bed with Awe –
> In it wait till Judgment break
> Excellent and Fair.
>
> [829]

Such vagueness can be shared where explicitness maybe cannot always be. She brings us into an unknown with her and holds our hand there. Or more. Awe is for her the ideal relationship—whatever that means—and the ideal relationship she wants the lover-critic to have with her—whatever that means.

We have laughed for a long time now that people should have thought of Emily Dickinson as "the myth of Amherst"—that is, the one entertainment to drive to see, the freak of the Valley. But why shouldn't we believe it? *She* created the role; *she* got people to believe it. It was show biz. But more than that, she wanted some awe out of people. One should learn from that how to go to see her: on her terms of awe.

Martha Graham was right to create two Emily Dickinsons in her classic "Letter to the World" in 1940, one who steps precisely and stands with dignity and comports herself with strictness, and one who is utterly free in her responses to life and death, ecstasy and fantasy. As the second Emily, she hopped around in multicolors, tied her foot to a scarf and pulled the foot ear-high as she lurched happily as "the little tippler leaning against the sun." Ned Rorem called her Emily Dickinson one of Martha Graham's "female monsters," her "female as female," her "more-than-criminal female as Royal Elect."

How easily the odd becomes awe, the awe becomes attraction, the attraction becomes, well, "sexual."

The plate for Emily Dickinson in Judy Chicago's *Dinner Party* is a pink-laced vagina. Of the plate Chicago writes: "Dickinson felt that her own poetry was dangerous, for it revealed feelings that society had taught women to repress. 'I took my power in my hand, and went out against the world,' she wrote, knowing that her intense creativity was hopelessly at odds with the prevailing ideas of what a woman was supposed to be. . . . Imagining a female creative genius imprisoned in all that lace evolved into my concept of Dickinson's runner and plate. We jiggered a plate with a thick center, which I then carved. Its strength is in stark contrast to the surrounding layers of immobile lace. . . . The soft but fleshy colors suggest a sensuality that nineteenth-century women were not supposed to have. . . . Lace borders over netting with ruffles on the back provide an incongruous setting for a poet whose voice was as powerful as her will."

A contrast to that. "Cotton Mather would have burnt her for a witch," concludes Allen Tate in what is probably the single most influential essay written on Emily Dickinson (1932), and one of the most blatantly chauvinist pieces of writing about her. Emerging at the moment of the breaking up of a culture ("born into the equilibrium of an old and a new order"), she did not have to think about things, only feel them: "brought down [see where the man puts her!] from abstraction to personal sensibility."

> "She cannot reason at all. . . ."
> "She could not in the proper sense think at all. . . ."
> "She never succumbed to her ideas, to easy solutions, to her private desires. . . ."
> "She did not reason about the world she saw; she merely saw it. . . ."
> "She has nothing to say. . . ."

In an effort "to live apart from a cultural tradition that no longer sustain[ed her]," she "withdr[e]w from life to her upstairs room" and wrote poems for us. Where a man, Hawthorne, faced up to the cultural changes and *thought* about them, a woman, Emily Dickinson, did what any sensible and sensitive woman would do, withdraw and *feel* the change going on, so there would be fine poems of tension for us to read. Again: "brought *down* from abstraction to personal sensibility." She was therefore of service to this "outsider" (i.e., this Southern man) who dislikes the things of New England, "threatening to tear them apart"—the female poet serving the male critic, and because of that service, she is "a great poet."

Another contrast. When Steve Allen made his series *Meeting of Minds,* he put Emily Dickinson in the company of Darwin, Galileo, and Attila the Hun. Although he introduces her as "America's greatest woman poet," he has her "enter[ ], somewhat timidly" and gives her pathetic, inconsequential lines to speak. She is a squeaker overshadowed by giants. To Attila the Hun she says, "How dreadful" and "Oh, my goodness" and

"How horrible!" To Darwin she says, "Oh, dear" and "I was one of those simple people, Dr. Darwin" and "Fascinating!" And to Galileo, she says, "No!" and "That must give you enormous satisfaction" and "How infuriating!" That is, little squeaks to the big ideas and events of history. She reads them some of her poems, to be sure, but about the only thing about herself that they seem to have any interest in is her reclusiveness. They call her "shy," "an enigmatic figure," "curious." Her answer to the charge is: "I felt that I had the right to live and die in obscurity. . . . I've been out with lanterns, looking for myself." Apparently only because pathetic does the woman write well. The men are bold and out conquering the world. The woman, like Milton's puritan, serves sitting/waiting/writing.

Of few poets can it honestly be said that the posture they strike (of necessity? creatively? perversely?) is destructive. Much of Emily Dickinson consoles, but much is unsettling. Much upsets assumptions. Much challenges. Much annoys. She is (often enough to believe it is really her) blatantly disturbing—at least to those who want poets as pillars rather than as bombs.

> The soul has moments of Escape –
> When bursting all the doors –
> She dances like a Bomb, abroad,
> And swings upon the Hours. . . .
>
> [512]

This women, in her more anxious moments, would, I believe, *kill*.

Were words a comfort to this "lonely, isolated woman"? (Who hasn't used the phrase and thought it really meant something?) Was language a compensation, an escape, a consolation, a comfort? Was it a completion, an extension, some kind of dramatic "letter to the [outside, larger, probably unreachable] world"? Well, she hunted down her words so carefully, even if sometimes inaccurately, and placed them so carefully, even if sometimes wrongly, and made such flashes of wit and wisdom out of them, even if sometimes poorly, that it seems askew to think it all such a private matter. Is language ever really private anyway? Her language seems more of an attack upon an imaginary world—loving it, laving it, stirring it, making it smart, stabbing—and so she overwhelms with it. I think she overwhelms. She is almost too much. Maybe *that* fact was comforting to her.

I doubt seriously whether Emily Dickinson was really a "*mad*woman in the attic" in any serious sense. Her agoraphobia is momentary like most of the roles she played and should not be made out to be a space made for her forever (by men?) nor a place of trial made for her forever (by her-self?). She knew how to go mad, to be sure, but she also knew how to get over it. That is the remarkable, and to a man (at least to myself) the in-teresting, part. Her little madnesses are more attractive than they are pathetic, more drawing than melodramatic, more scenic than serious. She was not determined to go "after great pain." Like everything else she wrote about, it came and went. What is wonderful to witness is her stoicism amid all the transience of things in her life. Three of her loveliest lines (paraphrasing the existentialist of *Ecclesiastes*) are:

> How much can come
> And much can go,
> And yet abide the World!
>
> [1593]

The Madwoman of Amherst was awfully sane about it, awfully coherent in telling about the "experience," awfully good at being bad/mad. When she went up into the attic of her "Haunted House," whether that was a haunted life or a haunted art, she went *wild*, not mad. She is up there now, dancing, not screaming. It was, remarkably, a place she could go when she wanted to; she was not locked in. In her own house, it wasn't the attic she went up into anyway; it was a cupola. From which she could see she was superior and into which came many of the things that gave her her Awe and Amplitude. (It is above the bedroom—well above.) If going up there makes one a madwoman, there's a hell of a good universe up there, let's go!

I lie here beside her not believing Emily Dickinson's disclaimer about wanting a large future for herself. "If fame belonged to me," she wrote to Higginson coyly/dishonestly in 1862, "I could not escape her." On the contrary, she very much wanted (from men) fame. "Could I make you and Austin – proud – sometime – a great way off," she confessed to her sister-in-law Sue in 1861, " 'twould give me taller feet." She is, in fact, one of the most ambitious writers I know of in the nineteenth century. That she did not know how to fuel (among men) her achievement is neither here nor there. Her many desires have about them the aura of ambition. To be sure, when she slipped into one of her larger views of existence, she belittled all worldly ambition; such was vanity and vexation of spirit. But she was not so nunnish or mad to hold this for long. She held, however vaguely, to a significance to human life and to the superiority of her own. Her touches of renunciation smack piquantly of hypocrisy; ambitious poet may be a contradiction in terms and in very poor taste, but Emily Dickinson did not let her little renunciations make a crippling ambiva-lence. She has a rather regular naive vulgarity about her hopes for her poetry. She was a go-getter even as she gradually became aware that there was precious little go to get. Her tragic view of much of life—which makes many other things look petty-spirited—she found she could *sell*. Devoted to triumph, she was not constricted by her own dark views of many things, but learned how to make products out of them, her poems. Maybe the world (of men) did not write to her much, as she said, but she did not anathematize the perks of fame it/they could give her. She lied her head off when she wrote to Higginson: "Publication is so far of the mind as firmament from fin." She would have *loved* to have been set among the stars. It has been sheer sexism to make Emily Dickinson one of our saints of failure. Ambition was, after all, one of the ways she defined herself, and one of the ways in which we must.

But I notice she has not noticed me here in bed with her at all. What should I do now?

JOANNE A. DOBSON **V**

"Oh, Susie, it is dangerous"

Emily Dickinson and the Archetype

To scan a Ghost, is faint –
But grappling, conquers it –

[281]

IN THE POETIC WORLD of Emily Dickinson there dwells a figure that is indeed something like a ghost, a figure that has long evaded precise definition and definite biographical assignment. I am speaking, of course, of that elusive masculine form, so long the occasion of conjecture and analysis. As has often been noted by Dickinson critics, a particularly intense constellation of images, situations, and statement in her poetry reveals an intriguing preoccupation with masculinity, and, more particularly, with a facet of masculinity that is perceived as simultaneously omnipotent, fascinating, and deadly.[1] In poem after poem we see the poet's persona presented as weak and insignificant, overwhelmed by the near presence of an arbitrary and rapacious masculine power. Whether that power be presented as God, death, or, seemingly, as some particular unnamed man, much can be learned about its imaginative function in both Dickinson's life and her poetry by viewing it as a single poetic construct, linked by significant similarities of tone and realization. Such an approach, concentrating upon the actual characteristics of the masculine figure as they are realized in the poetry rather than upon its "masculinity" per se, is necessary in order to counteract confusing and contradictory romantic speculations regarding the masculine, and allow us a clearer vision of the imaginative processes of this brilliant woman and poet.

The difficulty in studying the masculine construct arises from the elusiveness of the name behind the form, but Dickinson has given us a methodology for coming to terms with this phantom. Each poem in which it appears can be seen as a "scan," and the "grappling" that conquers occurs for both Dickinson and the critic in wrestling into identity the figure which the poetic as an entirety creates.

80

Both in patriarchal society and, as we will see, in that intimate and compelling world of the psyche that translates and enacts the conditions of the external world, Dickison was living in a masculine realm. Thus her perception of the nature of the masculine is socially influenced to a degree, but in many fascinating ways it is something wholly her own; both her life and her poetic stand in sharper relief when seen against the background of her imaginative reconstruction of the masculine.

The universe of Emily Dickinson's poetry is envisioned as a patriarchal place, curious and self-contradictory, and her relationship to it is ambivalent. On one hand, she can project her presence there as a mouse hidden snug in a permissive "Papa" God's "seraphic Cupboard,"[2] safe, satiated, and untouched (61). Conversely, she can envision herself as a daisy in a universe where an inexplicably "Approving" God measures off his days in the lengths of assassinated flowers (1624). It is an eroticized universe in which God is seen as a "distant – stately Lover" wooing humanity with legalistic pettiness (357) or, more passionately and with strangely oblique erotic imagery, as the mystical spouse (461, 817, 1072). The masculine power principle is at the center of this universe, and the conflicting and contradictory nature of its attributes is, of course, epitomized by Dickinson's protean God, her "Burglar, Banker – Father (49)," but these attributes are not restricted to divinity alone; in numinous and shifting fragments the masculine principle permeates a significantly large area of her poetic involvement, both as a vitalizing and as an inhibiting factor.

Although the configuration of deadly traits that can be seen to accrue to Dickinson's poetic mythos of the masculine migrates from subject to subject—God is seen in masculine terms, death is male, and certain poems seem to be written to an individual man—there are many poems where assigning a referent to the masculine pronoun is intriguingly impossible. It is in these poems of the indeterminate "He" that the pure energy of the *idea* of the masculine is most clearly observed, where we can see her fascination and her fear in their essence, without the distractions of biographical particularities.

> He fumbles at your Soul
> As Players at the Keys
> Before they drop full Music on –
> He stuns you by degrees –
> Prepares your brittle Nature
> For the Etherial Blow
> By fainter Hammers – further heard –
> Then nearer – Then so slow
> Your Breath has time to straighten –
> Your Brain – to bubble Cool –

> Deals – One – imperial – Thunderbolt –
> That scalps your naked Soul –
>
> When Winds take Forests in their Paws –
> The Universe – is still –

[315]

This poem, with its unspecified "He," depicts a force skilled in inflicting a maximum amount of pain with murderous efficiency. The victim is a full psychic and somatic presence in the poem; the torturer is only an energy. The pain is of her soul—it's an "etherial," psychic, blow—but many elements combine to stress the somatic. A distinctly sexual progression carries the poem from arousal to climax ("One – imperial – Thunderbolt") to terrified satiety. The hammers she hears are her own pulse booming in physical reverberation of the psychic shock. The straightened breath has been knocked askew or coiled in agony. The cooling blood has been bubbling in her fevered brain. The somatic nature of this imagery denotes a concrete and vulnerable involvement in the situation. It also serves to accentuate the contrast with the "He" of the poem, who is impersonal, who has no physical or psychic presence. As in many of Dickinson's poems, he is an abstract and indifferent force, a force without a name, to be embodied, significantly deified, in the metaphor of a storm against whose omnipotence even the universe does not struggle, and whose most tangible manifestation is the light and power of that phallic thunderbolt.

The intangibility of the masculine force is stressed in another poem of ambush and annihilation (338), one which also contains the indeterminate "He."

> I know that He exists.
> Somewhere – in Silence –
> He has hid his rare life
> From our gross eyes.
>
> 'Tis an instant's play.
> 'Tis a fond Ambush –
> Just to make Bliss
> Earn her own surprise!

The "He" is contained in "Silence" here, beyond the control of articulation, subjecting the speaker to assault. The poet experiences the masculine contact as initially playful, a "fond Ambush," as if the lover/god were an invisible, frisking cat. But in Dickinson's poetic universe possibility is commensurate with psychic reality, and the destructive potential inherent in interaction with the masculine leaps to the foreground of her mind and usurps the poem.

> But – should the play
> Prove piercing earnest –
> Should the glee – glaze –
> in Death's – stiff – stare –
>
> Would not the fun
> Look too expensive!
> Would not the jest –
> Have crawled too far!

[338]

This potential bliss is not worth its possible cost.

Ten years earlier, in 1852, long before Dickinson had begun her serious poetic endeavor, she wrote a letter to her good friend (and, ironically, in view of the nature of the letter, future sister-in-law) Susan Gilbert that reveals outlines of the psychic set with which she continues later in her poetry to confront the idea of the masculine. In an eloquent and devastating evaluation, she assesses the potential psychic cost of marriage ("Would not the fun / Look too expensive") and finds it "too dear."

> ... to the *wife*, Susie, sometimes the *wife forgotten*, our lives perhaps seem dearer than all others in the world; you have seen flowers at morning, *satisfied* with the dew, and those same sweet flowers at noon with their heads bowed in anguish before the mighty sun; think you these thirsty blossoms will *now* need naught but – dew? No they will cry for sunlight and pine for the burning noon, tho' it scorches them, scathes them; they have got through with peace—they know that the man of noon, is *mightier* than the morning and their life is henceforth to him. Oh, Susie, it is dangerous, and it is all too dear, those simple trusting spirits, and the spirits mightier, which we cannot resist! It does so rend me, Susie, the thought of it when it comes, that I tremble lest at sometime I, too, am yielded up.[3]

The psychic economy of marriage is evaluated and seen as too costly in personal expense. The fear of being overwhelmed, of having the self annihilated by the masculine is imagined here, once again, in a metaphor of an intangible natural force. This image of the sun, "the man of noon," lends mythic suggestiveness to Dickinson's configuration. He, too, is godlike, reminding us of Apollo, the god of light and the primordial man of noon. The Greek gods have been envisioned as being prone to amorous ambush, leaving their prey stunned or annihilated. One particular story, if she knew it, must have appealed greatly to Dickinson. Zeus, who seems to have been a dangerous lover for mortal maidens, revealed himself in human form to Semele, whom he loved. She desired to "see him in his full splendor as King of Heaven and Lord of the Thunderbolt . . ."; he obliged, "and before that awful glory of burning light she died."[4]

In this tale we find the same irresistible attractiveness, luminosity, and danger that exists in Dickinson's "man of noon." These "men are all gods; in some sense in her imagination being masculine is to partake of divinity. And the idea of cost is always there. Is not God seen as both "Burglar" and "Banker"? To trade with divinity is in some essential way to risk the loss of self; although the "man of noon" is the central dynamic power of the above passage, the author's attention is focused not upon him, but upon the pathetic reaction to him of the wilted flower/wives.

Certain qualities of her presentation of this destructive aspect of the masculine figure, its light and power, its intangibility, the protean nature of the surface referent, the static, enduring quality of the underlying traits, and Dickinson's predilection for the indeterminate "He," suggest that she was dealing not with God or death per se, or any particular man, although each seems to play its role in initiating certain of the poems and informing their characters, but with an enduring archetype lodged deep within her psychic makeup, envisioned in its compelling configuration by her unique imagination, and projected through a skilled welding of archetype and language as a poetic construct upon the phenomena of her literary universe. This primordial image of the masculine gathers unto itself all the inscrutability and emotional energy of any archaic symbol, deifying itself along the way, becoming a thunderbolt rapist, an invisible feline god, a scorching "man of noon," a Lord of Death. Carl Jung describes an archetype as an unconscious "tendency to form . . . representations of a motif."[5] This fascination/repulsion with the masculine is a strong motif in Dickinson's poetry, and the attention given it by readers and critics confirms both the energy of the archetype and Dickinson's ability to bring her particular vision to a skillful poetic realization.

What, however, is the meaning of the symbol? Where does it come from in her individual psyche? What does it mean for her poetry? Received definitions of concepts as abstract and prone to misrepresentation as "archetype" must be tested and at times adjusted according to the insights and reperceptions of our increased understanding of the components that go into making up a female psychology. As Adrienne Rich says, "the real question, given that the art of poetry is an art of transformation, is how this woman's mind and imagination may have used the masculine element in the world at large, or those elements personified as masculine—including the men she knew; how her relationship to this reveals itself in her images and language."[6] Therefore, rather than impose a preconceived idea of the archetype upon them, I will work outward from the individual poems, delineating the unique components of this particular masculine construct, and illuminating their significance by linking them when appropriate to the wider framework of archetypal criticism.

Mircea Eliade notes that "the authentic meaning of any archaic symbol shows a recognition of a certain situation in the cosmos."[7] In Dickinson's particular case I would use the term "perception of" rather than "situation in." Raised in a patriarchal religion and trained in the precepts of that religion, she naturally projected a masculine image upon the cosmic forces she felt restricted her soul and denied the ambitions of her brilliantly comprehensive mind. "Of Course – I prayed – / And did God Care? / He cared as much as on the Air / A Bird – had stamped her foot – (376)." But Dickinson's archetype of the masculine has also earthy, practical components. On a societal level she trembled before her psychic image of the masculine lest she should be "yielded up" in daily life, her identity subsumed in marriage, the possibilities of girlhood sacrificed to the narrow limitations of the proper wife; she once called marriage a "soft Eclipse." Furthermore, to compound her anxiety regarding the masculine, she, as a poet, was working within a tradition that was overwhelmingly masculine,[8] and which seemed to exclude her by virtue of her sex, the most intimate facet of her personal identity.

All of these factors combined and internalized, the religious, the social, and the literary, serve to reinforce for Dickinson an archetype of great power. A composite image of the very real powers of men in this world, and of her relation to them, plays a large part in shaping the surface of her exploratory map of the masculine. This combination by itself, however, this situation of external conditions and relationships, is not adequate to explain completely the particular numinous quality of the archetype, her fascination with, and revulsion against, its deadly attractiveness, as it shapes and energizes her poetic imagination. Something more powerful and more painful is at work here. As Rich says, "it is always what is under pressure in us, especially under pressure of concealment— that explodes in poetry."[9] The masculine construct in Emily Dickinson's poetic is not only an internalization of external verities but also an attempted realization in her poetic world of her own dimly perceived "masculine" self, the aspect of her psyche that had long been deprived in the "real" world of recognition and expression. Rich calls it a representation of the poet's relationship to her own power, which is exteriorized in masculine form."[10] This ambivalent, numinous figure, in Jungian terms, is Dickinson's animus struggling for life against deadly odds.

In a most convincing reading of that ambiguous and often-discussed poem, "My Life had stood – a Loaded Gun –" (754), Albert Gelpi also identifies the masculine figure as Dickinson's animus, "an image symbolic of certain aspects of her own personality, qualities and needs and potentialities which have been defined culturally and psychologically with the masculine."[11] His definition of the animus is apt and comprehensive, and I will adopt it as my own for this discussion, stressing the understanding that there is nothing innately "masculine" about this side of Dickinson's personality; the term must be recognized as being societal in origin. Gelpi goes on to discuss the powerfully explosive feeling of this poem, the sense of volcanic destructiveness that emanates from it, saying that the "archetype of the hero in the figure of the woodsman seems to her to necessitate a sacrifice of her womanhood."[12] This would in a very real sense mean the threat of psychic disintegration through the loss of social and personal identity. Gelpi concludes that "a woman in a patriarchal society achieves triumph through a blood sacrifice."[13]

The powerful emotional affect of the masculine figure in her poems, its intangibility, its godlike qualities, her fascination with it and her fear of it, and its tendency to exist in an absolute space and time—the grave, eternity, heaven, a "still" universe—all suggest the personal and internal makeup of the animus, with its energy and its autonomous existence in the timeless, spaceless realm of the unconscious. The shifting nature of the referents in the individual poems is explained by the dynamic of projection in which "the cause of the effect . . . appears to lie in objects and objective situations,"[14] rather than in subjectivity.

The components of Dickinson's masculine self are diffuse in her poetry, as they must certainly have been in her psyche. The very fact that she works in an oblique and slanted poetic renders them exceptionally difficult to isolate and define. However, in an early poem, "I have a King, who does not speak –," Dickinson gives unmistakable evidence of her awareness of a masculine presence in her psychic makeup.

> I have a King, who does not speak –
> So – wondering – thro' the hours meek
> I trudge the day away –
> Half glad when it is night, and sleep,
> If, haply, thro' a dream, to peep
> In parlors, shut by day.
>
> And if I do – when morning comes –
> It is as if a hundred drums
> Did round my pillow roll,
> And shouts fill all my Childish sky,
> And Bells keep saying "Victory"
> From steeples in my soul!
>
> And if I don't – the little Bird
> Within the Orchard, is not heard,
> And I omit to pray
> "Father, thy will be done" today
> For my will goes the other way,
> And it were perjury!

[103]

Here the animus is envisioned as split off from the conscious personality, from daily functioning, silenced, behaving, as Jung has put it, like a "part soul."[15] But it is a "part soul" with great power to grant or deny, by a mere glimpse, these most meaningful aspects of life, a sense of vitality, a capacity for joy, the capability of articulation. It is suggestive that the animus contact is seen as benign here—non-threatening. There is no danger of being assaulted and annihilated by the strength of a power that is glimpsed only obliquely in the polite parlors of a dream. This poem and the "king" poem that follows were written in early career, before Dickinson's masterwork, her great outpouring of passionate and brilliant verse in the early 1860s, and therefore it is significant that she employs her child persona here and portrays the animus figure in the following early poem as a ragged boy.

> I met a King this afternoon!
> He had not on a Crown indeed,
> A little Palmleaf Hat was all,
> And he was barefoot, I'm afraid!

This figure has physical realization of a sort, with his freckles, palmleaf hat and "faded jacket's blue." But the external embodiment fades into insignificance as the monarchal possibility beneath the surface is imaginatively realized.

> But sure I am he Ermine wore
> Beneath his faded Jacket's blue –
> And sure I am, the crest he bore
> Within that Jacket's pocket too!
>
> For 'twas too stately for an Earl –
> A Marquis would not go so grand!
> 'Twas possibily a Czar petite –
> A Pope, or something of that kind!

This monarch, freckled as was Emily Dickinson herself, transports the speaker slowly toward an unspecified destination in a vehicle she greets with amusement and astonishment.

> If I must tell you, of a Horse,
> My Freckled Monarch held the rein –
> Doubtless an estimable Beast,
> But not at all disposed to run!
>
> And such a wagon! While I live
> Dare I presume to see
> Another such a vehicle
> As then transported me!

The pokey horse and wagon of her "transport" are homely indeed compared with other vehicles in Dickinson's poetic travels. Death's stately carriage in poem 712, as we will see, impels an infinitely more sinister voyage. And the tone here is indulgent, even playful with its punning emphasis on the monarch who holds the "rein" as well as the reign.

The masculine figure is compounded in this poem, dividing his royal state with two other ragged "Princes."

> Two other ragged Princes
> His royal state partook!
> Doubtless the first excursion
> These sovereigns ever took!

He is not singular in power as he is seen in other poems, but capable of multiplicity and associated with innovation and origins rather than with paralysis and destruction. The presence of this equipage is delightfully and emphatically meaningful to the speaker.

> I question if the Royal Coach
> Round which the Footmen wait
> Has the significance, on high,
> Of this Barefoot Estate!
>
> [166]

Jung's understanding of the prophetic capacities of the unconscious is helpful here. "The unconscious is no mere depository of the past, but it is also full of germs of future psychic situations and ideas."[16] Poetry was to be Dickinson's royal coach, her vehicle for realization and transformation, and at some level that is so deep as to be yet unconflicted, she knows it here. Her masculine potential, her Logos, as Jung would have it, although his terms are open to question,[17] is immature but alive and functioning.

Why, however, should a positive component of the self, such as this animus-figure seems to be, come to elicit the anguished ambivalence that we have seen Dickinson display in "He Fumbles at your Soul," and "I know that He exists"? Joseph Campbell says, "symbols are only the *vehicles* of communication; they must not be mistaken for the final term, the *tenor* of their reference."[18] The starkly disparate tones of the two pairs of poems indicate two divergent referents, two antagonistic strands of a single unconscious dynamic that can be traced throughout the body of the poetry. Emily Dickinson had the potential to be a great poet; she *was* a great poet, and she must have known that. The psychic energy exuded by her unrealized capacities and the unconscious desire for the recognition of her poet/self must have been considerable. This would be reflected in the joyous image of the positive animus.

But the muse is a hard master and demands total allegiance, often requiring a renunciation of the active will with a resultant threat of disintegration. The promptings of the unconscious, the command of language, the relentless creation of the self in a medium that is alien to the concerns of a pragmatic society, all these demand isolation and radical integrity, selfishness and courage. In our society these traits have long been masculine prerogatives, and Emily Dickinson was a lady. She had been brought up and carefully nurtured in a society that demanded of her that she become a "Soft – Cherubic Creature." I think she was afraid. As Rebecca Patterson has so cogently noted, "She was the victim of an age that mutilated its gifted women."[19] I suggest that, initially, rather than accept the identity of poet with all its implications, she wavered—struggling against the realization of her masculine potential as such, and thus compounded the animus, inviting the anguished psychic influence of its negative face, the dark visage that the Jungian psychoanalyst Esther Harding calls the "Ghostly Lover." Harding describes this potent image as a woman's "animus, projected to the outside world, (which then) draws her irresistibly."[20]

An unconscious psychic strategy for repudiation of the heavy responsibilities of full personal realization, the concentration upon the ghostly lover is a disastrous form of denial of the self. It is not, however, an uncommon phenomenon among women. Some man in the external world, or the possibility of such a man, or the memory of such a man, or the fantasy of such a man, is made to carry the values of the masculine self, and they remain unrealized in consciousness. This second and complementary dynamic in Dickinson's poetry can be seen as co-existent with the first. In the peculiar tolerant manner of archetypes, the positive animus and the negative, destructive animus are simultaneously operative, and can be seen in various and shifting forms throughout her poetry.

Dickinson's radical ambivalence regarding the consequences of conscious identity with the masculine self is seen clearly in her fascination with the ghostly lover, or unrealized and unrealizable romance. In "Of course I prayed," an implied animus figure is externalized and reprimanded.

> Life –
> I had not had – but for Yourself.
> 'Twere better Charity
> To leave me in the Atom's Tomb –
> Merry, and Nought, and gay, and numb –
> Than this smart Misery.
>
> [376]

Here she projects the responsibility for her life upon the Other to whom she speaks. She may not be too far amiss in doing so. Jung suggests that such a projection often initiates the realization of the animus. Harding expands upon the idea as it affects women. "He (the ghostly lover) holds his power and exerts his lure because he is a psychological entity ... part of that conglomerate of autonomous, or relatively autonomous, factors which make up her psyche."[21] Harding goes on to discuss the danger that the values projected in such a form can never be realized in the conscious personality. Therefore the woman "*must* find him and consciously assimilate him if she is not to suffer the pain and distress of disintegration."[22] In the above poem, it seems to the poet that God, denying her the actual flesh-and-blood lover, leaves her no recourse but to exist in a painfully awakened state, conscious of incompletion but wildly and futilely longing for the fulfillment of the self in the Other, rather than in the transformation of the self and consequent realization of individual potential. Nullity looks like an attractive option. The dynamic and the danger are clear:

> The Drop, that wrestles in the Sea –
> Forgets her own locality –
> As I – toward Thee –

[284]

This destructive aspect of the animus, his compulsion as ghostly lover to act "as one who lures his victim away from reality by promises of bliss in another world,"[23] is fascinating to Dickinson. The Death as Lover configuration that is such an inextricable part of Dickinson's mythos of masculinity is vitally relevant to the understanding of this seductive aspect of her negative animus. Three major poems on this theme move with remarkably similar progressions—from the recognition of the suitor's rightful claim to mastery, to the triumphal voyage (almost, but not quite, an abduction) in a dark vehicle that stands in strong opposition to the ramshackle wagon of the freckled monarch discussed above. In a coach, a carriage, or a chariot the speaker is carried through the vanishing world of reality, to an unknown destination out of nature. Harding tells us that the ghostly lover always lures his victim away from reality by promises of bliss in another world. "Because I could not stop for Death (712)," and "Death is the supple Suitor (1445)," are explicit in their assignment of this characteristic of the masterful seducer to the death figure. But the naked motif can best be seen in a less well-known poem, one that does not refer specifically to death, but contains the so-significant indeterminate "He," with whom we have met before.

> It was a quiet way –
> He asked if I was his –
> I made no answer of the Tongue

But answer of the Eyes –
And then He bore me on
Before this mortal noise
With swiftness, as of Chariots
And distance, as of Wheels.
This World did drop away
As Acres from the feet
Of one that leaneth from Balloon
Upon an Ether street.
The Gulf behind was not,
The Continents were new –
Eternity it was before
Eternity was due.
No seasons were to us –
It was not Night nor Morn –
But Sunrise stopped upon the place
And fastened it in Dawn.

[1053]

There is an irreconcilable confusion of reference here. Who is this silent kidnapper? He seems to be death: "He bore me on / Before this mortal noise." But *is* he death? Not necessarily. "Eternity it was before / Eternity was due." This gnomic statement resists explication. Eternity is due at death, so it must be death. But it can't be, because eternity is not yet due. So, therefore, it must be a state something like death, but in what way? Possibly it is like death in that time is held in suspension, dawn becoming a temporal absolute. The speaker of the poem is lifted out of herself into a condition that may well be death or else a state of sexual, or even religious, ecstasy. It is the complete and deliberate lack of subjective comment in the poem that renders its ambiguity so complete. There is not one verb of emotion, not one adjective of emotive value. The "He" of this poem is indeed a strange companion to exert such a compelling influence upon the speaker, yet elicit such an autistic response. If he were death we would expect fear. If he were God or a lover we would expect awe or joy. She doesn't even speak, but answers mutely with her eyes. How significant that confusion of reference comes to seem when we look at it in the context of the underlying motif of the masculine in its archetypal manifestation as the ghostly lover. How significant that silence.

Dickinson exhibits a profound ambivalence; she is fascinated by the numinous presence of this animus figure, but extremely suspicious about the nature of the "bliss" to which he is leading her. What would it mean to be "fastened" in dawn? Would it mean to live always in potential, never in realization? Forever in a condition of stasis? This is the promise of the supple suitor in poem 1445 who leads her only to unlife, to "Kindred as responsive as Porcelain," and of the lover in poem 712 who takes the speaker out of the world of process represented by her journey:

> We passed the School, where Children strove
> At Recess – in the Ring –
> We passed the Fields of Gazing Grain –
> We passed the Setting Sun –

to a suddenly corrected perception, denoting a condition of stasis,

> Or rather – He passed Us –

The Lover Death image is an old one. The psychoanalyst M.-L. von Franz confirms that the animus has often been imaged as a "demon of death."[24] Significant here, of course, is Dickinson's treatment of this figure. The one is again remarkably flat. This suitor is described as kind, his "civility" is duly noted; however, the hopeful, pregnant swell of the grave, his destination, proves a barren and eternal disappointment, and that disappointment casts an ironic negation back upon the idea of an "civility" involved in any way with this interaction. For this eternal nothingness the speaker has put away her "labor" and her "leisure," in a futile and irreversible renunciation of the self.

I wish to make it clear that these last two poems are indeed poems about death, and that a condition of stasis, of suspension of being, is of course to be expected. What is significant, however, is that the poet has transferred, with such apparent ease, the values of the animus figures to these personifications of death, and, accordingly, the values of death to the animus figure. This indicates an awareness, conscious or unconscious, of the lack of self-realization (which to Dickinson came to mean realization as a poet) to be found in any relationship based upon the projection of the animus, upon hopeless and helpless romantic fascination.

The three letters that have come to be known as the "Master" letters, strange and intriguing as they are in their intense, hyperbolic, disjunctive avowals of passion and self-abasement, reinforce our understanding of this destructive dynamic of romance. Richard Sewall postulates a progression for these letters: the first one, which is hopeful in tone, he says, "represents the early stages of her love, the second the climax when she could still imagine herself as having hope, and the last a final cry of despair following a rejection which her Master never explained."[25]

In the first letter Dickinson images the world as "God's house," speaks of angels and of the gates of Heaven. Indeed, with its Sabbath Day setting the poem is located firmly in a context of Christian anticipation. "Each Sabbath on the Sea, makes me count the Sabbaths, till we meet on shore."[26] In religious parlance "shore" could well mean heaven, although I do not discount other, more corporeal, interpretations. The second letter, however, adds a more personal and anguished note, "I heard of a thing called 'Redemption' ... You remember I asked you for it—you gave me something else. I forgot the Redemption (in the Redeemed ...)."[27] Here "heaven" is subtly changed, achieved not through Christian redemption, but located in the "Redeemed," or in the Master himself. Her vision transforms redemption into "something else"—that promised state of bliss, perhaps, that Harding tells us is held out by the ghostly lover as he lures his victim from the world of reality. "So dear did this stranger become that were it, or my breath – the Alternative – I had tossed the fellow away with a smile,"[28] Dickinson continues in a passage she eventually crossed out in the manuscript. "Dear" is indeed a fitting adjective for a love that is purchased at the expense of breath, the cost of life itself. Consider the writer's willing self-abnegation in the final lines of the third Master letter:

> I will never be noisy when you want to be still. I will be ... your best little girl – nobody else will see me, but you – but that is enough – I shall not want any more – and all that Heaven only will disappoint me – will be because its not so dear.[29]

Maturity and autonomy are abdicated in favor of a passion that is now envisioned as surpassing the Christian heaven (that "difficult" grace) in "dearness."

Whether or not these letters were ever sent will most likely never be known for certain, but we can be confident that they were addressed to a particular man with whom Dickinson had in some way been romantically involved. Yet I agree with Richard Sewall when he says, "they raise innumerable question, of which the identity of the recipient, however intriguing, is among the least important."[30] What is important is the manner in which the letters reveal the anguished influence upon this brilliant woman of the projected animus, and the attendant denial of mature, independent responsibility—"I will be ... your ... little girl."

An intriguing aspect of this dynamic is that the negation of self, perversely, may well be the most profound and attractive component of the lure of the ghostly lover. It is the sublimated awareness of the greatness in her soul that Dickinson feels the partial need to deny lest it overwhelm her. Her continual profession of smallness and insignificance and nonentity, especially in conjunction with the masculine, is a not inconsiderable element of this dynamic: "I'm nobody! Who are you?" "I was the slightest in the House – / I took the smallest room –" "How noteless – I could die –." Her repeated use of the contrast between the lowly daisy and the mighty sun is especially suggestive, particularly in light of the "man of

noon" letter quoted above, and considering the fact that she referred
to herself in many poems and letters, including the Master letters, as
"Daisy."[31]

> The Daisy follows soft the Sun –
> And when his golden walk is done –
> Sits shyly at his feet –
> He – waking – finds the flower there –
> Wherefore – Marauder – art thou here?
> Because, Sir, love is sweet!
>
> We are the flower – Thou the Sun!
> Forgive us, if as days decline –
> We nearer steal to Thee!
> Enamored of the parting West –
> The peace – the flight – the Amethyst –
> Night's possibility!

[106]

Meek, common, insignificant, the daisy is hardly worthy of regard by the
magnificent sun. Yet, poetically, the daisy *is* a sun. With its golden center
and surrounding rays, there is a strong visual correspondence, and the
etymological derivation of the word from "daegesege," Old English for
"the day's eye," attests to the resemblance. The animus functions always
as a mediator between the unconscious and the conscious self. But Dickinson cannot acknowledge the correspondence here. What arrogance to
claim for herself the qualities of the man of noon! The divine characteristics of Apollo, of course, are those of the god of poetry as well as of the
god of light. Perhaps it is safer to continue to project the values and remain insignificant. What is "night's possibility" for a daisy after all? The
peace. The flight. Dickinson knows what happens to those who compete
with the gods.

But her fascination with the masculine remains, the archetype continues to exude its mediating energy, and the poet begins, as she must, to
explore the possibility of interaction on a personal level with the light and
power she sees as masculine attributes. What courage this must have
taken. "Oh, Susie, it is dangerous," she cries to her intimate friend, and
the risk is profound and real. In her perception, annihilation, disintegration, alienation, and anguish face her as possibilities in any dealings with
the masculine.

Emily Dickinson's poetry betrays a strong unconscious desire to deny
the masculine self, the nameless "He," to project it outward with a resultant self-negation of the poetic speaker. The strength and composition of
that projection, however, are extremely significant in terms of Dickinson's

desire for personal development. In an insight that is particularly revealing in light of the Master letters, grounded as they are in a "real," external, love, von Franz says, "passion that goes beyond the natural measure of love ultimately aims at the mystery of becoming whole."[32] "Teach her, preceptor grace – teach her majesty –" Dickinson begs her Master.[33] Ultimately, however, she is unable to abdicate the responsibility for her own individuation, her own acquisition of these transcendent qualities. Indifferent, or faced with an impossible love, her Master rejected her, inadvertently throwing her back upon the mastery of self as her only recourse for "grace." As Suzanne Juhasz says, "to command herself is the necessary condition for Dickinson to become a poet."[34] In order to begin to command herself, to become whole, she is forced to adopt an active rather than a passive stance in face of her masculine self.

The chronology of Dickinson's assimilation of the animus is not strictly sequential. While in poems such as "To my small Hearth His fire came –" (638) and "The Lightning playeth – all the while –" (630), there is the evidence of shifting image patterns and changing stances on the part of the poetic speaker to suggest at least a partial integration, it is in the nature of an archetype to endure beyond knowledge, to shift shapes, to exert powerful and conflicting impulses. Emily Dickinson's struggle with the "ghostly lover" who drained her strength and threatened her with silence and paralytic bliss took the form of a long and oblique poetic investigation of the various images that both embodied and obscured the pure energy of the archetype. For Dickinson the struggle was resolved in the process of resolution. While the masculine figure was a lover of a sort, whether in life or solely in imagination—his translation into language made him also a poem. Dickinson's self-realization involved her transformation into a brilliant and transcendent poet. Given the clash between the cruelly limited expectations for women in Dickinson's culture and the grand scope of her innate abilities, it is no great wonder that the impulse to realize those abilities generated an almost debilitating anxiety. It was in the grappling with the specter of that anxiety, with the intangible and terrifying ghost of her own stunning potential, that she found herself wrestling her true salvation, the angel, art.

NOTES

1. In particular, Clark Griffith, in *The Long Shadow: Emily Dickinson's Tragic Poetry* (Princeton: Princeton University Press, 1964), has focused on this issue. His reading concentrates on what he considers Dickinson's "dread of everything masculine, so that one of the bogies she fled from was nothing less than the awful and the implacable idea of *him*" (p. 166). Calling her the

"very prototype of the eccentric maiden lady . . . a figure much given to imaginary fears and to the practice of strange little meannesses" (p. 166), he states that she exhibited "a pathological loathing of the other sex" (p. 167). His discussion of the masculine figure in her poems, surprisingly astute in some specific ways, misses the mark widely in interpretation. In this paper I present an alternate reading of the masculine figure in Emily Dickinson's poetic that allows, through a shift in critical focus, a more sensitive interpretation of the strikingly complex and significant configuration of the masculine in Dickinson's poems.

2. I refer to all poems by the numbers assigned them in Thomas H. Johnson's edition of *The Complete Poems of Emily Dickinson* (Boston: Little, Brown and Company, 1955).

3. *The Letters of Emily Dickinson*, ed. Thomas H. Johnson (Cambridge: Harvard University Press, 1958), vol. 1, p. 210, #93.

4. Edith Hamilton, *Mythology* (1940. Reprint. New York: New American Library, 1969), pp. 54-55.

5. Carl G. Jung, "Approaching the Unconscious," in *Man and His Symbols* (New York: Dell Publishing Co., Inc., 1964), p. 57.

6. Adrienne Rich, "Vesuvius at Home: The Power of Emily Dickinson," *Parnassus* 5, no. 1 (1976): 56.

7. Mircea Eliade, *The Myth of the Eternal Return: or, Cosmos and History*, tr. Willard R. Trask (Princeton: Princeton University Press, 1954), p. 3.

8. Feminist critics have been recently exploring the implications of the masculine literary tradition for female poets. In " 'Come Slowly – Eden': An Exploration of Women Poets and Their Muse" (*Signs* [Spring 1978]: 572-87), Joanne Feit Diehl expands upon the implications of Harold Bloom's dynamic of the "anxiety of influence" for a feminist critique. Speaking of Dickinson, Rossetti, and Barrett Browning, she says that "the precursor becomes a composite male figure: finding themselves heirs to a long succession of fathers, these women share the vision of a father/lover that surpasses individuals. And so for them the composite father is the main adversary" (p. 574). She goes on to say, however, that he is also, as the masculine inspiriting power, envisioned as the muse. This doubly potent figure causes intense anxiety, she (Emily Dickinson) "wards him off . . . as she simultaneously seeks to woo him" (p. 576), fearing both the threat of dependency and the loss of inspiration. Sandra Gilbert and Susan Gubar also discuss this dynamic in *The Madwoman in the Attic* (New Haven: Yale University Press, 1979), pp. 48-49: "Thus the 'anxiety of influence' that a male poet experiences is felt by a female poet as an even more primary 'anxiety of authorship'–a radical fear that she cannot create, that because she can never become a 'precursor' the act of writing will isolate or destroy her."

9. Rich, p. 53.

10. Ibid., p. 57.

11. Albert Gelpi, "Emily Dickinson and the Deerslayer: The Dilemma of the Woman Poet in America," in *Shakespeare's Sisters: Feminist Essays on Woman Poets*, ed. Sandra M. Gilbert and Susan Gubar (Bloomington: Indiana University Press, 1979), p. 123.

12. Ibid., p. 126.

13. Ibid., p. 133.

14. Carl G. Jung, "Aion," in *Psyche and Symbol*, ed. Violet S. de Laszlo (Garden City, New York: Doubleday and Company, Inc., 1958), p. 15.

15. Ibid., p. 19.

16. Jung, *Man and His Symbols*, p. 25.

17. "The animus becomes a Logos . . . gives woman's consciousness a capacity for reflection, deliberation and self-knowledge" (*Psyche and Symbol*, p. 15). Dianne F. Sadoff discusses Jungian gender-based attribution of the qualities of individual consciousness cogently in "Mythopoeia, The Moon and Contemporary Women's Poetry," *The Massachusetts Review* 19, no. 1 (Spring 1978): 93-110. In my own mind I resolve a nagging dissatisfaction with these sexually defined categories of consciousness by accommodating them into a framework of societal deprivation and determination.

18. Joseph Campbell, *The Hero with a Thousand Faces* (Cleveland: The World Publishing Company, 1956), p. 236.

19. Rebecca Patterson, "Emily Dickinson's 'Double' Tim: Masculine Identification," *American Imago* 28, no. 4 (Winter 1971): 330-62.

20. Esther Harding, *The Way of All Women* (Rev. ed. New York: G. P. Putnam's Sons, 1970), p. 36. The idea of the ghostly lover in relation to Emily Dickinson is mentioned in passing by Theodora Ward in *The Capsule of the Mind* (Cambridge: Harvard University Press, 1961). "When the man she loved is withdrawn, a woman must redeem from her love the power and meaning it held for her, or she will be possessed by a ghostly lover whose hold prevents her from moving forward into a new phase." Ward does not, however, identify this figure in Dickinson's poetry, or investigate its qualities. Neither does she consider the possibility of its autonomous existence, pre-existing an actual love object.

21. Harding, p. 38.

22. Ibid., p. 38.

23. Ibid.

24. M.-L. von Franz, "The Process of Individuation," in *Man and His Symbols*, ed. Carl G. Jung (New York: Dell Publishing Co., Inc., 1964), p. 199.

25. Richard B. Sewall, *The Life of Emily Dickinson* (New York: Farrar, Straus and Giroux, 1974), p. 519.

26. Johnson, *Letters*, Vol. 2, p. 333.

27. Ibid., p. 374.

28. Ibid.

29. Ibid., p. 392.

30. Sewall, pp. 512-13.

31. Sandra M. Gilbert and Susan Gubar note this connection in their discussion of the "man of noon" letter, *Madwoman*, p. 596.

32. von Franz, p. 219.

33. Johnson, *Letters*, Vol. 2, p. 391.

34. Suzanne Juhasz, *Naked and Fiery Forms: Modern American Poetry by Women: A New Tradition* (New York: Harper & Row, 1976), p. 20.

ADALAIDE MORRIS **VI**

"The Love of Thee - a Prism Be"

Men and Women in the Love Poetry of Emily Dickinson

A FULL READING OF Emily Dickinson's poems and letters reinforces her striking suggestion that love is a kind of prism. In the poem where it first appears, the image attains an almost allegorical neatness:

> I see thee better – in the Dark –
> I do not need a Light –
> The Love of Thee – a Prism be –
> Excelling Violet –
>
> [611][1]

As a narrow beam of white light spilling through a prism breaks into bands of color, so, this image argues, energy passing through an experience of love reveals a spectrum of possibilities. While in many Dickinson poems love's prism discloses earthly colors, in this poem the possibilities cross time, the colors we know, and then, exceeding violet, probe into eternity. The value of a particular passion, as a later prism poem indicates, is not its romantic resolution, for

> Not of detention is Fruition –
> Shudder to attain.
> Transport's decomposition follows –
> He is Prism born.
>
> [1315]

What matters in passion is its prismatic quality, the range of its refraction. Always for Dickinson love is an opportunity for observation, for hypothesis, for experimentation, for revelation. It is no wonder, then, that this most exploratory of poets wrote poem after poem of love, poems that posit no final love or lover, poems that pour their considerable vision and vitality through very different kinds of passion.

All varieties of love fill Dickinson's work. It is clear that throughout her life she loved frequently, attentively, charmingly, loyally; she loved lightly as often as she loved gravely; and she made a practice of exceeding limits. Just as she often refused to resolve a poem by selecting among her many alternate word-choices, so she hesitated to choose any one habit of loving. She moves easily across moods and conditions, through the intensities of fantasy and flirtation, into and out of fully imagined love. She knew how to be an ardent friend, partner, lover, worshipper. As she told a girlhood friend in the last year of her life, she had known and still "this moment knew – /Love Marine and Love terrene – /Love celestial too –" (*L.*, p. 865): her love had explored every territory she could conceive.

This emotional mobility puts in doubt the either/or assumption of recent debates between those who argue that Dickinson's emotional and erotic ties were to men and those who insist that they were to women.[2] It is clear by now that throughout her life Dickinson was deeply, wholly compelled by men and women both. Her letters and poems suggest, moreover, that for her these two sorts of love varied greatly. To use her metaphor, they formed separate prisms and energy passing through them cast quite different spectrums. To examine the nature and intensity of this difference will be the purpose of this essay.

The list of Dickinson's possible attachments is long, and our confusion is augmented by the fact that many of her letters and no doubt many of her poems have been lost to us, both through carelessness and through deliberate destruction.[3] Two significant sets of writing to those she loved remain, however. The letters to the man she called "Master" are, as Richard Sewall points out, "among the most intense and fervent love letters she ever wrote,"[4] and they are supplemented by dozens of poems with similar vocabulary, rhythm, imagery, and symbolic pattern. The other group, addressed to her friend, sister-in-law, and next-door neighbor, Susan Gilbert Dickinson, consists of 154 extant notes and letters and 276 identifiable poems and poem fragments, probably a mere fraction of a lifetime's whole. The biographical details are gone: we don't know who her "Master" was, we know almost nothing of her sensual experience, we don't even know if those she loved loved her back. A plentitude of verbal detail remains, however, to allow us to compare the two prisms these loves formed and the very different spectrums they cast.

The rhetoric that describes the two relationships is surprisingly, even suspiciously similar, as if Dickinson were writing to the Master and Sue out of some peculiarly elliptic book of pattern letters. Both correspondences are highly compressed and heavily revised: the Master letters exist in drafts that hesitate over each choice of diction, syntax, and symbol, and rough drafts remain for even the most casual of notes sent across the lawn to Sue.[5] In both cases, the revisions make continuous minute adjustments between advance and evasion, excitement and control. Urgent and edgy, her writing teases, pleads, chides, jests, and sighs. The rhythms are by turns abrupt and sustained, gnomic and rhapsodic.

Both the Master and Sue evoke her passion; both are passionately solicited, courted with imagery chosen to convey their magnetic pull. Again and again she describes herself as bewitched, overwhelmed. The most revealing recurrence, however, is the linked imagery of sun, storms, volcanos, and wounds that she uses in both sets of letters and poems. Sue is "an Avalanche of Sun!" (*L.*, p. 733), a woman of "torrid Noons" (*L.*, p. 831); the Master becomes her "man of noon . . . *mightier* than the morning" (*L.*, p. 210). When the element of disturbance joins this imagery of huge heat and height, we have the thunderstorms described in so many poems sent to Sue. The setting is explosive, even volcanic: a sky sealed with "A Cap of Lead" (1649), wind rocking the grass (824), thunder piling and crumbling (1247), while

> Through fissures in
> Volcanic cloud
> The yellow lightning shone –
>
> [1694]

When explosion is withheld, Dickinson's image shifts from the thunderstorm to the silent, suppressed volcano vividly present in both sets of material. "Vesuvius dont talk – Etna – dont –," Dickinson reminds the Master, but so intense is the repressed force, she continues, "one of them – said a syllable – a thousand years ago, and Pompeii heard it, and hid forever" (*L.*, p. 374). This is the dangerous "Vesuvius at Home" (1705), the deceptively domestic surface she describes in a poem sent to Sue:

> On my volcano grows the Grass
> A meditative spot –
> An acre for a Bird to choose
> Would be the General thought –
>
> How red the Fire rocks below
> How insecure the sod
> Did I disclose
> Would populate with awe my solitude.
>
> [1677]

The red, rocking, inner fire of this poem is unreleased passion, passion that endangers everything around it. The heat, intensity, and destructively deep interiority this image stresses connect it with the last of the series: the image of the profound inner wound. This is the hurt Dickinson describes to Sue as a sting (156), a stab (238), the gash that "wantoned with a Bone" (479), and to the Master as a stab (*L.*, p. 392), the "bullet" which "hit a Bird" (*L.*, p. 373), the "Tomahawk in my side" (*L.*, p. 392).

The linked imagery of intensity, explosiveness, suppression, and mutilation suggests the extravagance of Dickinson's commitments. Her awareness of such excess is evident in the second major similarity in the rhetoric of these relationships: both sets of material are self-consciously idolatrous. Both toil to set the loved one in the place of divinity; both struggle to maintain wholehearted, blind devotion to someone not usually worshipped, to someone in fact probably not worthy of worship.

Dickinson uses several strategies here. One defines the beloved as a better heaven than heaven itself. "This [union]," she tells Sue, "is the lingering emblem of the Heaven I once dreamed" (*L.*, p. 306); after death, "all that Heaven," she tells the Master, "only will disappoint me – . . . because it's not so dear" (*L.*, p. 392). Another stratagem is to set a scene of salvation and give the beloved a better part than Jesus. In the poem "Dying! Dying in the night!" for example, the Savior arrives but the sufferer still cries for Sue, here summoned by her nickname:

> Somebody run to the great gate
> And see if Dollie's coming! Wait!
> I hear her feet upon the stair!
> Death wont hurt – now Dollie's here!
>
> [158]

The singsong, sideways rhythm reinforces Dickinson's wry play with the trope of Christ the Bridegroom, a figure she returns to in a similar scene of midnight rescue where the Bridegroom is her other lover:

> Softly – my Future climbs the stair –
> I fumble at my Childhood's Prayer –
> So soon to be a Child – no more –
> Eternity – I'm coming – Sir –
> Master – I've seen the Face before –
>
> [461, 2nd variant]

A third strategy, implied in the others, is to ask the beloved for the gift which is Christ's to give. "I heard of a thing called 'Redemption' – which rested men and women," she reminds the Master. "You remember I asked you for it – you gave me something else. I forgot the Redemption [in the Redeemed]" (*L.*, p. 374). The letters to Sue are full of such deliberate forgetting: others go to meeting, for example, but she summons Sue to "the church within our hearts, where ... the preacher whose name is Love – shall intercede" (L., p. 181); others said " 'Our Heavenly Father,' " Dickinson recalls, "I said 'Oh Darling Sue' " (L., p. 201). Such language celebrates an idolatry of love, the faith that, as she explains to Sue in a late poem, "to be undone/Is dearer than Redemption" (1568, 3rd variant).

This is an intense—and intensely familiar—discourse. Sun, storms, volcanoes, wounds, rescue, redemption: all emerge from that catalogue of romantic generalities Adrienne Rich calls "the language of love-letters, of suicide notes."[6] This language seems to fit so easily into both sets of letters and poems that we might suppose it signifies a mode of loving Dickinson solicited from men and women both. Such a suspicion is bolstered by the existence of love poems with alternate sets of pronouns: in a particularly apt example, one variant of poem 494 begins "Going to Him! Happy letter!" while the other starts, "Going – to – Her!/Happy – Letter!" We would be wrong, however, to conclude that similar rhetoric describes a similar sort of love. The kind of love Dickinson desires and develops with a woman is very different from the love she desires and develops with a man. The similarities in rhetoric mask deep dissimilarities of structure.

Romantic rhetoric permits only one set of relations, the paradigm of disturbance and idolatry that is everywhere consonant with the structures of her love for Sue. Western traditions offer no developed discourse for love between women and thus, in need of a precedent, Dickinson may have used conventional romantic rhetoric in the letters and poems to Sue as a linguistic formula signifying an intensity (love) rather than a structure (dominance/submission). The most intriguing aspect of the writing to Sue is the consistency with which the clichés of romantic love are undermined by a revolutionary revision of love's possibilities.

The differences in structure are coded into the names Dickinson assigned her lovers: a "Master" can exist only in a world of difference and hierarchy; a "Sister," on the other hand, inhabits a world of similarity and equality. The structures of the Master's world are predominantly vertical and its dramas are largely dramas of positioning: the prostration of the woman, the exaltation of the man. She is forever "a tiny courtier" as the pageant of his tremendous glory (151). By contrast, the structures of the sisters' world are horizontal, not a universe but a neighborhood. Its dramas detail the flexible push and pull, the coming and going of those who live day to day, side by side. Against the abstract dignity of stasis in the Master material, the two figures in the poems and letters to Sue demonstrate a scrappy spontaneity: they are alternately large and small, far and near, magisterial and coy.

The difference between Emily Dickinson's envisioning of her love for men and her envisioning of her love for women is radical enough to suggest her sense of herself as a participant in two separate yet simultaneous universes. Not simply the separate social worlds detailed in Carroll Smith-Rosenberg's important work,[7] these are two opposed conceptual realms. They constitute the world differently. In one the supremacy of the patriarch informs the rituals of courtship, family, government, and religion; in the other, the implied equality of sisterhood is played out in ceremonies of romantic, familial, social, and even religious reciprocity. When he appears, the male is Lover, Father, King, Lord, and Master, and the woman, metal filing to his magnet, accordingly takes a complementary position. It is only when the male does not signify—as he does not in the letters and poems to Sue—that the woman can take her position as Lover, Sister, reigning Queen, and deity.

In the couples the letters and poems construct, the initial premise is difference from the Master, similarity to Sue. "Have you the Heart in your breast – Sir," one letter plaintively inquires, "– is it set like mine – a little to the left – has it the misgiving – if it wake in the night – perchance?" (*L.*, p. 374). Any affinity —emotional, philosophical, even anatomical—is open to question. The Master is clearly one of the men who said "What" to Dickinson (*L.*, p. 415), and much in her letters struggles to respond. The Master cannot comprehend her poems: "You ask me what my flowers said," she notes, "I gave them messages" (*L.*, p. 333). He will not acknowledge her declarations of love: "One drop more from the gash that stains [my] bosom –," she asks, "then would you *believe*?" (*L.*, p. 373). He apparently even refuses to credit her sincerity: "You say I do not tell you all –," she protests," [I] confessed – and denied not" (*L.*, p. 374).

The expectation with Sue, on the other hand, is immediate comprehension. The poems she sent received, from all appearances, quick, full, critical response,[8] and the almost daily notes the two women exchanged indicate a richly constant attentiveness. As one message suggests, far from wondering whether Sue had a heart, Dickinson felt free to locate, measure, and apprehend Sue's heart by her own:

> For largest Woman's Heart I knew –
> 'Tis little I can do –
> And yet the largest Woman's Heart
> Could hold an Arrow – too –
> And so, instructed by my own,
> I tenderer, turn Me to.

[309]

Between them there is often mystery and pain, but there is always some fundamental certainty. "Sister," as one letter redundantly puts it, "We both are Women" (L., p. 445). On this basis much of the writing to Sue builds, rising sometimes into such elaborate imagery of identity as this earlier offering: "Here is Festival – Where my Hands are cut, Her fingers will be found inside" (L., p. 430).

The metaphors Dickinson selected to describe her relationship with the Master repeatedly link her sense of otherness to her feeling of subordination. She is small, passive, dependent: *"His little Spaniel"* (236), his hunting gun (754). Her existence is contingent, to be located only in relation to his encompassing power. If she is a "minor stream" then he is "the awful sea" (506), but if she is a sea then he becomes the tide-controlling moon:

> Oh, Signor, Thine, the Amber Hand –
> And mine – the distant Sea –
> Obedient to the least command
> Thine eye impose on me –
>
> [429]

Unlike the imagery of fused hands, these are images of domination. They stress the speaker's sense of difference and diminishment.

The name Dickinson takes for herself throughout the Master material is "Daisy," and this is the image she uses most consistently to present her place in their relationship. His beard makes him rough, but her petals are soft, pliant (L., p. 374). Where she is humble and low, he remains proudly remote. Though she emerges predictably "in white" to please him, he has a self-generating, vast, various sweep and in his grandeur he is generally oblivious to her (L., p. 374).

Dickinson places the Daisy in a number of pairings, all of which emphasize imbalance. Some poems juxtapose the Daisy and the "Immortal Alps" (124) or the Daisy and "The Himmaleh" (481) to stress the flower's evanescent diminuitiveness. Other poems pair the Daisy and "Great Caesar" (102) or the Daisy and "Her Lord" (339) to portray the flower's luxurious bending to a masterful will. But the most telling juxtaposition is the major iconographic pattern of the Master material: the relation between the Daisy and the Sun.

The poem "The Daisy follows soft the Sun" gives best access to the significance of this pattern, for it reminds us that the daisy, or day's eye, is named for its tropism, its involuntary orientation to the sun:

> The Daisy follows soft the Sun –
> And when his golden walk is done –
> Sits shily at his feet –
> He – waking – finds the flower there –

> Wherefore – Marauder – art thou here?
> Because, Sir, love is sweet!

The Master's question—"Wherefore – Marauder – art thou here?"—is the puzzle the imagery is designed to solve. A marauder is one who roams in search of plunder, and the daisy, though bewitched by the sun's huge sweet gold, is neither roamer nor raider. "We are the Flower – Thou the Sun!" the poem explains, "Forgive us, if as days decline – /We nearer steal to Thee!" (106). The daisy's "stealth" is not arrogation of another's being or belongings but rather a furtive, secret, all but imperceptible movement. It would be useless to withhold forgiveness, for the daisy cannot help following the sun. Tropism is an image that at once explains and condones her unquestioning subservience. Beyond reason or right, beyond reciprocity, the daisy's love has the inevitability of a reflex.

A poem that begins by quoting another of the Master's questions— " 'Why do I love' You, Sir?"—proceeds with a series of analogies to mock his rational inquisitiveness. "The Wind does not require the Grass/To answer – Wherefore when He pass/She cannot keep Her place," Dickinson notes; "The Lightning – never asked an Eye/Wherefore it shut – when He was by." The final example, tropism, clinches her argument:

> The Sunrise – Sir – compelleth Me –
> Because He's Sunrise – and I see –
> Therefore – Then –
> I love Thee –
>
> [480]

The overdetermined "Therefore – Then –" gives away the game. The drama of the love of a daisy for the sun could never be logical, no more than it could be various or reciprocal. It is a love enacted in steady, compelled subjection.

If the term "Master" all but names the other member of the couple "slave," there are many ways in which this designation is apt. The speaker of the Master material relinquishes control, embraces the terms of living set by another entity, and accepts domination. "So say – if Queen it be – / Or Page – please Thee –," one poem affirms:

> I'm that – or nought –
> Or other thing – if other thing there be –
> With just this Stipulus –
> I suit Thee –
>
> [738]

"What Thou dost –," as a related poem declares, "is Delight – /Bondage as Play – be sweet" (725).

To use Simone de Beauvoir's terminology of subject and object, self and other, the Master letters and poems offer the spectacle of a self willing itself to be an inessential other. Sometimes the speaker merely pretends inferiority to glorify the Master's primacy: she plays "Backwoodsman" to accent "his finer nature"; she calls herself "Slow (Dull)" so he may seem quick and gracious (L., p. 391). At other times, however, her role as object seems necessary to define his as subject, a moment most clearly signalled by the speaker's appearance as "it." In one poem, for example, for his "dear – distant – dangerous – Sake" she poses herself as a thing: "Why make it doubt – it hurts it so –," the poem begins, only to end, "Oh, Master, This is Misery –" (462). In just the process de Beauvoir describes, the woman has become "the incidental, the inessential as opposed to the essential. He is the Subject, he is the Absolute—she is the Other."[9]

The poems and letters to Sue, though they participate in the rhetoric of exaltation and abasement, suggest a fundamentally different struggle: the asking and giving, accusing and apologizing of autonomous beings. Where the Master material presupposes helpless subservience, the poems sent to Sue present exchanges between willful equals: they are two pilots (4), peasants (66), pirates (11), two mountain-dwellers (80) or mountain-climbers (446), even two millionaires (299). The hierarchies the poems to the Master are written to establish, these poems attack with withering sarcasm. "Unworthy of her Breat," one poem sputters,

> . . . by that scathing test
> What Soul survive?
> By her exacting light
> How counterfeit the white
> We chiefly have!
>
> [1414]

The speaker's insistence on her own worth gives these poems a very different stance: in them she refuses to be a party to romantic formulas, declines to play the Other, and resists what Simone de Beauvoir calls "the temptation to forgo liberty and become a thing."[10]

The letters and poems to Sue often stretch after metaphors for a love outside conventional romantic patterns. One of the most intriguing attempts imagines her relationship with a woman as a "Dimpled War," a loving contest between powers who fight "Without a Formula":

> 'Tis Seasons since the Dimpled War
> In which we each were Conqueror
> And each of us were slain
> And Centuries 'twill be and more
> Another Massacre before
> So modest and so vain –

> Without a Formula we fought
> Each was to each the Pink Redoubt –
>
> [1529]

Jotted on a scrap of paper originally attached to another sheet, this poem has the edginess of many of Dickinson's reprimands to Sue. Whether or not it was actually sent to Sue, it suggests the two related rules which seem to have governed their relationship: variousness and reciprocity. Too protean to be stylized, the figures in the poems to Sue both take each role in love's dramas: each is to each conqueror *and* slain, massacre *and* "the Pink Redoubt" which protects against massacre. In this material, for every celebration there is a complaint, for every cry of the conqueror there is a cry of the wounded, for every aggression a desire to soothe and shelter. The one requirement is reciprocity, the rule that privileges by mutually exchanged and that each take her turn in sheltering the other. By this rule when Dickinson writes,

> Sue
> Could *I* – then – shut the door –
> Lest *my* beseeching face – at last –
> Rejected – be – of *Her*?
>
> [220]

the answer, of course, must be no. In a relationship of equal responsiveness, neither participant can completely close her heart to the other's needs.

The stasis of the Master material, where he is perpetually conqueror and she is perpetually slain, gives way here to rhythms of cyclical recurrence. This is especially evident in the shift in Dickinson's poetic use of the sun. When the Master letters and poems emphasize the sun's scorching dominion over the daisy, the scene is the universe and the time span is eternity. The solar poems to Sue celebrate a local, daily, neighborhood event: the setting of the sun behind Sue's house. Almost a tenth of the poems remaining in Sue's possession were sunset poems, and these include some of Dickinson's finest work. In poems like "Blazing in Gold and quenching in Purple" (228), "The Sun kept stooping – stooping – low!" (152), or "She sweeps with many-colored Brooms" (219), Dickinson matches her poetic power against the sun's display and, as one playful piece asserts, it is she who emerges the winner:

> I send Two Sunsets –
> Day and I – in competition ran –
> I finished Two – and several Stars –
> While He – was making One –

His own was ampler – but as I
Was saying to a friend –
Mine – is the more convenient
To Carry in the Hand –

[308]

Carried by Timothy, the handyman who each evening brought the milk first to the Mansion, Emily's house, and then, with her messages, next door to the Evergreens,[11] sunset poems like these accompanied Dickinson's notes to Sue and helped her celebrate the daily intensities of blazing and quenching which linked the two women. The sun that set over the Evergreens rose over the Mansion. It came to stand not for dominion but for a daily sharing, the joining of the two houses in a moment of radiance.

The imagery of the sunset, because its gist is intensity, cannot clarify the structures of Dickinson's relationship with Sue in the same way the daisy/sun imagery clarifies her relationship with the Master. A more comparable code in the letters and poems to Sue is the imagery of birds and nests. The daisy/sun and bird/nest images address the same problem: the balancing of attraction and autonomy. The daisy/sun imagery resolved this dilemma by eliminating one element: within the terms of tropism, autonomy is not possible. The terms of the bird imagery, however, suggest another kind of solution.

The symbolic function of birds is first predicted in an early letter of crisis. "Sue –," the letter begins, "you can go or stay – There is but one alternative – We differ often lately, and this must be the last" (L., p. 305). This curt, either/or ultimatum yields, at the letter's end, to a different formulation, one mediated by the image of the bird. In an allegory of reconciliation, Dickinson writes,

Then will I not repine,
Knowing that Bird of mine
Though flown
Shall in a distant tree
Bright melody for me
Return.

[5]

The imagery allows the kind of both/and solution Dickinson needs and can only seem to achieve within the letters and poems to Sue. The bird is both its own and "mine," both distant and devoted, both autonomous and attentive.

Birds perch, sing, soar, disappear, migrate to some distant land, and then return to nest. The emphasis here, as in the sunset imagery, is on cyclical rhythm. The bird will migrate, yet the hope expressed in poem after poem is that through love's attraction it will reappear and, in a final extension, that it will choose to nest within the lover's heart.

A telling aspect of the imagery of nesting is that, unlike the daisy/sun system, it can work reciprocally. In some poems it is Sue who "as a bird her nest,/Builded our hearts among" (14). In others the speaker herself enacts the allegory:

> Her heart is fit for *home* –
> I – a Sparrow – build there
> Sweet of twigs and twine
> My perennial nest.
>
> [84]

Whichever the builder, Dickinson's concern is for the nest's careful construction, its sweet snugness, and its function as a base for flight and return. These characteristics epitomize that world of mutual nurturance that exists side by side in Dickinson's work with the harsher world of the Master. The signals of this world are words like *heart*, *home*, and *nest*, and a necessary, if not sufficient, condition for its appearance is the presence of women who create for each other an intimate and sustaining shelter.

The two very different sets of relations constituted within Dickinson's love poetry are neither isolated nor self-generating. They correspond in significant ways to larger social and metaphysical structures. In Dickinson's male/female couple, the supremacy of the Master replicates nineteenth-century American patterns of courtship, family, government, and religion. Because the male/female couple is symmetrical with other parts of the patriarchal system, Dickinson can use familial, civic, and religious metaphors to describe the couple or, conversely, use intersexual metaphors to describe social and metaphysical systems.

Nina Baym's hypothesis that the relationship between Dickinson's speaker and her male lover is governed by the same rules that govern the relation between the speaker and her father and the speaker and God is fully supported by the Master material.[12] In it, social structures fit neatly one inside the other: as the speaker is to the Master, so a child to its father, so a subject to its King, so a petitioner to the Lord. The Master is the Father for whom she becomes the "best little girl" (L., p. 392); he is the judge before whom she "kneels a culprit" (L., p. 391); he is the "wheeling King" who confers or withholds status (232); he is her God, the origin and end, the Unmoved Mover of her fate.[13] Throughout this material, Dickinson speaks with the apprehensive voice of a child or supplicant. Despite her edges of irony, she accepts and works within the conditions of a patriarchal universe.

This is not the case in the letters and poems to Sue. They come as from a different universe. Because the female/female couple stands outside conventional structures, the metaphors Dickinson selects are more exploratory and subversive. When they draw from familial, civic, and religious structures, they do so in order to oppose and even collapse them. The voice throughout is predominantly that of an adult speaking to an adult or, more precisely, a woman addressing a woman.[14] In the symmetrically expanding metaphorical contexts, each setting replicates the effort toward equality in the original relationship: as the speaker is to Sue, the series runs, so sister is to sister, so queen to reigning queen, and so, finally, a petitioner to something like a cosmic nurturing principle.

From her very first letter to Sue, Dickinson chose the word "sister" to describe their bond (L., p. 101). This metaphor gathers Sue into the most enduring unit Dickinson knew, the family. "Why Susie – think of it –," she explains, "you are my precious Sister, and will be till you die, and will be till you die, and will be still, when Austin and Vinnie and Mat, and you and I are marble – and life has forgotten us!" (L., p. 315). Such intense bonding is traditionally associated with a mother, the figure who might be expected to take in the womanly universe the elevated position the Master/father holds in his. Dickinson never places Sue in a maternal position, however, because to do so would negate an element crucial to the relationship she desired: the assurance of equality.

When Dickinson speaks to Sue of sisterhood, she seems to have in mind a family without fathers, a world of women apart from male authority. As Dickinson's imagery of female governance reveals, authority in this world belongs to female rulers. Although queens exist in the Master material, only kings signify. The sole excuse for a queen in that universe is her devotion. "If I wish with a might I cannot repress – that mine were the Queen's place –," Dickinson assures the Master, "the love of the Plantagenet is my only apology" (L., p. 374).

The poems to Sue present queens without kings, reigning monarchs who across some distance salute each other's splendor and sovereignty. Dickinson's use of this image is, for the most part, straightforward. Sue is majestic (L., p. 880), she is "royal" (L., p. 813), she is "Power . . . Glory . . . and Dominion, too –" (L., p. 432), she is Emily's Cleopatra (L., p. 533). Before her, Emily, the Queen Recluse,[15] does not demean herself. There are, however, two obscure and rather desolate poems—"Like Eyes that looked on Wastes" (458) and "Ourselves were wed one summer – dear" (631)—which complicate the image. These poems explore the idea of a royal marriage between queens.

The first poem seems to portray a situation in which neither woman can free herself to accomplish a union both women want. The poem ends in multiple ambiguities:

Neither – would be absolved –
Neither would be a Queen
Without the Other – Therefore –
We perish – tho' We reign –

Several implications open out of the word "absolve": neither can absolve herself of the obligations of power (therefore, "We reign"), neither can be absolved of the consequences of guilt (therefore, "We perish"), neither can be absolved from her compulsion toward the other (thus, "So looked the face I looked upon – /So looked itself – on Me –"). It is clear that unlike the union of king and queen this marriage would be mutually empowering, that "Neither would be a Queen/Without the Other," but it is also clear that the union cannot be achieved. It remains "A Compact/ As hopeless – as divine."

The second poem—"Ourselves were wed one summer – dear" (631)— substantiates the first poem's hopelessness. It tells the story of the reabsorption of one queen into the universe of the fathers. Whether or not this poem treats Sue's marriage to Emily's brother, Austin,[16] it builds on the contrast between a summer wedding that unites two queens and a June marriage that separate them. Paradoxically, the second wedding is both a "crown[ing]" and a diminishment: it legitimizes the bride and yet it marks the moment "when [Her] little Lifetime failed." To describe this failure, the poem turns from an energetically subversive vision of a marriage between queens to the most domestic of clichés: "Your Cottage – faced to the sun"; "Your Garden led the Bloom"; your marriage was "in June." The poem, like the queen, subsides into a harmless and predictable banality.

Patriarchal rituals, whether domestic, social, or religious, never effectually threatened the bond between Sue and Emily. Much of the material Dickinson sent Sue, in fact, shows that they engaged to the end in a conspiracy against patriarchal pretensions and rigidities. What the Master letters and poems take seriously, this material pokes fun at. There are poems which laugh at fathers who yank you from bed at dawn (13), at scientists who "Compute the stamens" of flowers (70), at ministers who aren't what they seem (1453) and solemn patriarchs who scuffle with angels (59). There is even a poem that takes on "Papa above," the one who presides pompously over the cosmic cycles (61). Papa above, like the Master, like the Father, like the King, is serenely oblivious to the struggles of those below.

Perhaps Dickinson felt free to mock this hierarchy because her interchanges with Sue—as with her sister Lavinia, with Kate Scott Turner Anthon, with Mrs. Holland and the Norcross sisters, and with the other women who were important to her—suggested the possibility of constituting the world differently. Unlike Papa above, the deity belonging to this system would be both maker and cunning caretaker of the mortal world. She would not be too elevated to notice birds and nests, nor would she be too abstracted to note the fall of a sparrow. Her concern is immediate and intimate:

> Mama never forgets her birds,
> Though in another tree –
> She looks down just as often
> And just as tenderly
> As when her little mortal nest
> With cunning care she wove –
> If either of her "sparrows fall,"
> She "notices," above.
>
> [164]

In recapitulating the imagery of the earliest poems to Sue, this poem indicates how consistent the patterns in this material are. The spectrum cast through the prism of her love for Sue, as it moves outward from the intimate to the infinite, from the couple to the cosmos, consistently reveals possibilities unimaginable in the terms of the spectrum cast by her love for the Master.

If love poems written for a Master almost inevitably reproduce paradigms sanctioned by the dominant culture, one of the appeals of the poetry written for Sue must have been the release it offered from such reiteration. The letters and poems sent to Sue yearn towards, explore, and celebrate a very different world. Perhaps this is what Dickinson meant when, toward the end of her life, she dashed off one of her enigmatic notes to Sue, who had apparently just left or perhaps just returned to town: "That Susan lives –," Dickinson declared, "is a Universe which neither going nor coming could displace" (*L.*, p. 659).

NOTES

1. *The Poems of Emily Dickinson*, 3 vols., ed. Thomas H. Johnson (Cambridge: Harvard University Press, 1955). Poems are cited by the number Johnson assigned to each. References to Dickinson's letters (*L.*, followed by the page number) are to *The Letters of Emily Dickinson*, 3 vols., ed. Thomas H. Johnson (Cambridge: Harvard University Press, 1958).

2. The most revealing confrontation between these positions occurred in the pages of *Signs* where Joanne Feit Diehl in her essay " 'Come Slowly – Eden': An Exploration of Women Poets and Their Muse" (*Signs* 3 [Spring 1978]: 572-87) argues that Dickinson perceived a mythic male as the source of her poetic power and Lillian Faderman and Louise Bernikow rejoin by arguing that Dickinson's muse was a female power (*Signs* 4 [Autumn 1978]: 188-

94). Adrienne Rich's essay "Vesuvius at Home: The Power of Emily Dickinson" (*Parnassus* 5 [1976]: 49-74) treats the male muse as an inner daemon, the creative spirit Keats called "The Genius of Poetry."

Informative discussions of Dickinson's love for the Master include Richard B. Sewall's chapter on "The Master Letters" in volume two of his *Life of Emily Dickinson* (New York: Farrar, Straus and Giroux, 1974), Nina Baym's essay "God, Father, and Lover in Emily Dickinson's Poetry," in *Puritan Influences in America*, ed. Emory Elliott (Urbana: University of Illinois Press, 1979), and the chapter entitled "A Woman – White: Emily Dickinson's Yarn of Pearl" in Sandra M. Gilbert and Susan Gubar's *The Madwoman in the Attic: The Woman Writer and the Nineteenth-Century Literary Imagination* (New Haven and London: Yale University Press). Useful discussions of Dickinson's love for a woman include Lillian Faderman's essays "Emily Dickinson's Letters to Sue Gilbert" (*Massachusetts Review* 18 [1977]: 197-225) and "Emily Dickinson's Homoerotic Poetry" (*Higginson Journal*, no. 18 [1978]: 19-27) and Jean McClure Mudge's essay "Emily Dickinson and 'Sister Sue' " (*Prairie Schooner* 58 [1978]: 90-107).

3. On the deliberate mutilation of the manuscripts by Susan's husband, Austin, see R. W. Franklin, *The Editing of Emily Dickinson: A Reconsideration* (Madison, Milwaukee, and London: The University of Wisconsin Press, 1967), pp. 78-81.

4. Sewall, *Life of Emily Dickinson*, vol. 2, p. 512.

5. See, for example, *Letters*, vol. 3, p. 743.

6. "Trying to Talk with a Man," in *Diving into the Wreck: Poems 1971-72* (New York: Norton, 1973), p. 3.

7. "The Female World of Love and Ritual: Relations between Women in Nineteenth-Century America," *Signs* 1 (1975): 1-29.

8. A good example of Sue's familiarity with and critical response to Emily's work is the correspondence they carried on about the early poem "Safe in their Alabaster Chambers," quoted in Johnson, *Poems*, Vol. 1, pp. 151-55.

9. *The Second Sex*, trans. H. M. Parshley (New York: Bantam, 1961), p. xix.

10. *The Second Sex*, p. xxiv.

11. Martha Dickinson Bianchi, *Emily Dickinson Face to Face: Unpublished Letters with Notes and Reminiscences* (Boston and New York: Houghton Mifflin, 1932), p. 8.

12. See Baym, "God, Father, and Lover in Emily Dickinson's Poetry," passim.

13. "Unmoved Mover" is the wonderfully apt term used by Gilbert and Gubar, "A Woman – White," p. 663.

14. The exceptions are poems in which Dickinson, using an appropriately childish voice, summons Sue by her nickname "Dollie." See poems 51, 156, and 158.

15. "The Queen Recluse" is a nickname Samuel Bowles, the Austin Dickinsons, and perhaps the rest of the family used fondly to refer to Emily. See Samuel Bowles's letter to Austin Dickinson, quoted in Jay Leyda, *The Years and Hours of Emily Dickinson* (New Haven: Yale University Press, 1960), vol. 2, 76.

16. This is John Cody's argument in *After Great Pain: The Inner Life of Emily Dickinson* (Cambridge: Harvard University Press, 1971), p. 394.

"Oh, Vision of Language!"

Dickinson's Poems of Love and Death

EMILY DICKINSON AS A woman poet enters in a non-traditional way into the ongoing dialogue in Western literature and metaphysics over the dualism of subject and object.[1] It would seem that Emerson's claims to overcoming Cartesian dualism might have liberated any subsequent American poet from the burden of entering this dialogue, but Emerson's claims do not fully apply to or help Dickinson. To oversimplify enormously, he performs this overcoming from the point of view of a strong subject exerting power over and internalizing everything he sees, or as he writes in *Nature* of the figure whom he calls man,

> More and more, with every thought, does his kingdom stretch over things, until the world becomes, at last, only a realized will,—the double of the man.[2]

The term "Man" does not appear to be as inclusive for Dickinson as it is for Emerson. As a self-consciously female writer she engages the issue of dualism in a non-traditional way, because the feminine is traditionally identified with what Emerson terms "all things" and "the world," not with that powerful self whose thought may be victorious. Woman as category is traditionally the object, not the source of that power. A dualism of presence and absence, of subject and object, of self and other, structures everything thinkable, yet women do not participate in it as subjects as easily as do men because the feminine self is said to be categorically on the same side of that dualism with what is traditionally the other, and that "said to be" has always carried a burdensome authority. Feminist theory argues that our most basic formulations of dualism and of subject-object relationships originate in gender difference, and that wherever dualism is present, which may be every time a word is spoken, the question of the objectification of women is raised. Various reasons, both from literary and from psychological theory, have been proposed for this alignment of the feminine with the object; suffice it to say that a woman growing up in Dickinson's historical and literary context would have learned that men say *I* and that women do not.[3]

Dickinson's earliest extant poems, the poems in which she first tests the possibility of being a poet, are love poems: the verse valentines of 1850 and 1852 and the rhyming close of an 1851 letter to Austin that Thomas Johnson transcribes as her second poem.[4] Interpersonal relations are structured as subject-object relations in the manner I've been discussing. The poems share both an extravagant metaphoricity and an unsurprising conception of desire as distance and of romantic love as the bridging of that distance. The first valentine consists largely of an exuberant series of analogies for human love drawn from "earth, or sea, or air," and the love thus pictured is seen as the meeting of opposites or complementary parts, or, as the speaker puts it, as "unity made of twain":

> Oh the Earth was *made* for lovers, for damsel, and hopeless swain,
> For sighing, and gentle whispering, and *unity* made of *twain.*
> All things do go a courting, in earth, or sea, or air,
> God hath made nothing single but *thee* in His world so fair!
> The *bride,* and then the *bridegroom,* the *two,* and then the *one,*
> Adam, and Eve, his consort, the moon, and then the sun;
>
> . . . .
>
> The high do seek the lowly, the great do seek the small,
> None cannot find who *seeketh,* on this terrestrial ball;
>
> . . . .
>
> The *worm* doth woo the *mortal,* death claims a living bride,
> Night unto day is married, morn unto eventide;
> *Earth* is a merry damsel, and *heaven* a knight so true,
> And Earth is quite coquettish, and beseemeth in vain to sue.
> [1]

Similarly, the rhymes for Austin develop the conventional metaphor of a garden for the beloved woman, and in such a way that love is the male voyager's crossing of a distance from there to here:

> Never mind faded forests, Austin,
> Never mind silent fields –
> *Here* is a little forest,
> Whose leaf is ever green;
> Here is a brighter garden,
> Where not a frost has been;
> In its unfading flowers
> I hear the bright bee hum;
> Prithee, my brother,
> Into *my* garden come!
> [2]

Although a female persona is speaking in these love poems, her subjectivity is called radically into question by the fact that she continues to subscribe to the paradigm in which subjectivity is male and the object is female. This does not mean that the female identifies her subjectivity as male, but rather that she compromises her subjectivity by seeing herself as the object; as, for example, the static, objectified garden to be sought out by the voyaging and beloved brother. In the valentine, all of the examples of what it sought are stereotypically female, and when the poem turns to the subject of its polemic, the male addressee, it is of course the girls who are to be sought by the man:

> *Six* true, and comely maidens sitting upon the tree;
> Approach that tree with caution, then up it boldly climb,
> And seize the one thou lovest, nor care for *space*, or *time*!

The pattern of subject-object relations forms the theme of heterosexual romance, and its problematic arrangement of male and female is echoed, by design, in the central rhetorical structure of the two poems, extended and extravagant metaphor. Some general remarks about the significance of this connection between romance and metaphor may suggest why this connection adds to the challenges that Dickinson faces as a woman poet. Accepting the Lacanian assertion that subjectivity is constituted of and by language, and that to internalize language is to internalize social and cultural laws, especially those that reflect patriarchal power, the French feminist critic Luce Irigaray argues that the hierarchically organized structure of language, of signifier and signified, repeats and reinforces both the objectification and the repression of women.[5] As in the model of subject-object dualism, an order of priority is unavoidably assigned in any binary system: reading a written text, we are with the signifier, and the signified, the thing actually referred to, is, like the object, somewhere else, absent and secondary to the signifier. One thing, the word, stands for or in the place of something else, the object. And the signified is categorically feminine, just as the object is categorically feminine. For Irigaray, metaphor is the rhetorical figure that typifies this structuring of language, because of all kinds of figuration metaphor involves the most arbitrary relationship and the greatest possible distance between vehicle and tenor; metaphor also depends on and reproduces a hierarchical power structure in which one term claims the authority to define the other term—or, in its implications for the personal, one person claims the authority to define another person. Irigaray agrees with Freud's and Lacan's descriptions that woman's place in a heterosexual system has been to be categorically absent, a lack, and that the structures of language that repeat structures of presence and absence repeat that exclusion of women. When Dickinson uses metaphor and the thematics of heterosexual romance together in her early verse, she raises precisely the issue with which Irigaray is so concerned. Metaphor and heterosexual romance stand in a mutually dependent and even determinate relation to one another in the early love poems, since the bridges built by the structure of metaphor show how romantic love is supposed to work. That is, metaphor gains its effects through coupling unlikely pairs and subordinating one term to another: where human lovers are said to be like earth and heaven or night and day, the metaphor is operating to limit one term to the needs of the other. The romantic making of twain into unity follows this pattern in presupposing an original opposition or dualism in which presence seeks out absence, and, where the male lover is to "seize the one thou lovest," this thematic coupling repeats the assertion of power by one term over the other found in metaphor.

That her community held something of an established place for poetry in the form of valentines, even when written by young women, may be one reason why the first poems she was willing to show to others and to keep were love poems, but these poems are significant as a starting point for her poetry also because of their interdependency of metaphor and love. Poetry for her begins with romantic love and specifically with the model of love that metaphor generates, where difference and subject-object relations structure what it is possible to say and to feel.

When Dickinson began to write more seriously several years after the date of the early love poems, she produced, more or less simultaneously, poems that confirm and poems that critique the hierarchical relationship between lovers that the earliest poems introduce. Most readers' predominant impression is of the first group, in which the self is figured as small, frail, and feminine in relation to a series of powerful, clearly male figures; as, typically, in "Mute thy Coronation –" (151), in which the speaker as a "meek" and reverent "tiny courtier" imagines herself, on the occasion of his coronation, enfolded in the Master's "Ermine."[6] In poems of this kind, Dickinson imagines a possibility for placing herself as a woman that is at once seductive (because traditional and comfortable) and dangerous (because it defines her as silent). Like the lowly and the small sought out by the high and the great in the first valentine, the tiny courtier takes her place with the object and the absent tenor in a hierarchical structure of romantic relations that is like the structure of metaphor. But in other poems written at the same time, Dickinson initiates a radical critique of conventional romantic relations between the sexes, through a simultaneous critique of the dualistic structure of language and of metaphor. The relation between subject and object necessary to the structures both of metaphor and of romantic love obtains as well and most fundamentally for Dickinson (as well as for contemporary criticism) in language's relation between signifier and signified, but as I have argued elsewhere,[7] in her endeavors to transcend or correct this oppositional structure of language, Dickinson pushes language to the border of meaninglessness. Her efforts to undo the subject-object structure of romantic love encounter similar obstacles. One group of poems appears to follow the pattern of the conventional love poems, the pattern begun in the earliest poems and continued in poems such as "Mute thy Coronation –." In this group of poems the powerful male figure (who incorporates attributes both of God and of the father) is figured as the sun, while the fragile female self is figured as a daisy. This conventional polarity, recalling the genuinely conventional male-female relations in the earlier love poems, is set up in these particular poems in order to be collapsed. At the same time, metaphor is shown to be integral to the structure of that relation, and is undercut as well.

In the love poem that begins, "The Daisy follows soft the Sun" (106), at the level of the theme of romantic love the daisy reverses the two figures' apparent relation of authority and humility, while at the level of rhetorical structure the metaphor that underlies both the poem's and the relationship's structure is exposed as illusion.

> The Daisy follows soft the Sun –
> And when his golden walk is done –
> Sits shily at his feet –
> He – waking – finds the flower there –
> Wherefore – Marauder – art thou here?
> Because, Sir, love is sweet!
>
> We are the Flower – Thou the Sun!
> Forgive us, if as days decline –
> We nearer steal to Thee!

As in the poem about Master and the tiny courtier, it is the distance and disparity between the sun and the daisy that structures their relationship, which is then acted out as the effort to bridge that distance. At the same time, as in the earliest valentine, their relation is structured by and as metaphor. As sun and moon are like lover in the valentine, here daisy and sun are like each other because of a minimal visual resemblance that is privileged by and formulated in her name: day's eye. The daisy's name makes her like the sun: a flower called a day's eye is being defined not as itself but in comparison to the sun. The bridging of the tremendous discrepancy between them in status and size structures both their romantic attraction and the metaphor that governs the poem. The perspectival illusion that, as the sun approaches the horizon, the daisy steals close to him visually enacts the way metaphor and romance are working here: she only seems to look like him, and their relation only seems intimate because of an optical illusion.

Through a strategy of mock humility the daisy gently dismantles the sun's pretensions to absolute power, but she can increase her power only by decreasing his. The transcendent third term beyond them both that would benefit both by permitting an escape from a closed system of opposed and relative power is found in the poem's final lines, where the daisy descries what she really wants:

> Enamored of the parting West –
> The peace – the flight – the Amethyst –
> Night's possibility!

"Night's possibility," gorgeous and compelling as it is, both removes the basis of their relationship (visual resemblance and optical illusion) and indeed requires the absence of the beloved sun himself. In moving away from the binary system in which two terms are related by opposition, by distance, and by illusory resemblance, toward the single term of night, the poem collapses its thematics of romance. It also collapses its own rhetorical structure: "Night's possibility" is beyond ordinary communication, which depends on the rhetorical dualism and on the tension between disparity and resemblance that this image rejects. "Night's possibility" is a theoretically ideal but effectively unhappy solution to the problem of hierarchical relations between genders.

The alternative to this self-defeating end to rhetoric, however, where a conventionally heterosexual paradigm is retained, is for Dickinson a silence that represents no improvement. When Dickinson turns to the more conventional conclusion of a male-female love relationship, she figures marriage as a "soft eclipse" (199). Having imagined herself leaving "the Girl's life" behind, the speaker concludes,

> This being comfort – then
> That other kind – was pain –
> But why compare?
> I'm "Wife"! Stop there!

Being wife means stopping, both in the sense that the woman's life stops growing and in the sense that the poem comes to an end. Like the night that closes the poem about the daisy, heterosexuality is imaged as leading to an end to communication. The poem calls a halt to comparisons, especially the obviously disadvantageous one between being a wife and being a girl; but the alternative to comparisons is not to speak at all: "I'm 'Wife'! Stop there!" Without the possibility for the measurement of difference—which is the basis of metaphor as well as of this poem's thematics—language dwindles into silence.

Yet Dickinson of course does not stop there. She is continuously searching for ways to expand the limits of the speakable and the imaginable, both in experience and in language, which for her, living her experiential life almost wholly in the mind, are practically the same. Poetry for Dickinson begins with love as the attraction of opposites and it begins with metaphor's unresolvable dualism of presence and absence. Love becomes a form of oppressive power and the foundation of a rhetoric that reinforces that power. In seeking a way around the bind presented both by romantic love and by metaphor, she arrives at the kind of solution represented in the poem about the daisy and the sun, where to choose night as transcendence is also to choose obscurity of articulation. If heterosexuality models a rhetoric founded on metaphor's hierarchical relation of difference, it may be reasonable to speculate that a love relationship between women might conceptually offer a paradigm for a happier thematics of experience and for a more capacious language. Recent feminist criticism of Dickinson has raised this issue primarily as a biographical and thematic one, and I would like to add to this discussion by looking at the way in which the structure of rhetoric both contributes to and is shaped by the thematics of love between women.[8] Adalaide Morris argues, in her essay elsewhere in this volume, that the relation between a powerful male and a fragile female, based as it is on distance and inequality, is always presented as static, while the love relationship between women, structured horizontally on the basis of similarity and equality, is not static and offers richer imaginative possibilities. I have been trying to suggest that the hierarchical structure of heterosexuality is not always static and that the poems that question and subvert that structure are among her most daringly imaginative. I will also argue that the non-hierarchical structure of exact equality presented in the poems about two women does not always or necessarily offer the kind of positive solution Morris claims for it; in fact, it can lead to the kind of problematic stasis that trouble us, though for different reasons, in the most clearly hierarchical of the heterosexual love poems. Yet the rhetorical and thematic possibilities are suggestive and deserve serious consideration.

The persona Dickinson presents in the letters was clearly capable of being as passionately attached to women as to men, or to the idea of a woman as much as to the idea of a man. However, it is making the transition from letters to poems that is problematic. In addition to 154 notes Dickinson sent 276 poems to Susan Gilbert Dickinson, her friend and later sister-in-law. The case for a sizable amount of homoerotic verse is based on the assumption that these poems also refer to Sue, as if they were no different from the prose messages that are clearly personal in reference.[9] Many of them are framed as messages, headed "Sue" and closed "Emily," but many were sent without elaboration, as if simply for approval or criticism; and many exist in packet (or fair) copies as well as in the versions sent to

Sue. Though a poem's frame of reference may be altered in complex ways by its context, in the absence of conclusive evidence that any given poem originated as a message to Sue, I would prefer to allow these poems the independence from biographical determination usually granted to lyrics.

Looking only at internal evidence, in only a small proportion of the poems sent to Sue (and in a few poems apparently not sent to Sue) is a relation of equals or a subversion of hierarchy explicitly identified as referring to a relationship between two women, but these poems demand close consideration. Where two lovers are categorically the same by gender rather than categorically different or opposite (as in the early valentine and the love poems about Master), their relationship presents a model of language built on contiguity, that is, a possible proximity or identity between signifier and signified rather than a definitive separation and difference. The thematic emphasis in the poems that do refer to two female figures is on similarity and equivalence, indeed on sameness, as characteristically the two figures share the same name or names. As I have argued elsewhere, a number of poems depict the self as composed of two elements that neither form one unified whole nor are separate: they share one name but they are neither the same nor different as entities.[10] There is no hierarchy organizing any difference between these identical elements, so that neither has more power than the other, but instead of the peaceful equilibrium that might be expected in such a situation, these poems are characterized by an intense violence to which there is no forseeable end because of the precise equality of the warring sides. In poem 642 "We're mutual Monarch," and yet "Myself – assault Me –." In poem 683

> The Soul unto itself
> Is an imperial friend –
> Or the most agonizing Spy –
> An Enemy – could send –

Many of the poems involving two figures of women appear to follow the same pattern. Where the relation between two individuals, like the relation between elements of the self, is structured not by oppositeness and hierarchy but by sameness and equality, the resulting stasis often becomes a violent stalemate. Although there are a few poems about women's relationships that are positive in tone or outcome, in what follows I will be considering the poems that present another view.

Among the love poems that are gender-marked in such a way as to define both speaker and addressee as female, "Like Eyes that looked on Wastes" (458) presents both the advantages and the disadvantages of such a strategy both for life and for language and verse. The poem's penultimate lines

> Neither would be a Queen
> Without the Other –

identify this poem as a transaction between two female figures, although the poem is not among those sent to Sue. The relationship in the poem is certainly non-hierarchical, since both either are or are not queens, but what replaces hierarchy is a vision of terrifying absence. The poem begins with an extended comparison between "Eyes that looked on Wastes" and the way the two figures look at each other. There is a perfect reciprocity of looks and looking:

> So looked the face I looked upon
> So looked itself – on Me –

Both are subject, both are object, unlike the heterosexual love poems in which the speaker sees herself as purely the object. But what they see when they look at each other, as in mirrors, is

> Blank – and steady Wilderness –
> Diversified by Night –
>
> Just Infinites of Nought –
> As far as it could see –

The poem ends with a set of paradoxes issuing from this mutual and equal looking:

> The Misery a Compact
> As hopeless – as divine –
>
> Neither – would be absolved –
> Neither would be a Queen
> Without the Other – Therefore –
> We perish – tho' We reign –

The compact here, from which neither would be absolved, is, I take it, the shared absence in both. It is as hopeless as divine for the same reason that "We perish – tho' We reign": the two are both queens, and that is exactly what is terrifying. Queens of misery, they see nothing in each other to relieve or change their mutual state; it is precisely the lack of differentiation between them, the fact that they are equally queens, that causes them to be hopeless and to perish. A state without difference seems (in this poem at least) to be a state like death.

While metaphor has elsewhere been invidious as a structure of mind and of rhetoric, now it is sought out, perhaps as a kind of relief from

sameness. Though the poem's first two stanzas are ostentatiously metaphoric, "Like Eyes . . . / So looked . . . ," the extended comparison offers
no saving difference, since the logic of its content collapses the difference
that its structure might offer. If the eyes are "Incredulous of Ought / But
Blank," then they do not believe the blank, but to disbelieve in a blank is
not yet to put anything in its place but only to counter one negative with
another, as the lines' convoluted chain of negatives suggests. It is very precisely impossible to say whether the "Eyes that looked on Wastes" are
being compared to the speaker's way of looking or to the way of looking
of the face the speaker is looking at. The metaphor serves only to collapse
the distinction between seer and seen, a collapse that is underscored by
the verbal repetitions of the lines

> So looked the face I looked upon –
> So looked itself – on Me –

One of the few other poems that at all clearly refer to a relationship
between women is "For largest Woman's Heart I knew –" (309). In it the
speaker, identifying her own heart as indistinguishable from that of the
other woman and recognizing that it "Could hold an Arrow," chooses a
matching arrow for herself. The poem that opens "She dealt her pretty
words like Blades" (479) is more simply violent; the speaker appears to be
the victim in a situation in which the two women's positions are not equal,
although the violence here is just as disturbing as it is elsewhere. (Poem
479 exists only in a packet copy; poem 309 exists both in a packet copy and
in a copy addressed "Sue" and signed "Emily –.")

Finally, a very late poem that was neither copied into a packet nor,
apparently, sent to Sue, identifies the two actors as participants in a
"Dimpled War" (1529), which suggests, though not definitively, that
they are women. The experience of one exactly duplicates that of the
other:

> we each were Conqueror
> And each of us were slain
> · · · · · · · · ·
> Each was to each the Pink Redoubt –

The equilibrium achieved by this mirroring has produced a stalemate or
statis so complete that time stands still:

> 'Tis Seasons since the Dimpled War
> · · · · · · · ·
> And Centuries 'twill be and more
> Another Massacre before

In addition to the characteristic common to this kind of poem of a violent stalemate leading to stasis, this poem shares with "Like Eyes that looked on Wastes –" an insufficiency of terms, owing to, or causing, the identity between the protagonists. The poem closes:

> Without a Formula we fought
> Each was to each the Pink Redoubt –

To fight "Without a Formula" is to suggest that language might have provided but did not provide rules for combat or for relationship. And to define the lack of formula as "Each was to each the Pink Redoubt" is to say that language's insufficiency in this regard is due to the uncomfortable but obligatory sharing of one term between two individuals. Without different terms, without hierarchy, the two figures are too much the same. As in the reduplication of "looks" in "Like Eyes that looked on Wastes –," there are not enough names to go around, and language fails to prevent what seems now to be the wholly undesirable collapse of one identity into the other.

If heterosexual love relations tend to result in an invidious polarity and hierarchy between genders, and to rely on and reinforce metaphor's inscription of disparity and distance, the most intense relations between members of the same gender seem to result in an equally unappealing situation, if unappealing for opposite reasons. Where metaphor preserves a relationship of distance and hierarchy between the two elements of a comparison, while seeming to bring them together, the poems about two women are characterized by a lack of distance so complete that there is only one identity and one set of terms for the two figures. This rhetoric of sameness may be considered a form of metonymy, in which each figure could be said to be the name of the other, as when the two faces that look at one another are identical and also stand for each other. But this rhetoric of sameness points ultimately towards a lack of language: for each to be the other's "Pink Redoubt" is to be "Without a Formula." The sense of silent closure in the poems about two women suggests that it is the overcoming of hierarchy, not the absence of it, that is conducive to poetry.

What possibilities remain, among relationships that might model new kinds of language to respond to dualism's bind? An alternative to the relationship between two women appears in a series of poems about two lovers (who are sometimes specified as male and female, though more often gender is not specified at all) one or both of whom are imagined as dead. The rhetorical mode again could be categorized as metonymy, but unlike the poems about two women, the poems about love after death use metonymy not to limit the two figures by causing them to share one name or set of terms, but, starting from an assumption of original difference, to make them more present to each other. Rather than reducing language these poems open up new kinds of linguistic meaning. A late poem rather cryptically identifies love, poetry, seeing God, and death in one apocalyptic vision:

> To pile like Thunder to it's close
> Then crumble grand away
> While Everything created hid
> This – would be poetry –
>
> Or Love – the two coeval come –
> We both and neither prove –
> Experience either and consume –
> For None see God and live –

                                        [1247]

Love and poetry are both apocalyptic because both are visions of God and to see God is to die. The poem leaves us with the paradoxical definition of poetry as post-linguistic (hence the necessary difficulty of reporting on or verifying these experiences) and of love as post-experiential. The moment at which language becomes poetry is precisely the moment when we cease to be able to understand it, and that is the same moment when love occurs: just as we cease to be able to experience it. That it is only in death that these imagined solutions occur tacitly acknowledges the impossibility of a solution practicable in mortal life. Like many later poems, this one gives us a result without the process leading up to it; I would like to look back at some poems about love, death, and language from the early 1860s, poems that may suggest some of the sources of this equation.

Many of these earlier poems concentrate, apparently rather gruesomely, on the image of the recently dead body of the beloved. Between lovers who have been separate all their lives communication just now begins— paradoxically, it would seem, as the possibility for it ends. The speaker has spent her life at a distance, occupied with "guessing" the lover's "translated faces" (253). The lover is a text and this separation is for Dickinson analogous to the structure of language and of metaphor: it is built on the absence of the signified. The touch and direct vision possible at or after death in these poems represent a different structuring of language by metonymic contiguity rather than by difference or absence; they model a less dualistic language. Death diminishes all differences, including language's necessary difference. As the lovers are reunited, signifier and signified become one and the boundary between life and death vanishes. That these poems may be about language as much as they are about love and death diminishes the shock of their necrophilia, but their violation of language's decorum is no less startling than their apparent violation of the decorum of the grave.

In the poem that begins "If I may have it, when it's dead" (577), "it" appears to refer to the lover's body and the speaker imagines with delight what she will do when "It shall belong to me –."

> Think of it Lover! I and Thee
> Permitted – face to face to be –
> After a Life – a Death – We'll say –

The speaker appears simply to be reversing the terms for life and death here, but instead of completing the reversal by calling death life, she substitutes for death a pure, referentless presence:

> For Death was That –
> And this – is Thee –

This presence is insistently physical. In possession of the body, face to face at last, the speaker pictures herself telling the lover what she experienced immediately after the lover's death. After describing the initial stoppage of time and of sensation, she will "tell Thee"

> Then how the Grief got sleepy – some –
> As if my Soul were deaf and dumb –
> Just making signs – across – to Thee –
> That this way – thou could'st notice me –
> > [variant: speak to me]

The turn to purely visual signs at this point suggests a model of language involving the greatest possible contiguity. These signs depend for their communication of meaning on the lovers' being face to face, while written or even spoken signs could travel some distance. The signs made here have no identifiable content separate from the fact of sign-making itself, nor need they have. Language here signifies only its own process, without difference. Simply to communicate with the dead, to make signs and be noticed (or, according to a variant, even to be spoken to), is what is desired. Similarly, in the poem that begins "I've none to tell me to but Thee" (881), in which the speaker constitutes herself as a text, the death that seems to have taken the lover "Beyond my Boundary –" is negated when the speaker assumes that the lost lover can hear and answer a question that she poses, and that she

> the Answer may pursue
> Unto the lips it eddied through –
> So – overtaking Thee –

Again, *what* the lover answers is not as important as *that* he answers. The speech that crosses the boundary between life and death is a language in which the physical properties of the sign are as important as what it signifies: at the end of the search for the source of speech there is a kiss. What it signifies is that and how it signifies: the act of communication is itself the love. Whether aural as here or purely visual as in "If I may have it," this sign-making after death denies the distance between signifier and signified.

One of the signs the speaker will make when the lovers of "If I may have it" are face to face is

> A smile, to show you, when this Deep
> All Waded – We look back for Play,
> At those Old Times – in Calvary.

Dickinson frequently uses Calvary as a general term for human suffering, especially the pain of living apart from the beloved. But Calvary also has meaning among Dickinson's terms about language. In the probably very late poem "A Word made Flesh is seldom" (1651) she uses the image of the Incarnation as God's "condescension" to criticize patriarchal religion and patriarchal language use; the poem proposes the revision of that condescension into the relationship of "consent" implied by the definition of language as "This loved Philology." If the Incarnation is the Word stooping to assume the burden of human flesh, Calvary is the agonizing reversal of the Incarnation, when the suffering and now wholly human flesh of Jesus is left to cry out "Sabachthani" (313) while the Word, now wholly spirit, departs to heaven. The look back on a life of separation from the beloved as Calvary is to define a lifetime's separation from the lover as an extended severing of "Word" from "Flesh." Suffering will necessarily accompany any relationship (within words or between lovers) founded on the Incarnation's faulty premise that the Word must condescend to assume the flesh. Calvary is the consequence when either language or love is structured as a hierarchy. The old language tore word from flesh, the old life tore lover from lover. Now, through the apparently gruesome concentration on the lover's body, the flesh, the signifier, is restored to a position of importance. "Face to face," making visual signs that are what they signify, the speaking lover insists that Calvary is over—both that the lovers' agonizing separation is over and that language's difference is no longer necessary for the production of meaning. The poem closes,

> Forgive me, if the Grave come slow –
> For Coveting to look at Thee –
> Forgive me, if to stroke thy frost
> Outvisions Paradise!

With her emphasis on looking and touching, this speaker's Paradise is explicitly antithetical to the heaven of the orthodox, which is always by definition just out of reach and always non-physical.

Meeting slightly less unconventionally when both are on the other side of the grave, the lovers of the poem beginning " 'Twas a long Parting – but the time" (625) are described as "Fleshless," and their meeting seems, on the model of the Incarnation and its reversal, a meeting of words without flesh, of two signifieds without signifiers. Yet the description of their meeting insists on literal vision. Meeting for "The last – and second time,"

> These Fleshless Lovers met –
> A Heaven in a Gaze –
> A Heaven of Heavens – the Privilege
> Of one another's Eyes –

The poem goes on to assert that they are all new, as if unborn, except that they bring with them from life the visual memory of a mutual gaze:

> No lifetime set – on Them –
> Appareled as the new
> Unborn – except They had beheld –

The insistence on a visual remainder, and the apparent identity between what "They had beheld –" and what they gaze at now, undercuts the implications of their being described as "Fleshless." Death is not a simple confirmation of dualism, a separation of the limitless spirit from the limiting flesh. The poem joins "If I may have it" in its argument against the notion of an antithesis between body and soul. The pure gaze, like the kiss that answers "I've none to tell me to but Thee" or the silent signs of "If I may have it," images a language where signifier and signified are becoming one.

"A single Screw of Flesh" (263) also begins with the notion of a dualistic boundary to be crossed by a transformation in language. The poem opens with a conventional dualism of flesh and soul:

> A single Screw of Flesh
> Is all that pins the Soul
> That stands for Deity, to Mine,
> Upon my side the Vail –
>
> One witnessed of the Gauze –
> It's name is put away

The soul that stands for deity, the lover (who elsewhere replaces God in the speaker's unorthodox worship: " 'Your Face / Would put out Jesus' "

[640]), remains connected to the speaker only by the fact of his living flesh; once he is glimpsed on the other side of the veil or gauze he is dead. But this soul curiously becomes its own name as it vanishes in death:

> It's name is put away
> As far from mine, as if no plight
> Had printed yesterday,
>
> In tender – solemn Alphabet,
> My eyes just turned to see,
> When it was smuggled by my sight
> Into Eternity –

In other poems as well the beloved's precious face becomes a name as one or the other lover vanishes into death. In poem 336, "The face I carry with me – last –" will assure her a high rank in heaven. By the last stanza, the face appears to have become the Master's name, and yet its effects remain insistently visual:

> he'll turn me round and round –
> To an admiring sky –
> As one that bore her Master's name –
> Sufficient Royalty!

Vision and language are one here. The speaker in "A single Screw of Flesh" struggles to keep hold of the vanishing name, and seems to succeed, because the poem ends with the speaker's refusal to let it go:

> So greater than the Gods can show,
> They slink before the Clay,
> That not for all their Heaven can boast
> Will let it's Keepsake – go

The conventional, dualistic heaven of "the Gods" would separate the two souls, presumably the now purely spiritual beloved from the still embodied speaker. But the speaker affirms her superiority to "their Heaven" in her denial of separation, both of body from soul and of lover from lover. A keepsake, like a name, is something that is valued not so much for what it is in itself as for its metonymic associations. But the poem insists that as metonymy rather than metaphor, the name, as a keepsake, is not just an arbitrary signifier or representation; a name that can be held does not just "stand for Deity" but is tangible and valuable in itself through its contiguity to the beloved. The Gods think human bodies are merely "Clay," but the poem insists that names are more than mere incumbrances that conceal the soul. At the end of the poem, "Clay" is holding "Keepsake," in place of the dualistic and frangible pinning of soul to soul with a screw of flesh with which the poem began. As the notion of "standing for," or metaphor, becomes metonymy (in the figure of the name as keepsake), a dualistic heaven is revised into a perpetual breaking of boundary.

These poems break down the disturbing hierarchy between Master and the tiny courtier (or other diminutive female figure) without falling into the trap of total lack of differentiation that the poems about two women encounter in proposing their solution to hierarchy. Where the imagined state of death creates a possibility for the overcoming of hierarchical differ- ence, it is valued and celebrated; but where no difference appears, it may be that a stasis that is like death to the imagination is already occurring. That a structure of mutuality makes the two women perish, while the al- ready dead can, in the imagination, gain from such a structure, suggests Dickinson's perfect, if perhaps ironic, willingness to accept the idea that the best experience can take place only in the realm of the imagination. The poems about death imagine an impossible point of suspension or equilibrium just before or just as oppositeness passes into sameness and perhaps as gender difference passes into sameness and as language passes into silence. Pushing out the boundaries of possibility for love relation- ships and for language, Dickinson locates a point where communication is as close to perfect as possible without denying the necessity for her own remade and yet still fully intelligible language, in fact for poetry.

Although I have earlier insisted on maintaining a decorum between personal and poetic utterances, so as not to risk making wrong inferences about the poetry from information in-the letters, it may be worth noting a suggestive moment in the letters that provides an analogy for, and thus may underscore, much of what I have been arguing in this paper about the relation between language, love, and death. The cryptic exclamation "Oh, Vision of Language!" closes a letter of 1882 about her mother's re- cent death, and obliquely as she puts it, in context she seems to have in mind, as she does in the poems discussed above, that an apotheosis of language, not its extinction, takes place in a world beyond death.[11] The line just before this exclamation expresses the hope "that all is safe in your unspeakable home." The letter is addressed to Mrs. Sweetser, whose parents-in-law had been the Dickinsons' neighbors and who had both died earlier in the year; and a passage earlier in the letter links them to Dickin- son's mother:

> Wondering with sorrow, how we could spare our lost Neighbors, our first Neighbor, our Mother, quietly stole away. [L. III, p. 748]

An unspeakable home is one from which loved ones have departed; when the letter writer exclaims "Oh, Vision of Language!" she seems then to be tracing the departure of language with the loved from the home to the heavens.

The letter's central theme, arising from an account of the mother's death and from thanks for the recipient's kindnesses, has been the relationship between death and symbolism, and it is in this context that her exclamation is especially relevant to our concern with rhetoric. The following passage appears earlier in the letter:

> The last Token but one, on which her dear Eyes looked, was the Grapes from you. The very last, a little Bird, from thoughtful Mrs. Hills.
> Grapes and Birds, how typic, for was she not on her sweet way to a frostless Land?

A letter from about the same time to the Mrs. Hills referred to in the last letter repeats the same theme:

> The last Gift on which my fleeing Mother looked, was Mrs. Hills' little Bird. I trust this Morning, a Bird herself, she requires no Symbol.
> [L. III, p. 746]

And finally to Mrs. Holland she writes:

> The dear Mother that could not walk, has *flown*. It never occurred to us that, though she had not Limbs, she had **Wings** –
> [L. III, p. 746]

The departure of language from the home to the heavens coincides with the shift from understanding these objects (grapes, bird) as tokens of friendship, to the poet's converting them into symbols of death and immortality, to, more startlingly, a leveling of difference in death between symbol and symbolized. The dead require no symbol, she says, because for Dickinson death is the place where symbols come true, where words become things and where the distance between the thing symbolized and the symbol, between tenor and vehicle, collapses into pure presence. The diction of the exclamation, "*Vision* of Language" indicates that language is made visible or literal at the same time that it becomes visionary or transcendent.

Dickinson's textual responses to her two parents' deaths differ enormously, and they differ along the lines of the gender differences that appear in the poems. The father that emerges from the letters remains to the end the awesome patriarch. Her epitaph for him, "His Heart was pure and terrible and I think no other like it exists" (L. II, p. 528), reminds us that he was one likely model of the hierarchically defined male figures in the poems. Her narrative of her last moment with him underscores this similarity:

> The last Afternoon that my Father lived, though with no premonition – I preferred to be with him, and invented an absence for Mother, Vinnie being asleep. He seemed peculiarly pleased as I oftenest stayed with myself, and remarked as the Afternoon withdrew, he "would like it not to end."
>
> His pleasure almost embarrassed me and my Brother coming – I suggested they walk. Next morning I woke him for the train – and saw him no more.
>
> [L. II, p. 528]

Like the daisy and the sun, the crucial dynamic of this relationship is the formal distance between the two figures; to endeavor to mitigate that distance is joyous, but when that effort threatens to become too successful, the intimacy dismantles itself. The narrative of the mother's death is entirely different. Dickinson celebrates an exact leveling of differences that occurred towards the end of her mother's life:

> We were never intimate Mother and Children while she was our Mother – but Mines in the same Ground meet by tunneling and when she became our Child, the Affection came –
>
> [L. III, pp. 754-55]

The interchangeability of terms, and the fact that it was a prelude to the mother's death, here recalls the poems about two women in which, without hierarchy of any kind, the two figures are both queens, and both conqueror and slain. The "Vision of Language" in which words become things as they and the mother vanish into death follows in time and both thematically and rhetorically supersedes both the hierarchical relationship with the father and the relationship of equivalence with the mother. The history in the letters may then provide a compact image of the sequence I have been tracing in the poems. Beyond a thematics of hierarchy and a rhetoric of metaphor, beyond a thematics and a rhetoric of sameness—and beyond men and women—Dickinson identifies in an imagined state of death a vision of language that opens new vistas of possibility both for language and for love.

NOTES

1. A version of this essay was read at the special session on Dickinson organized by Suzanne Juhasz at the MLA Convention, 1980; I am very grateful to the panelists for their helpful comments.

2. Ralph Waldo Emerson, *Nature, Addresses, and Lectures*, ed. Robert E. Spiller and Alfred R. Ferguson (1849; Cambridge: Harvard University Press, 1971), p. 25.

3. Various versions of the dualism of subject and object are fundamental to a wide spectrum of feminist readings of culture and society. See for example Simone de Beauvoir's use of the philosophical terms Self and Other in *The Second Sex* (1949; New York: Knopf, 1952); Dorothy Dinnerstein's psychological analysis of the mother as every infant's first experience of an object separate from the self in *The Mermaid and the Minotaur* (New York: Harper and Row, 1976); or the analysis of women's place in literary categories in chapters one and two of Sandra Gilbert and Susan Gubar, *The Madwoman in the Attic* (New Haven: Yale University Press, 1979).

4. All quotations from Dickinson's poetry are from *The Poems of Emily Dickinson*, 3 vols., ed. Thomas H. Johnson (Cambridge: Harvard University Press, 1955), cited by the number Johnson assigned each poem.

5. Women's exclusion from language has been the general subject of Irigaray's work for some time; see especially the essays "Ce Sexe qui n'en est pas un," "Cosi fan tutti," and "Quand nos lèvres se parlent" in *Ce Sexe qui n'en est pas un* (Paris: Minuit, 1977) and "Women's Exile: Interview with Luce Irigaray" in *Ideology and Consciousness* 1 (1977): 62-76.

6. For the most salient discussion of Master and the other male figures of power, see Joanne Feit Diehl, *Dickinson and the Romantic Imagination* (Princeton: Princeton University Press, 1981), ch. 1: " 'Come Slowly – Eden': The Woman Poet and Her Muse," pp. 13-33.

7. Margaret Homans, *Women Writers and Poetic Identity* (Princeton: University Press, 1980), pp. 176-88.

8. See for example Lillian Faderman's "Emily Dickinson's Letters to Sue Gilbert" (*Massachusetts Review* 18 [1977]: 197-225) and "Emily Dickinson's Homoerotic Poetry" (*Higginson Journal*, no. 18 [1978]: 19-27); Jean McClure Mudge, "Emily Dickinson and 'Sister Sue' " (*Prairie Schooner* 52 [1978]: 90-107); and Adalaide Morris, " 'The Love of Thee – a Prism Be': Men and Women in the Love Poetry of Emily Dickinson," ch. 6 in this volume.

9. The case for Dickinson's attachment to women is argued, with respect to the letters, with varying degrees of persuasiveness by Faderman, Mudge, and Morris (cited above). There are a few poems that use Sue's name, as for example poems 14, 51, 156, and 158, and a few that I would admit sound as though they are very personal in reference, as for example poems 220 and 631. But it is simply not justifiable to assume (as does Mudge, pp. 101-2) that in poem 159 "A little bread – a crust – a crumb" refers to a crumb "presumably of Sue's love," or that "Your Riches – taught me – Poverty" (299) is addressed to Sue (or to anyone in particular); or to assume (as does Morris, p. 106) that the "Pilot" in poem 4 or the other figures of addressees that are not specified even as to gender are the same Sue addressed by name in the correspondence.

10. Homans, *Women Writers*, pp. 208-14.

11. Quotations from the letters are from *The Letters of Emily Dickinson*, ed. Thomas H. Johnson and Theodora Ward (Cambridge: Harvard University Press, 1958), cited as *L.* followed by volume and page numbers.

How "Low Feet" Stagger
Disruptions of Language in Dickinson's Poetry

EMILY DICKINSON SEES AND understands her world through her manipulation of words. According to her logic, if one is to be anything more than a passive observer of the world, one must exercise some essential control over those words, and for Dickinson this control often takes the form of a linguistic violation. Violating the norms of language is nothing new in poetry; poetic language has even been defined as a language that aesthetically violates a standard language or a poetic norm.[1] For a nineteenth-century woman, however, the necessity is more complex. To participate in the control of social or personal relationships, a nineteenth-century woman had to disrupt, to some extent, existing (male) authority structures. Similarly, to gain some control over structures of language, a poet had to work free of existing (implicitly male) patterns of poetry and language. Dickinson fundamentally identifies these two necessities. Consequently, at least in some poems, she sees the archetypal poet as a woman; she substitutes a female poet for the traditional male norm.[2] In her poetry about female creators and their creations, Dickinson disrupts or undercuts standard linguistic and poetic forms in order to disrupt normative ideas about creation and about women. In all of her poems, Dickinson uses disrupted norms of grammar, syntax, and typography to question or criticize assumed knowledge.[3] Dickinson manifests her (female) poetic freedom in undermining traditional patterns of language.

Dickinson attempts to build up the possibilities of personal choice and control in her poems, not to create a female-dominated hierarchy of power. To her mind, powers, like meanings themselves, do not remain stable or balanced for long; nonetheless, her ideal seems to be a kind of balance. The poet attempts formally to create that fragile equilibrium in which two forces—a man and a woman, a personal weakness and a strength, the norm and the singular, or a word's grammatical, lexical rules and its metaphorical meanings—attain a temporary reciprocity.

Poetry results from and creates such a balance, and in Dickinson's poetry the delicacy of the balance is often central to the poem.

Dickinson generally restructures hierarchies of power or role associations through a parallel disruption of some word's normal use or meaning. For example, the "low feet" of the tired housewife in "How many times these low feet staggered" (187) become the burning words of a secret poet when we remember that a housewife's "feet" may also be iambic, and note that "low" also means "flame" in Dickinson's 1841 Webster's dictionary.[4]

> How many times these low feet staggered –
> Only the soldered mouth can tell –
> Try – can you stir the awful rivet –
> Try – can you lift the hasps of steel!
>
> Stroke the cool forehead – hot so often –
> Lift – if you care – the listless hair –
> Handle the adamantine fingers
> Never a thimble – more – shall wear –
>
> Buzz the dull flies – on the chamber window –
> Brave – shines the sun through the freckled pane –
> Fearless – the cobweb swings from the ceiling –
> Indolent Housewife – in Daisies –lain!

> [187]

The idea of flaming poetic feet in line one helps to explain the "soldered mouth" of the second line: poetic feet are spoken, and flame solders; poetry burns the reader, or poet, into silence. Further, this reading of "low feet" makes us reread "staggered"; the housewife's poetic feet may have staggered us as often as her laboring feet have staggered through her chores. The poem of death becomes a poem of celebration: death brings the housewife rest, and staggering poetry removes its reader, or creator, from the world of housekeeping as absolutely as death does. The flame solders; this private staggering of the soul cannot be shared. The secret poet is as awesomely undisturbed by our nagging and prying as the corpse is by our perversely curious touch. Although this poem's reversal hinges on word play and etymology rather than on grammatical or syntactic disruption, its pattern is typical of those disruptions. The staggering "low feet" of weakness, read differently, become the staggering "low feet" of poetic power. The harried and then "Indolent Housewife" becomes a prototype for the secret poet.

Dickinson restructures role associations perhaps most clearly through an unconventional use of pronouns. For example, although both the moon and the sea are traditionally given female attributes in English poetry, in poem 429 Dickinson begins by casting the sea as a male.[5]

> The Moon is distant from the Sea –
> And yet, with Amber Hands –
> She leads Him – docile as a Boy –
> Along appointed Sands –
>
> He never misses a Degree –
> Obedient to Her Eye
> He comes just so far – toward the Town –
> Just so far – goes away –
>
> Oh, Signor, Thine, the Amber Hand –
> And mine – the distant Sea –
> Obedient to the least command
> Thine eye impose on me –

The sea is at first a "Boy"—docile, obedient and strictly confined; he comes and goes only "so far" along his mistress's "appointed Sands." In the final stanza of the poem, Dickinson reverses what she has presented as the natural roles of authority. Here a Signor has the (female) moon's ruling "Amber Hand" and the speaker (presumably a woman) becomes the obedient attentive (male) sea. However, the lovers' reversal of command and obedience seems to be willed by the female speaker. Furthermore, insofar as the speaker creates the metaphor, she appoints the bonds of the relationship and thus, like the female moon, continues to lead her Signor. The relationship of the first two stanzas and the poem and the depth of the speaker's humility at the end also suggest that her absolute obedience to her lover is more apparent than real. Whether as sea or moon, she seems to be calling the shots, and another reversal, realigning her with the female heaven, could occur at any time.

The central metaphor of the poem further suggests the speaker's unadmitted strength. By using the cycles of the moon and the tides to signify control and obedience, Dickinson indicates that neither party is in control. The patterns of their movement are synchronized, but neither the moon nor the sea has any choice in, or any potential to vary from, those prescribed movements. Obedience and control are the reciprocal gifts of the relationship, whether control is attributed to the distant lady or the distanced Signor.[6]

In other poems, Dickinson repeats the tide or sea metaphor to much the same effect. For example, in poem 643, "I could suffice for Him, I knew –/He – could suffice for Me," the woman/"syllable" and "He" begin in equilibrium. Each is a "Fraction" that could suffice to make the other whole, although the woman fraction rebels at the man's proposal to

become so. In the last lines of the poem, she questions whether she must
accept the sea's answer as her own: must she, too, "adjust her Tides –
unto –" his proposal?

> The Answer of the Sea unto
> The Motion of the Moon –
> Herself adjust Her Tides – unto –
> Could I – do else – with Mine?

Even if, in answering her question, we suppose that she cannot do otherwise, the adjustment remains her personal "Decision" and it occurs entirely under her control. No one else may adjust her tides.[7]

Poems 249 and 732 take a different twist on the sea metaphor in reversing expected sex roles. In "Wild Nights – Wild Nights!" (249), the
woman is the ship that seeks to "moor – Tonight –/In Thee!"—an activity more representative of male than of female social and sexual behavior.
It is stereotypically the woman who is "port" to the wandering, promiscu-
ous male. "She rose to His Requirement" (732) compares the mind of the
"Woman, and . . . Wife" to the sea, with its "Pearl, and Weed" buried
so deep that only "Himself" (logically also the wife) would know of them.
In her "unmentioned," past or perhaps potential, inner life of tremendous
richness and expansiveness, the meekly obedient "She" assumes the masculine role of control and power: Himself.[8]

In poem 481, Dickinson again undercuts expected hierarchical and
gender relationships by using an unexpected pronoun, although this poem
is about a flower instead of the sea. "The Himmaleh" that is "known to
stoop/Unto the Daisy low" is presumably male, and presumably more
powerful than the "Daisy" or "Doll" below. However, the poem's final
lines lead us to conclude either that the Himmaleh is a "Her" or that the
"Universe" that snows on both of them is the daisy's:

> The Himmaleh was known to stoop
> Unto the Daisy low –
> Transported with Compassion
> That such a Doll should grow
> Where Tent by Tent – Her Universe
> Hung out it's Flags of Snow –

[481]

Because Dickinson's mountains in her flower poems are usually male, and
because *Himmaleh* is so suggestively masculine, we conclude that the universe is probably the daisy's. Thus, the mountain's condescension to the
"Doll" at his feet is entirely inappropriate to the majestic force and control of her "low" power—reminiscent of the housewife's in poem 187. The
mountain 'transports' itself downwards in "Compassion," but meanwhile

the daisy's universe caps the mountain with her celebratory "Flags of Snow."[9]

Dickinson's parallel disruptions of both a linguistic and a thematic norm do not by any means always relate to gender associations, nor do her unorthodox uses of language always correspond directly to a disrupted thematic norm. However, most of Dickinson's disruptions of language function in ways similar to each other and similar to the unorthodox pronouns examined above; they have a thematic relevance to her poems whether or not they operate thematically in a particular poem. The poet may have been simply confused, for example, about whether one wrote the possessive 'its' with or without an apostrophe (see "it's" in poems 481, 754, 858 quoted in this essay),[10] but she clearly intends her deviations from other norms, and her poems suggest similar motives for these deviations, thereby also suggesting that her deviation from language rules as a whole stems from a single, general poetic principle. Examining the logic behind these repeated, deliberate deviations leads me to conclude that there is such a principle, and that its manifestations pervade all levels of her poetry.

The immediate effect of the poet's unorthodox uses of language is to subvert our sense of a word's or poem's single association, meaning or reference. A person is both he and she, weak and powerful; action occurs but in no time, with no agent, thus it cannot be located but it goes on indefinitely; figures are simultaneously singular and collective; language patterns are used to create meaning and at the same time misused. An expected, traditional association or reference exists and it does not, just as the housewife's feet are humble and powerful. The standard form or association is cracked, allowing a less fixed, often paradoxical, association to join it. Dickinson's use of unorthodox language does what she claims a woman must do and a poet should do: escape the restrictions of old form by undercutting it in radical but relatively unobtrusive ways and thereby suggest at least temporary new possibilities of form and meaning.

Perhaps the most unusual of Dickinson's syntactic disruptions is her use of uninflected verbs, or verbs unmarked for tense and person, used most often in place of third-person singular verb forms. Critics have agreed to some extent in interpreting her use of this ungrammatical form as an attempt "to universalize her thought" or to reach the essence of meaning.[11] In a poem about essential meaning, Dickinson uses four uninflected verbs in eight lines:

> Essential Oils – are wrung –
> The Attar from the Rose
> Be not expressed by Suns – alone –
> It is the gift of Screws –

> The General Rose – decay –
> But this – in Lady's Drawer
> Make Summer – When the Lady lie
> In Ceaseless Rosemary –
>
> [675]

Here Dickinson substitutes "Be," "decay," "Make," and "lie" for their expected forms to demonstrate how one enables meaning—whether as scent or as poetry—to remain vital. Essence "Make Summer" endlessly. The verb is detached from all limitation of person or time; it, like the rose, is reduced to its purest and most potent form. As the poem tells us, essential meaning is not wholly natural; it is not "expressed" alone by the natural producers of either flowers or poetry: the daily repeated "Suns" of summer or, perhaps, the succeeding generations (sons) of male poets. Instead, essential meaning requires both the efforts of suns (sons?) and Screws; it is the secret poetry of "Lady's Drawer," the "gift" of Dickinson's manifestly torturing the language of nature or established growth.

Dickinson's distortion of these verbs also suggests that the poem is not a single finished thing. Although the sachet, or poem, has been completed, the emphasis is on the process of expressing, or being expressed, a process that continually involves both the poet's "Screws" and the facts or "Rose" of language. Reading a poem returns us to the roses of summer. Dickinson's uninflected verbs manifest this continuous recreation. They present their root meaningfully but leave their action unfinished: the "Essential Oil" is continuously "expressed"; it "Make Summer"; the process does not end.

Similarly, in another poem, Dickinson writes:

> No Crowd that has occurred
> Exhibit – I suppose
>
> [515, ll. 1-2]

There we stop. It should be "No Crowd . . . has exhibited," we think; these past crowds seem still to exist.[12] And for the purposes of the poem, they do. Apparently, just as Dickinson accepts no limitations of tradition or expectation on the actions of men and women in the first group of poems discussed, she will accept no limitations of person and time (tense) on the truths or abstract relationships she proposes in other poems. She sees the fluidity of agent and time suggested by unmarked verbs as the "Essential Oil" of a poem or of one's life. Each reader at each reading, or each poet at each new creation, returns to the "Screws" and "Rose" of expression.

Dickinson's truncated participial adjective "create" in poem 664 also suggests both infinite potential and incompleteness.

Of all the Souls that stand create –
I have elected – One –
When Sense from Spirit – files away –
And Subterfuge – is done –
When that which is – and that which was –
Apart – intrinsic – stand –
And this brief Tragedy of Flesh –
Is shifted – like a Sand –
When Figures show their royal Front –
And Mists – are carved away,
Behold the Atom – I preferred –
To all the lists of Clay!

[664]

Leaving "create" without an "ed" gives the first line of this poem the proper number of syllables, but it also suggests that the 'soul' may be creat*ed* or creat*ing* or itself creat*ive*.[13] The soul "create" is an "Atom," the basic building component of all solid structure. Like the protean atom, it exists in the limbo of infinite potential but only temporarily specifiable form. Thus, in isolation, at any particular time, it can only be conceived as the essential element of that process leading to completion; it is "create"—a verb without the grammatical marker of acting person or infinitive presence and without the closure of a participial, gerundial, or adjectival ending. Because it is open-ended, the word seems to have dynamic and infinite potential. The poet's choice of this open-ended adjective over the more common, closed "created" points to the word play in the speaker's choice in the poem. The speaker prefers an "Atom" to all the "lists of Clay"/Adams, suggesting that Adams do not stand up to this sort of "shift" or apocalyptic change of the rules. Open-ended, the word seems to have dynamic and infinite potential. Even if the speaker's preferred "Atom" is in fact a man, the emphasis is on its/his lack of fixed, finite form. Her atom/Adam is outside history.

Dickinson frequently omits the "ly" suffix of adverbs in the way she omits the adjectival suffix of "create." "Perception" costs "Precise the Object's loss" (1071); "Slow tramp the Centuries" (160); "I tug childish at my bars" (77); "Martyrs" trod "even" instead of evenly (792); and readers are instructed to "Step lofty" (1183). Adjectives used as adverbs have the effect of returning a description to its most essential elements, and of giving it broader range. Like "ed," the suffix "ly" marks a word's grammatical status; it does not change the word's basic, semantic meaning. Thus, for example, the adjective adverb in "They might as wise have lodged" (613) provides a flavor that is both more essential and less restrictive than "wisely" would have. Because "wise" does not take the more specific, adverbial, form, it may modify "They" as well as "have lodged." In turn, this grammatical identification of "They" and "have lodged" identifies "They" morally and personally with their 'lodging' of the "Girl" in the closet of "Prose": they are only as wise as this action makes them.

Omitting the suffix of an adverb may also focus uncommon attention on the verb the ungrammatical adjective modifies. Modifying a verb with an adjective disrupts our sense of movement because it makes that verb seem like a noun: "Martyrs – even – trod" becomes, ambiguously, *the* even trod of the martyrs. Action is partially objectified; it becomes substantial. Paradoxical as it may seem, Dickinson objectifies action through the truncated adverb for much the same purpose as she seeks a fluid, simultaneously essential and universal type of action in other disruptive forms. Just as the poet's 'expression' resists becoming a static thing, noun-like verbs both are and resist becoming as substantial as nouns. Using "even" instead of 'evenly' stabilizes the martyrs' trod. Grammatically speaking, we could say martyrs never escape the "strait pass of suffering" through which they march because in its local, phrasal context their action ceases to be clearly an action. On the other hand, in its larger context, "trod" remains syntactically a verb, and the disruptive adjectival modifier, by suggesting the static or nominal form of the action, only makes the action seem hesitant or incomplete. The martyrs trod endlessly because the verb itself is called somewhat into question; the action, like the adverb, is incomplete.

In another of these pervasive, minor but disruptive maneuvers, Dickinson makes nouns function as adjectives. This form-class deviation has an effect similar to that of adjectives functioning as adverbs. To call a prayer "more angel" or a fright "So over Horror" is to modify that prayer and fright with the syntactically simplest and therefore strongest or most essential form of the meaning possible. Adding adjectival endings to "angel" or "Horror" weakens the words, insofar as it makes them less concrete and more grammatically restricted: "angel" is the primary form, the root, of 'angelic.'[14]

Dickinson also disrupts our expectations that words will carry fixed, restricted reference to some time, quality, or thing in her repeated liberties with the standard singular or plural number of nouns. The poet writes to her sister-in-law, "Emily is sorry for Susan's Day – To be singular under plural circumstances, is a becoming heroism" (*L.*, p. 615). Perhaps it is with the same idea of unobtrusive heroism in individuality that Dickinson particularizes the collective and wishes she were "a Hay" (333) and has a bird on her walk drink "a Dew/From a convenient Grass" (328). The singular indefinite article gives no particular identity here but it suggests that it could. It creates a world of clarity and distinction or what Dickinson, in her letter to Susan, calls "heroism," in the midst of a mass or collective unit where we do not expect such distinctions to exist. The common mass-word "Hay" fails even grammatically to distinguish any one of its parts, yet were Dickinson "a Hay" it is hard to imagine that she would be absolutely undifferentiated from collective hay, even if the point of the differentiation existed only in her own consciousness of singularity. Dickinson balances the collective and the particular: she is not a stalk but "a Hay." Instead of rejecting or denying the plural (collective) circumstance, she celebrates it but reserves herself a small space there inside.

On the other hand, Dickinson's use of a singular ending with a reflexive plural (ourself, themself) seems to undermine individuality (and thus, again, the possibility of reference) by identifying all people in a symbolic one. In a poem ending with the first person singular "And so I bear it big about/My Burial," Dickinson writes:

> If we demur, it's gaping sides
> Disclose as 'twere a Tomb
> Ourself am lying straight wherein
> The Favorite of Doom.
>
> [858, st. 2]

The speaker includes her lover, and perhaps implicitly the reader, in her experience ("Ourself") without departing from the narration of her singular position ("am lying"). Using the same technique but reversing the process, Dickinson begins with the plural "we" and "Our selves" in "Those fair – fictitious People" (499) and ends with the stanza:

> Esteeming us – as Exile –
> Themself – admitted Home –
> Through gentle Miracle of Death –
> The Way ourself, must come –
>
> [499, st. 6]

"Themself" and "ourself" here, as in the previous poem, emphasize that although we all die, each instance of death involves only one solitary 'self.' Similarly, we "deem ourself a fool" (320) and "We" question, "if, Ourself a Bridegroom" (312). Conventional reference is destroyed because there is no conventional referent for a word which is simultaneously singular and plural or collective. The disruption of number places these poems in the spectrum of common human experience but maintains the particularity of an immediately active and experiencing "I." "Ourself" like "a Hay" suggests the heroism of "singularity under plural circumstances" but also the comfort and assurance of collective form.

Dickinson emphasizes this collective side of the balance between the individual and the mass or communal in other poems. Here, she makes a weak or unremarkable (often female) figure plural to balance it against a powerful (generally male) authority.[15] The disruption of number in these poems, like the unorthodox use of pronouns in the poems discussed earlier, corresponds directly to the explicit thematic concern of the poem and thus to some extent provides us with its own interpretation. For example, in "The Daisy follows soft the Sun" (106), the singular, lowly "flower" sitting "shily at his feet" proclaims "We are the Flower" and anticipates a kind of independence: the sun's "parting" and "Night's possibility." The sun addresses the daisy as singular, "Marauder," but she replies graciously in the collective and with sufficient strength of assurance to love both the rude sun and the "peace" of his departure. The speaker of "In lands I never saw – they say" (124) contrasts the "Immortal Alps" with "A Myriad Daisy" and then questions: "Which, Sir, are you and which am I/ Upon an August Day?" The singular daisy is "meek" at the feet of the plural alps, but the daisy is also "Myriad": the endlessness of her quantity clearly balances that of his ("Immortal") size. Furthermore, she retains the strength of the personal and individual in her collectivity as the "Alps" do not.[16] The male no longer has any advantage of power in remaining the alps; the "Sir" had just as well be a daisy.

Although in "To hang our head – ostensibly" (105), we cannot tell the sex of either the "You" or of the plural I, the poem again concentrates collective power in an otherwise weak or subordinate singular and contrasts that figure with some person (or, "You" plural, persons) of authority.

> To hang our head – ostensibly –
> And subsequent, to find
> That such was not the posture
> Of our immortal mind –
>
> Affords the sly presumption
> That in so dense a fuzz –
> You – too – take Cobweb attitudes
> Upon a plane of Gauze!
>
> [105]

Our solidarity of "head" and "mind" provides the strength of confidence for our "presumption." The weak and uncertain self adopts the royal "We" to undermine (God's?) authority. Dickinson's liberties with the number of nouns allow the self to be both faceless and personal in a supporting but grammatically undifferentiable crowd. As "a Hay" or "ourself," the unidentifiable becomes particular or the unremarkable becomes powerful, frequently thereby subverting the expected relations of authority or command.

The powerful collective self of Dickinson's weaker parties suggests something like the ongoing action of her uninflected verbs, and both reflect her strategy of using innumerable minor disruptions of association or syntax to present her meaning. The grammatical variations illustrate in small, as it were, her larger intention of continuous disruption. The stress is on repetition, on the power a thing or a poem gains from being continuously repeated or from repeating variations of itself—whether in forms identical with itself (like "a Hay" or "Myriad" daisy), in a process of continuing form (like "Essential Oil"), or in autonomous but similar new forms (like a pervasive continuation of language disruptions or an ongoing series of individual poems). Each singular collective, each disruption of language finds strength in continuity or repetition as well as in the singular (heroic) product or act. Like the housewife/poet's silent repetition of her "Ceaseless" chores, but flame or "Oil" of secret poetry, each turns its apparent weakness and anonymity to strength.

Dickinson may also, surreptitiously, be contrasting a female "we" to a "Man"/authority in poems that contain no disruption of number. For example, in "Publication is the Auction – /Of the Mind of Man" (709), the "We" contrasted with this "Man" could be female: unlike the publishing "Man," "We – would rather/From Our Garret go/White – Unto the White Creator–/Than invest–our Snow." Although one can interpret "Man" as 'mankind,' this generic "Man" would include all people and thus presume no contrary "We." If, on the other hand, "Man" is specifically male (instead of mankind) the opposing "We" would logically refer to women. Dickinson's practice in other poems at least suggests that we ask this question here.

"Myself was formed – a Carpenter" (488) operates in much the same way. This poem identifies a poet with his/her "Tools" and then suggests they may be female by referring to the reductive and authoritative builder they oppose as "the Man":

> My Tools took Human – Faces –
> The Bench, where we had toiled –
> Against the Man – persuaded –
> We – Temples build – I said –
>
> [488, st. 3]

Capitalizing "the Man" here and in poem 709 strengthens the suggestion that we are to interpret this word both specifically and representatively, therefore not only as one specific man and not only as the general 'mankind,' but as specifically 'men.'[17] Certainly, however, whether or not "We" are women in the two poems, "We" are the weaker and collective party, and the businesslike seller, auctioneer or builder is "the Man."[18]

Before returning to a broader explanation of Dickinson's disruptive language, let me summarize briefly the conclusions we may draw from the poems examined above. Different types of language disruptions have different specific effects, but there is a common principle, a general pattern in these effects. First, each unorthodox pronoun, collective singular, unusual word association, and so on, disrupts the standard of an orthodox or grammatical form. A restriction is broken; a form is cracked, no matter how minor that restriction or expected form may be. Second, the manner of the break or disruption often points to a thematic concern of the poem, generally also a disruption of some expected norm. Thus the deviations are subversive; they overthrow our expectations in order to set up and illustrate the new, less restrictive equilibrium of meaning that is the point of the poem. These subversions are also repeated; most poems containing an uninflected verb contain more than one; an unusual pronoun or singular mass-word finds its disruption repeated in the metaphors or larger patterns of the poem. Finally, although I have called these forms subversive, their effect is not to destroy rules or forms but to experiment with them. Suggesting that a "Wife" may be a "Himself" does not erase all distinctions between the sexes but directs the reader to see that the boundary between their relative degrees of freedom and power is arbitrary and superficial. The poet disrupts language to allow herself greater personal control in her creation and expression of new form and understanding.

Dickinson indicates that this is the way she intends us to understand her irregular grammar and word choice in her poems on female creators and poets, where the principles and strategies of creation are the explicit topic of the poems. In these poems, we find the same disruption of old forms as we do in the poet's unorthodox uses of language. We find subversive or secret kinds of creation—often corresponding to escapes from some confinement, reminiscent of the language disruptions themselves. In other parallels, we see that creation is repetitive, ongoing, and that a symmetry evolves in the relation between the poet's new form and her environment or what she is disrupting. For Dickinson, these qualities are apparently characteristic of all creation, all poetry, but they are peculiarly characteristic of women insofar as the tradition or authority being disrupted in these poems, as in the poems containing a singular collective figure, is often explicitly male. Dickinson presents the strategies of poetic creation as the strategies of the nominally weak and therefore, in her time, of the female. The generic poet, for Dickinson, is not restrictively female, but she is archetypally so.

Most of Dickinson's poems on poetry leave the sex of the poet unspecified. They refer to plural "poets" ("they" or "we"), the poet "I," or avoid pronoun reference altogether.[19] A few of her poems make the poet specifically male, notably "This was a Poet – It is That" (448). Some of her poets may be female, as I have argued above with "Myself was formed – a Carpenter" (488) and "Essential Oils" (675). But Dickinson also wrote a number of poems specifically about female creators.

Among these poems on female creators are some of Dickinson's most violent and most anarchic poems on poetry and language. The poet seems to be saying in these poems that one cannot attempt to experience or harness the power of language without risking complete lack of control and destruction. For example, in "She dealt her pretty words like Blades" (479), it is "not Steel's Affair" that language pierces to the "Nerve/Or . . . Bone." To be involved in communication with this speaker at all is to risk being deeply wounded; "To Ache is Human – not polite." The speaker of another poem is "a Loaded Gun" who hunts the weak (female) "Doe" and smiles volcanically in her terrible pleasure:

> And do I smile, such cordial light
> Upon the Valley glow –
> It is as a Vesuvian face
> Had let it's pleasure through –
>
> [754, st. 3]

In "The Soul had Bandaged moments" (512), the shackled poetess, with "staples, in the Song" escapes from her repressive, male "Horror" and "dances like a Bomb."[20]

However, Dickinson generally has her poets escape or disrupt expected forms less destructively, and often the disruption remains a mental act of the poet.[21] In "I cannot dance upon my Toes" (326), "No Man instructed" the speaker, but "oftentimes, among my mind,/A Glee ['song' as well as 'joy'] possesseth me"; following the same pattern, none "know I know the Art/I mention – easy – Here," yet she claims it is "full as Opera," the grandest, public form. The unspecified "They" of "They shut me up in Prose" (613) try to keep a "little Girl . . . 'still' " in the "Closet" of prose, not realizing she carries the tumult of poetry in her mind and can always "will" her escape. The poems recall the corpse of "How many times these low feet staggered" (187) and the "Lady's Drawer" of "Essential Oils" (675). Perhaps, as I speculated earlier, "Only the soldered mouth can tell" how often the poetry of "low feet" has staggered thought because the very act of writing, or of reading, poetry condemns the "housewife" to death. In an alternative reading, if it is the poem's, not the writer's, "mouth" that is "soldered," a woman's poetry itself remains metaphorically as secret and silent as a tomb. Meaning is an escape in these poems, reenacted at each experience of the poem and impossible to communicate other than through that experience. Both readings remind us of the "Lady" poet of poem 675, who suffers the "Screws" of expressing poetry from the "General Rose" of her life while living, the poem perhaps puns, a "lie" except in that secret "Drawer" of "Summer." It is difficult to read this poem without thinking of Dickinson's own drawerful of unpublished poems, and without seeing her as the embodiment of the poet she describes.

The constricted realms of these last poems, however, like the "Closet" of poem 613, do not imprison either the writer or her poem:

> They might as wise have lodged a Bird
> For Treason – in the Pound –
>
> Himself has but to will
> And easy as a Star
> Abolish his Captivity –
> And laugh – No more have I –
>
> [613, 11. 7-12]

These confinements do not ultimately confine. Dickinson seems to choose secrecy and apparent confinement to allow herself increased freedom; her "still" disguise apparently allows her a more radical power. Escape and freedom are matters of will, and Dickinson wills her escape; she laughs when she cracks the rules of language, then uses both its traditional and altered forms to express her meaning.

"It would never be Common – more – I said" (430) takes that moment of escape and transformation as its theme. The poem tells a Cinderella story in which the speaker is her own fairy godmother. She turns herself from a "Common" woman into a poet, and her magic gifts and husband Prince are all words:

> It would never be Common – more – I said –
> Difference – had begun –
> Many a bitterness – had been –
> But that old sort – was done –
>
> Or – if it sometime – showed – as 'twill –
> Upon the Downiest– Morn –
> Such bliss – had I – for all the years –
> 'Twould give an Easier – pain –
>
> I'd so much joy – I told it – Red –
> Upon my simple Cheek –
> I felt it publish – in my Eye –
> 'Twas needless – any speak –
>
> I walked – as wings – my body bore –
> The feet – I former used –

Unnecessary – now to me –
As boots – would be – to Birds –

I put my pleasure all abroad –
I dealt a word of Gold
To every Creature – that I met –
And Dowered – all the World –

When – suddenly – my Riches shrank –
A Goblin – drank my Dew –
My Palaces – dropped tenantless –
Myself – was beggared – too –

I clutched at sounds –
I groped at shapes –
I touched the tops of Films –
I felt the Wilderness roll back
Along my Golden lines –

The Sackcloth – hangs upon the nail –
The Frock I used to wear –
But where my moment of Brocade –
My – drop – of India?

[430]

Here the woman poet overcomes her "old sort" of "bitterness" and "pain" and creates a state of "Difference," "words of gold." This moment follows "Golden lines"; it is "Brocade"—a fine weave of cloth, incorporating into its "Common" ("Sackcloth"?) stitch a differentiable pattern of silk threads. In lines 9-12, we see again the play on "feet," here boot-less because useless to the old life of "Sackcloth" and because they are composed of poetic trochees and iambs. "As boots – would be – to Birds" is even divided by its dashes into perfect iambic feet, the only line so divided in the poem. The speaker's "Golden" moment is a moment of creating poetry.

Creating poetry or 'dealing' words for this woman appears to be synonymous with creating a world. The progression of verbs in the poem indicates that to "deal" a word of gold is to participate actively in the world: in stanzas 4 and 5, the speaker becomes the agent of the action she describes and the verbs become primarily specific and active.[22] "Frock" and "Sackcloth" suggest a religious penitent and celibacy, consequently that, in her old life, the speaker had no fertile relation to the world. Like the "gift" of screws making ripe "Summer" in poem 675, her golden words become a gift of the most intimate communication, a wedding 'dower' the bride-to-be gives her world-husband. By the same taken, the speaker's lost "dew" and "drop" suggest that losing the word of active communication results in infertility. The speaker directly contacts things outside her own perception only through her use of these poetic words. Formerly, she spoke with "it" (presumably her previous self or the "old sort" of bitterness), and later she meets a goblin (that fairy-tale excuse for whatever evil we cannot understand); here she meets creatures and deals words to them. If this is not explicitly a conversation (as the alternative dealing "with" would imply), it is at least immediate contact.

Losing "Difference," on the other hand, brings necessity, passivity, commonness, a loss of communication (both of words and of her partners) and the inability to distinguish sounds or shapes in the world: without words one perceives only "Wilderness." In poem 430 we see what is perhaps an early stage of the dilemma that culminates in the dead "housewife" and "Lady" of poems 187 and 675. The poet has discarded her "Sackcloth," or "old sort" of life, but she cannot control or stabilize the moments of authority and active participation in the world that accompany the creative moments of what she has decided to make her new life. In the metaphor of the poem's last stanza, the speaker has lost her brocade but she does not resume wearing the sackcloth; she prefers what would be complete nakedness to her former state and leaves the frock "upon the nail." The speaker's opening exclamation now rings as a vow: it will "never be Common – more." Continuing to reject the old forms at least offers the possibility of recurring moments of creativity and generous, powerful life.

"Bloom upon the Mountain – stated" (667) repeats the concerns of Dickinson's other poems about women poets, this time in implicit contrast to a male creator and male audience.

> Bloom upon the Mountain – stated –
> Blameless of a Name –
> Efflorescence of a Sunset –
> Reproduced – the same –
>
> Seed, had I, my Purple Sowing
> Should endow the Day –
> Not a Tropic of a Twilight –
> Show itself away –
>
> Who for tilling – to the Mountain
> Come, and disappear –
> Whose be Her Renown, or fading,
> Witness, is not here –
>
> While I state – the Solemn Petals,
> Far as North – and East,

Far as South and West – expanding –
Culminate – in Rest –

And the Mountain to the Evening
Fit His Countenance –
Indicating, by no Muscle –
The Experience –

[667]

The flower that 'states' herself and sunsets is "Blameless of a Name" and the tiller, because no one witnesses her "Renown" ('renaming' in Latin), also remains nameless. This is private, anonymous, implicitly but not exclusively female art. We assume the speaker is a women because she has no "Seed," yet flowers reproduce themselves from seeds and tillers must have seeds to till. By the same token, although in stanza 2 the speaker implies that, in her lack of male "Seed," she cannot "endow the Day" with a permanent tropical twilight, in stanza 4 she 'states' and apparently thereby does create "Solemn Petals." Poets, here create with or without "Seed." They "state" their poetry, in a process that identifies the artist with her art (like the "Bloom" creating "Petals" of sunset, or the housewife's and the poem's "low feet"). Dickinson isolates "stated" at the end of the first line to emphasize it: the flower has "stated" creations, and it is, or has been, "stated" itself. Even in this bold 'stating,' however, the flower/woman/poet's art is silent. She remains nameless, or 'disappears'. Furthermore, she cannot prevent the day from 'culminating' in the "Rest" of night, or death. Nonetheless, in this anonymous silence, she does bypass the assumed prerequisite for creation ("Seed") to create a poetry that is endless at least in its daily recurrence and that is indistinguishable from herself.

As Dickinson implies in her uninflected verbs and in other forms and poems, the product of a (woman) poet in poem 667 is not an iconic, single form, event, or thing. It is countless flowers and sunsets, like staggering footsteps or perfume. It is a repeated, daily event, presented silently in full view of the male Mountain's impassivity. This poetry is the "Snow" of "Publication is the Auction" (709) or the "unmentioned . . . Pearl, and Weed" of the "Wife" who "rose to His Requirement" (732). Also, as in the poems examined above, this ongoing or collective event equalizes the balance between the poet and her, apparently dominant, outside world. Although "the Mountain" will not acknowledge that the "Experience" has even occurred, he is moved by it to the extent that he must now "Fit His Countenance" to the new world, or sky, of her creation. His pretense of indifference is only a pretense. The poet's 'stating' moves the man/ Mountain; her "Petals" dower ("endow") the sky and will do so every day whether he admits it or not.

Dickinson presents women poets and their poems largely in terms of what they are not. She works from contrast. In "Bloom upon the Mountain – stated –" (667), the "Bloom" creates by assertion, by 'stating', instead of by what would appear to be the more natural, but male, "Seed." Similarly, in "Essential Oils" (675), the poet requires "Screws" as well as the growth of "Suns." The housewife of poetic "low feet" (187) finds her screws in her own willed but condemned secrecy: she hides behind the façade of a tired woman's daily chores and, in the text of the poem, behind word plays. The escapes from a "Closet" (613), the "Common" (430) and "Horror" (512) indicate that the poet's art is essentially one of subverting given, imprisoning forms. The escape is incomplete; one cannot control the ecstatic communication of golden words, or "Glee," or dancing like a "Bomb"; one cannot write poetry except through the restrictive words of 'their' "Prose." However, the decision to escape those restrictions as far as possible—never to be "Common – more"—can be complete, and it is clearly so in Dickinson's continuous disruption of the accepted patterns of language.

As we have seen, subversion entails risk. One's mouth is "soldered" by the volcanic or bomblike power of one's own poetic thought. The gamble is for one's life. Yet to have succeeded in creating freer, fuller form by insisting on the reexamination of old roles and meanings is a gift of gold. By reading these poems as a group, we learn that one can rise out of "Wilderness" by meeting "His Requirements," but one rises much higher by meeting goals that are entirely one's own.

> She staked her Feathers – Gained an Arc –
> Debated – Rose again –
> This time – beyond the estimate
> Of Envy, or of Men –
>
> And now, among Circumference –
> Her steady Boat be seen –
> At home – among the Billows – As
> The Bough where she was born –

[798]

"Staking" your only support in the risky middle air can make you as at home in the "Billows" as in the lower, humble "Bough" (Bow) of everyday.

Repeated, relatively minor, personal "Arcs," extraordinary moments of creation, perhaps typify all lyric poetry. Certainly, to some extent all poets reject, or rebel against, forms of the past in order to create forms of their own. However, Dickinson's insistence that poetry manifests the universal and collective while the poet remains unobtrusively, even indistinguishably, singular also identifies the act of writing poetry with what she sees as the pattern of a woman's life in a male-dominated world. Dickinson uses the relative insignificance of writing short ("little") poems and of repeating small disruptions in basically traditional forms to explode traditional ways of thinking and to replace those ways with her own. She "eases the lightning" of her "Truth" (1129) by balancing subversive tactics with the simplest of metrical designs and rhyme schemes. Dickinson does not seem herself to know if there can be a lasting balance between the personal and the conventional, the self and the public role. She does know, however, that the conventional alone is inadequate. As a poet, Dickinson can only reach her "Billows" by risking that old form.

NOTES

1. ". . . For poetry, the standard language is the background against which is reflected the esthetically intentional distortion of the linguistic components of the work, in other words, the intentional violation of the norm of the standard." Jan Mukarovsky, "Standard Language and Poetic Language," rept. in *Linguistics and Literary Style*, ed. Donald C. Freeman (New York: Holt, Rinehart & Winston, 1970), p. 42.

2. Sandra Gilbert and Susan Gubar discuss Dickinson's use of traditionally female activity (especially sewing) to represent her work, and they stress the secrecy and unobtrusiveness of a woman's art. See "A Woman – White: Emily Dickinson's Yarn of Pearl" in *Madwoman in the Attic: The Woman Writer and the Nineteenth-Century Literary Imagination* (New Haven: Yale University Press, 1979), pp. 581-650. Other critics who discuss the deliberately female qualities or strategies of Dickinson's art include Suzanne Juhasz, *Naked and Fiery Forms: Modern American Poetry by Women, A New Tradition* (New York: Harper Colophon, 1976); Joanne Feit Diehl, "Come Slowly Eden: An Exploration of Women Poets and Their Muse," *Signs* 3, no. 3 (1978): 572-87; and Vivian R. Pollak, "Thirst and Starvation in Emily Dickinson's Poetry," *American Literature* 51, No. 3 (1979).

3. Dickinson is not alone in this strategy. Elaine Marks and Isabelle de Courtivron in *New French Feminisms: An Anthology* (University of Massachusetts Press, 1980) describe a French women's group that believes there can be no meaningful change without the disruption of bourgeois language; "only by dislocating syntax, playing with the signifier, punning outrageously and constantly can the old language and the old order be subverted" (pp. 32-33). Recently, Edwin Newman has claimed that many Americans who knew better "deliberately misused language in the 1960s in an effort to disassociate themselves from the Establishment, to mark themselves as anti-Establishment." People restricted their vocabularies to manifest a "political position and, as they saw it, a humanistic position" (quoted from David Shaw's "The Use and Abuse of Language," *Los Angeles Times*, 19 April 1981). Dickinson chooses a different mode of misusing language, but her motivation may be much the same as that of these more recent French and American protesters.

This argument could also perhaps be made for Dickinson's distortions of traditional poetic forms—meter, rhyme, stanzaic regularity—and the argument has been made for her reinvention of poetic themes and images. See, in this regard, Margaret Homans's *Women Writers and Poetic Identity* (Princeton: Princeton University Press, 1980), pp. 162-215.

4. "Flame" or "blaze" was an accepted meaning of 'low' throughout the nineteenth century. For example, according to the 1971 *Oxford English Dictionary*, Charlotte Brontë uses it with this meaning in 1849, and Rudyard Kipling in 1892.

5. Dickinson's sea is male in other of her poems, too. See in particular, "I Started Early – took my dog" (520); "Escaping backward to perceive" (867); and "The Sea said 'Come' to the Brook" (1210).

6. Dickinson creates the same kind of balance in "He was weak, and I was strong – then" (190); the partners' weakness and strength are interchangeable in this poem.

7. In "Like Eyes that looked on Wastes" (458), we again see two persons (presumably lovers) in a balance of separation, although this time they are being loyal to each other instead of fractional. Again, the "Cause" for the "Misery" is the speaker's, and she makes the general position of authority and power they each hold female, even though it is possible that the other "face" is male: "Neither would be a Queen/Without the Other –".

8. People today at times similarly perceive women who take positions or attitudes of authority as male. For example, in Charles Schulz's comic strip, *Peanuts*, Marcy calls Lucy "Sir" out of respect.

I am indebted to Gilbert and Gubar for this reading of poem 732 (see *The Madwoman*, pp. 588-91).

9. Homans (*Women Writers*, pp. 201-7) discusses this and other "Daisy" poems in the context of Dickinson's use of nature in her poetry.

10. Perhaps, on the other hand, Dickinson uses "it's" instead of 'its' to substantiate the possession by identifying the possessor with its object: the "Universe" *is*, or becomes, "it's" (it is) "Flags of Snow" (481); the "Chasm" becomes even more clearly defined by "it's" (it is) "gaping sides" (858). Johnson corrects "it's" and Dickinson's other consistently faulty contractions (does'nt, dont, has'nt, have'nt, wont) in *The Complete Poems Of Emily Dickinson* (Boston: Little, Brown and Company, 1951). On such points, individual readers must decide for themselves.

11. See Thomas H. Johnson, *Emily Dickinson: An Interpretative Biography* (Cambridge: Harvard University Press, 1955), p. 93. David Porter claims Dickinson attempts "a verbal, and indeed visual (for the inflections are visibly pared away), correlative for the insight into *essences* at the core of meaning and experience," and states that the poet does not confine this technique to the verb form (*The Art of Emily Dickinson's Early Poetry* [Cambridge: Harvard University Press, 1966], p. 139).

12. The pattern of timelessness continues for the rest of the poem. In twenty lines, Dickinson uses ten uninflected verbs: for example, "The Dust – connect – and live"; "All Multitudes that were/Efface"; "Solemnity – prevail" and so on. As befits a poem describing resurrection, there is no clear sense of time or of number here. Singular "Dust" and plural "Multitudes" refer to the same crowd of dead and both take the same unrestricted but incomplete verb form. Those crowds do still exist, and resurrection is not clearly an event of the future or of any other single time.

13. As Brita Lindberg-Seyersted explains, "create" is a poetic archaic usage. Whicher and Anderson call it Shakespearian; Chase suggests the poet may have adopted it from Reverend Wadsworth's habit of truncating past participles. Sherrer reminds us that it was still an accepted poetic form in the nineteenth century, and the *Oxford English Dictionary* substantiates her claim. The question, however, is not who else may have used this unidiomatic form but why Dickinson chose to use it. See Lindberg-Seyersted, *The Voice of the Poet: Aspects of Style in the Poetry of Emily Dickinson* (Cambridge: Harvard University Press, 1968), p. 115; George Whicher, *This Was a Poet: A Critical Biography of Emily Dickinson* (New York: Scribner's Sons, 1939), p. 235; Anderson, p. 33; Richard Chase, *Emily Dickinson* (New York: William Sloane, 1951), p. 79; Grace Sherrer, "A Study of Unusual Verb Constructions in the Poems of Emily Dickinson," *American Literature* 8 (1935): 40-41.

14. Dickinson's use of adjectives, verbs, and adverbs as nouns also makes the abstract concrete; examples are "We talk in careless – and in toss" (663), "There are . . . a Must," "a Shall" (1618), and "In Death's Immediately" (1420). However, because in these types of form-class experiments the nominal adjective, adverb, or verb itself suffers—and suggests—no disruption of its own form, there is no subversive implication in the usage. When used as a noun, "Immediately" is unusual and highly suggestive, but it does not call the rules of grammatical categories into question as the use of "angel" for angelic, "even" for evenly, and "create" for create*d*(?) do.

15. Poem 312, quoted from above, appears to reverse this pattern. In speaking of how she can honor Elizabeth Barrett Browning, Dickinson concludes:

> Be it's Grave – sufficient sign –
> Nought – that We – No Poet's Kinsman –
> Suffocate – with easy woe –
> What, and if, Ourself a Bridegroom –
> Put Her down – in Italy?

Here the collective husband seems a mere 'groom' of the "Ducal" woman poet; the weak collective singular is male. However, the bridegroom is the privileged authority over the dead woman's body. Furthermore, the poem suggests that "What, and if" applies only to those who are "No Poet's Kinsman," that is perhaps, to women poets. In this case, Dickinson would seem to be implying that if women could be the powerful "Bridegroom" in charge of Barrett Browning's burial, the grave would indeed be worthy of her greatness, and the poem would fit her pattern of granting the weaker, woman figure increased authority through the singular collective, "Ourself."

16. I am indebted to Homans (*Women Writers*, pp. 203-4) for my reading of these poems.

17. Dickinson's use of the singular and her definite article, "the Man," encourage the effect of specific reference but representative force I have attributed to the capital letter.

18. The suggestion that "We" may be female in this poem is particularly disruptive because traditionally one associates a Carpenter/poet with Christ. Seeing the poet exclusively as a Christ figure (therefore at least implicitly as male) weakens the contrast between him and "the Man" because Christ is also referred to as a man and generally in capitalized titles and pronouns. On the other hand, seeing the poet as both a Christ-like Carpenter and a woman—and

as both the singular individual and the collective "Tools" and worker—enables us to distinguish her "Temples" sharply from the man's "Boards": she is then distinguished by being forcibly excluded from the normal structures of authority (the temple builders) as well as by rebelling against their condescension in the strength of her vision—just as Christ himself was and did.

19. These poems include 544, 569, 883 (although the word "disseminate" here might suggest that these poets are masculine), 1247, 1292, and 1472.

20. For a reading of 754 as a poem about poetry, see Gilbert and Gubar, pp. 608-10. Dickinson also refers at least indirectly to her speaker as a volcano in poems 175, 601, 1677, and 1705.

21. Dwight Eddins, in "Emily Dickinson and Nietzsche: The Rites of Dionysus" (*ESQ* 27, no. 2 [1981]: 96-108), claims that Dickinson anarchistically obliterates boundaries of all kinds. Although it is true that the poet considers boundaries fallible and impermanent, her repeated concern with particular practical boundaries indicates that she believes in the possibility of generating new forms rather than in the meaninglessness of all bounds. If boundaries respond to the manifestos of personal control, as I think Dickinson shows they do, then they may have the potential to be both temporary and meaningful. Dickinson, I find, subverts or denies form only to recreate it.

22. In the first three stanzas the verbs are stative or generalized (be, have, do) and action is done to the speaker or independently of her. In stanza 6, the verbs are active but again the speaker is their object instead of their subject. In 7, the speaker acts in confusion; the verbs are active and specific but they denote generally tentative or abortive movements. Stanza 8 is written in the present tense and, like the first three stanzas, describes conditions surrounding the speaker. She is again watching, feeling, waiting.

JOANNE FEIT DIEHL IX

"Ransom in a Voice"

Language as Defense in Dickinson's Poetry

I dwell in Possibility –
A fairer House than Prose –

"LET US SIT AT HOME with the cause," admonished Emerson in his seminal essay, "Self-Reliance." Of all the ambitious young Americans who took this essay to heart, none followed his advice so literally as Emily Dickinson or adhered to its demands more rigorously. See defined her version of the "cause" as a desire to reveal, through her poems, a responsive, wholly alive consciousness. No matter how frequently ignored or misunderstood, Dickinson continued speaking into the void. Whatever the particular origins of her sense of estrangement (and we need not look far to discover its most overt forms: absence from the ongoing cultural life of Boston and Concord, spiritual exclusion from the orthodoxy sweeping mid-century Amherst, misunderstanding by those she hoped would recognize and nurture her genius), the austere originality of Dickinson's poetry develops from the tenor of her reaction to such exclusions, from her conversion of a potentially crippling alienation into a conception of language that serves as a defense against what she perceived not simply as an antipathetic society, but also as an adversarial nature and an inscrutable, if not fundamentally hostile, deity. From this estrangement, Dickinson develops a deeply skeptical, indeed, an antithetical approach toward the world beyond the self. Her pervasive skepticism toward both the world and language, moreover, foreshadows a distinctly modernist alienation. Although the reasons for Dickinson's and other nineteenth-century women poets' sense of exclusion from both nature and culture necessarily differ from the origins of rejection that fuel the modernist writers of our century, the character of their poetic responses presents a strong, albeit surprising resemblance. How Dickinson converts her estrangement into verbal power, just how her sense of alienation informs her vision of a defensive language that pushes the word ever closer to indecipherability, are questions that lead back into her work and forward to a consideration of the possible ties between a feminist poetics and modernism.

156

The greatest danger facing a poet is, of course, the danger of silence. That Dickinson resists this temptation is proof of her energies; that she makes her alienation the subject of many of her most brilliant poems, thus transforming estrangement into a source of power, testifies to the strength of her imagination. No poet can accomplish this transformation in a single gesture, nor is the transformation of estrangement into power, once accomplished, permanently assured. Thus, Dickinson's poems, not unexpectedly, document a cyclical process in which the "I" initially experiences a rejection that provokes rage followed by resentment.[1] This anger on the poet's part climaxes in the poems' assertion of a fiercely won independence from the very force or substance that she had originally been denied. Despite her disavowal of such appetite, "Art thou the thing I wanted?/Begone – my Tooth has grown –" (1282), no final resolution or poetic satiety can be achieved because of the very nature of the conflicts generated by repeated banishment and denial. In her attempts to marshal internal power against such continued threats to her autonomy, Dickinson makes language her strongest weapon. The Word becomes her defense as she assigns it sufficient force to devastate her adversaries and exercise her will even against Divine power. In response to the exclusionary silence of a hostile, or at best, incomprehensible, world and a threatening poetic adversary, Dickinson invokes the powers of language, asserting that her word may vie with the Divine for authority over herself and her experience. If the word becomes a weapon, it also possesses, as Dickinson is well aware, the capacity to find its victim within the self. To assert that what determines survival or destruction resides within the self is simultaneously to acknowledge internal authority while denigrating the threat of any and all external forces.

Dickinson appropriates power for her own linguistic purposes by, among other ways, drawing upon the authority orthodox Christianity ascribes to Christ. Adopting qualities associated with the Christian deity, and transforming these into a linguistic process that she describes as both more humane and equable than the Christian, Dickinson creates an alternative power potentially subversive of any external authority based upon the sovereignty of a male-identified divinity or predicated upon the supremacy of those within the religious fold. In her boldest poetic statement of these alternative powers—the choosing of her words over against the force of God—Dickinson explores the possibilities for a poetics that yields nothing to forces beyond the self.

> A Word made Flesh is seldom
> And tremblingly partook
> Nor then perhaps reported
> But have I not mistook

> Each one of us has tasted
> With ecstasies of stealth
> The very food debated
> To our specific strength –
>
> A Word that breathes distinctly
> Has not the power to die
> Cohesive as the Spirit
> It may expire if He –
> "Made Flesh and dwelt among us"
> Could condescension be
> Like this consent of Language
> This loved Philology.
>
> [1651][2]

One experiences a power commensurate with the Divine depending upon one's own capacity; the Word lives, the human word, as the Spirit. That Dickinson here chooses the power of the human word over the power of the Divine becomes apparent in the closing lines. The "condescension" of Christ, with that word's concealed arrogance of *descent* does not approach the mutuality of relationships expressed by "consent," the power of a human word to meet the reader on equal terms. As I have argued elsewhere, this poem can be viewed as Dickinson's central statement about language, her role as poet, and her relationship to the Divine.[3] The process of transubstantiation here serves as a trope investing the poet's word with godlike authority. In a stunning inversion of orthodoxy, Dickinson takes the Word of God and makes it her own, which then serves as the criterion for measuring all power outside the self. Transubstantiation thus becames a trope for poetic inspiration. Combined with this discourse of religion is the language of appetite, which Dickinson frequently identifies with the poetic enterprise. This transference of authority—"The Word made Flesh"—describes an alternative drama of mutuality between desire and fulfillment absent in the relations that exist within a hieratic Christianity. So sweeping is the usurpation of orthodox powers into the self that by the poem's final stanza, traditional incarnation can only hope to match the reciprocal relationship that informs "beloved philology." The closing words echo their own meaning in a circle of love (*philo-logos*), the beloved love of the word.

Yet, if here the poetic word triumphs over LOGOS, elsewhere it assumes no such absolute or benign power, but is, instead, identified as functioning within an adversarial relationship, as a weapon used to defend the self against the self's own powers. Once such power resides solely within the single consciousness, once the poetic self attempts to replace external authority, the dangers for poetic identity grow more intimate and acute. As Dickinson remarks, "Jacob versus Esau, was a trifle in Litigation, compared to the Skirmish in my Mind –".[4] Language, the usurping power of the imagination, becomes, then, both a weapon of salvation and the means for potential self-destruction. Dickinson underscores the lethal relationship between the potentially brilliant show of her Word (its destructive possibilities) in "She dealt her pretty words like blades," where language "glitters" and "shines" while it exposes, like a surgeon's knife, the nerves or "wantons with a Bone –". Such surgical "wanton"-ness may prove lethal to its victim. But this is a risk Dickinson must take if she is to direct her linguistic energies toward a confrontation with her personal and literary isolation, if she is to provide herself with a means for overcoming the strictures of circumstance.

The ground of poetry, alone, offers Dickinson the freedom to articulate her independence. Choosing to write from her perception of this alienated consciousness, she projects an inviolate territory where words, even if potentially self-destructive, are her weapons against limitation, orthodoxy, and a hostile world. Such an alternative territory emerges in the early poem, "There is a morn by men unseen –" (24). Here Dickinson describes a pastoral landscape but with a difference: process ceases, temporality fades, and, as in poem 1056, "Consciousness – is Noon." Characterizing this "mystic green" in terms of her own ambition, Dickinson seeks there a "morn by men unseen." Whether she is using "men" in the generic or the more specific, sex-related sense, she attests to an enchanted ground inhabited by "maids" who engage in their own "dance and game," those who participate in secret rituals of delight during their "holiday" (holy day).

> There is a morn by men unseen –
> Whose maids upon remoter green
> Keep their Seraphic May –
> And all day long, with dance and game,
> And gambol I may never name –
> Employ their holiday.

Whether the poet "may never name" these rituals because she does not know them or because she will not or cannot disclose them affects the interpretation of the remaining stanzas. However one decides to read the poem, and I will not attempt a full reading here, it is significant that Dickinson is invoking an alternative, sacred ground toward which she yearns to travel. Wishing to join that company of fairy maids who do not inhabit the earth, she finds in their magic "ring" a ground secure from the antipathetic forces that drove her from the daylight world of men and women. In a poem that itself describes a form of sacred play, one must take into account Dickinson's own play with words throughout the text. Puns and associative images create a complex web of meaning that reinforces the overall vision of the poem as a counter-revelation, another way for the poet to be, as opposed to the commonly received notion of poetic vocation and the daylight world of masculine orthodoxy. Not only is the holiday also a holy day, but the Chrysolite that shines in her alternative landscape is, perhaps, an alternative to Christ's light; the revels of the magic "maids" are a kind of play that replaces traditional "revelation."

> Like thee to dance – like thee to sing –
> People upon that mystic green –
> I ask, each new May Morn.
> I wait thy far, fantastic bells –
> Announcing me in other dells –
> Unto the different dawn!

Despite the jubilation of the closing stanza, this "different dawn" remains in the realm of ambition. The luminous powers of the "mystic green" are not yet experienced by the poet who *waits* for her call to election, to this counter-revelation of a natural, free-spirited, exuberant circle of otherworldly "maids."

As this "different dawn" has yet to be attained, so Dickinson recognizes that she cannot stay in her self-made world of language forever. Her most impressive poems thus derive their energy from the conflict between the poetic self and a world she perceived as estranged, or "other." Yet, if nature is alien, society without comprehension of her poetic powers, the language Dickinson inherits is also, she recognizes, not fully her own. Language as she knows it is defined primarily by a long line of male poets—to rid her words of their literal meaning would be an act of liberation that would free her from a confining tradition, a gesture that would allow her access to a new mode of signification. Her quest for such a revision of language itself becomes a major subject for a number of her most remarkable poems and the beginning of a feminist poetics that treats the difficulties of a woman poet who struggles for the integrity of her own voice. By describing her experience of rejection in terms that only serve to deepen its ambiguities, Dickinson demonstrates the precariousness that governs her relationships to all outside the self, especially to nature and to God—the chief adversaries she must resist if she is to survive as woman and as poet. The terms of Dickinson's encounter with the world go beyond mere antagonism as God and nature turn against and actively pursue the inquisitive self.

Nature and God – I neither knew
Yet Both so well knew me
They startled, like Executors
Of My identity.

Yet Neither told – that I could learn –
My Secret as secure
As Herschel's private interest
Or Mercury's affair –

[835]

Here the ambiguities in Dickinson's relationships with external forces reveal themselves in a series of curiously inverted linguistic structures. First, note that the poem speaks of the I's relationship with nature and God in the past tense; whether this means that the relationship has subsequently altered or whether she is speaking of herself in the past in a eulogistic vein remains an open question. Although apparently a simply statement of her ignorance concerning God and nature, and their intimate knowledge of the "I," the poem is really more complex. For instance, after the opening lines assert that nature and God possess this knowledge, while she remains ignorant of them, she defines the character of this knowledge in terms of her response: "They startled, like Executors / Of My identity." In her choice of "executors," Dickinson begins the dichotomy that will set the poem against itself, for "executor" suggests both one who puts to death (perhaps explaining the posthumous tense of the poem), carrying out the verdict of society, and/or one who carries out the wishes of the deceased as expressed in her or his Will. Although the second alternative incorporates within its definition the sense of one who obeys, who thus subordinates himself to the wishes of an other, this acquiescence is precipitated by the death of the person who wrote the "will" and who now exercises that will through the very act of dying. "Executor" can, then, be either the agent of the victim's death or the one who protects her rights, sustains her will, after she has succumbed to other forces—most compellingly, the word may retain both these meanings and so operate dualistically, in an apparently antithetical relationship to itself. Thus, "executor" simultaneously contains both protective and potentially lethal meanings. The ambiguity associated with nature and God intensifies as Dickinson further complicates these relationships through additional syntactic complexities, the most obviously being her use of dashes and the pronoun "that," which discourages any single reading of the poem's final lines.

Yet neither told – that I could learn –
My Secret as secure

As Herschel's private interest
Or Mercury's affair –

The clause, "that I could learn" again operates in two ways: first, as a parenthetical clarification—to the best of her knowledge, and second, nature and God did not tell their secret in ways so that she could learn. The reader cannot, moreover, be certain just what nature and God are refusing to disclose. The options might be these: either they will in good faith not reveal the "secret" information about the poet which would, she suggests, in some unnamed way, damage her were it told (thus she is protected by them as the deceased's wishes would be respected by her executors) and/or nature and God will not reveal *to her* what they know, preserving instead an inviolate secrecy. Within this second reading, "secure" functions as an ironic term, for the "I" cannot learn directly about either God or Nature, let alone about what they know of her; the secret is thus secured just because it is hidden from the self. What Herschel's private interest might be she cannot know, as Mercury's affair remains a mystery. These closing lines are themselves enigmatic in their brevity, but equally suggestive as well. The reader does not know, for example, to which Herschel the poem refers—to the distinguished astronomer, William, or to his remarkable sister and collaborator, Caroline, who discovered eight comets in her lifetime, or to William's son, John. Each of these names does, however, recall not simply an astronomer, but a scientist who discovered a celestial body hitherto unknown. A conjectural reading of "As Herschel's private interest" suggests that if Herschel's (any of the Herschels) public interests were so vast, how great might his/her secret interest have been; the speaker's secret is as secure as Herschel's because it also is cosmological in scope and as much a part of the hitherto unknown. The closing line with its reference to Mercury makes both the astronomical connection to Herschel and the link back to the Roman god, a pagan deity as opposed to the Judeo-Christian presence with whom the poem opens. But Mercury has other important connotations for this context as well: the planet is closest to the sun and extremely hard to view from the earth. (In what was most probably an apocryphal story, Copernicus on his deathbed reportedly stated that his one regret was never to have observed Mercury.) Moreover, because of its position in relation to the sun, one side of Mercury is constantly in light, the other in total darkness. Thus, Mercury could keep its secrets in two senses—as the planet so hard to see from the earth and as one that keeps half its form in constant night. The allusion to the pagan identity of Mercury functions ironically: as the messenger, the one who brings news, Mercury would disclose rather than withhold secret knowledge. In larger terms, two meanings operate antithetically here; the first more overt, perhaps, than the second, but both equally sustained through the poem's syntax and diction, creating an unresolvable tension rather than a resolution of interpretation. Such interpretative indeterminacy, moreover, places the reader in a position analogous to that of the "I" of the poem. Dickinson informs us of the terms in which she understands her predicament but gives no clear notion of exactly where her power or knowledge might reside.

Such interpretative ambiguities, brilliant as they may be, are a sign of a deeper ambivalence that manifests itself in the linguistic and syntactic complexities informing Dickinson's often richly multivalent texts. And yet, the extremely delicate process of articulating such indeterminacy is in itself the source of authority that surpasses nature's mystery by naming it. Whether such obscuring strategies have their origin in a deliberate desire to obscure or in an ironic evasiveness, or in both, no reader can ascertain; more alarming, such indeterminacy of language, despite the authoritative force of individual poems, may signal the potential breakdown of the word's capacity to bear the pressures of simultaneous, antithetical meanings that deconstruct each other.

Confronting her own awareness of the deconstructive possibilities in language, Dickinson finds that her weapons, her words, are double-edged. If language may serve as defense against an alien world and a rejecting father-God, it may, in the very act of its expression, further expose the sources of conflict that war within the self. Respect for the word and recognition of its power lead to a concomitant fear the language may turn precipitously, unannounced, against its author. If to "hurt" is "Not Steel's Affair" (479), when steel is the synechdochal knife of language, the word can be trusted neither to spare nor to protect; language may not only captivate—it may, alas, also condemn.

II

Such a vision of language leads Dickinson to an understanding of the world and her epistemological relation to it that is at once potentially dangerous and dangerously modern, for her poems speak repeatedly of a sense of a dislocation that neither depends upon nor assumes a ground of common or shared experience. The roots of such an alienated imagination draw their sustenance from isolation—both intellectual and physical.[5] But the result of such depleting circumstances is, remarkably, a poetry that not only manifests a penchant for ambiguity (the double-edged ironic mode) but reveals as well experimentation with the possibilities of language to convey mutually conflicting meanings as the word pushes toward, and indeed at times *over*, the limits of communal understanding. Exclusion thus offers Dickinson the occasion to adopt a radical approach to experience that prompts her to invent a startlingly modernist poetics. In a world where nothing is certain, all relationships can be shifted, reversed, subverted, or kept indeterminate because they rely for their definition upon an isolate, rebellious consciousness, which itself is in a state of flux. Such radical solipsism often leads to a vertiginous freedom, what Dickinson herself names "that precarious Gait/Some call experience." Dickinson's skeptical investigation of experience combined with her abiding sense of exclusion translates into poems that assert their defiance against the existing order and articulate a willful rejection of the very things she has most desired, what she has been denied. In this way, Dickinson's poems potentially free her to become "executor" of her own identity.

Although engendered by different anxieties, the skepticism often bordering on despair that precipitates so many of the major modernists' experiments finds a kindred manifestation in Dickinson's work. If the modernists turn to radical experimentation with language to reclaim poetry for contemporary experience (one thinks of Pound, of Eliot, of H. D.), to fashion a language adequate to a deeply altered, forever changed world, so, too, Dickinson, albeit in isolation and without the support gained from the knowledge of others striving toward a common goal, pits her language against the world in a gesture as defiant as that of any of those twentieth-century poets who were to follow. As a woman poet she experiences cultural rejection and isolation *earlier* than the male poets who will later feel themselves exiled by cataclysmic historical events beyond their control—the most fatefully being the turbulent changes wrought by the First World War and the cultural disruption that was its aftermath. These changes forced writers to confront an historical discontinuity between themselves and an irretrievable past. So, too, women poets had, generations earlier, felt themselves cut off from the post-Miltonic poetic tradition, which had never been theirs. Thus, one may begin to account for some of the indeterminate quality of Dickinson's poetics by viewing her as a proto-modernist whose radical ways were formed, in part, by a feminist impulse.[6]

Dickinson's sense of dislocation emerges with an austere clarity in the following poem, with its strong Stevensian tone:

> Four Trees – upon a solitary Acre –
> Without Design
> Or Order, or Apparent Action –
> Maintain –
>
> The Sun – upon a Morning meets them –
> The Wind –

No nearer Neighbor – have they –
But God –

The Acre gives them – Place –
They – Him – Attention of Passer by –
Of Shadow, or of Squirrel, haply –
Or Boy –

What Deed is Their's unto the General Nature –
What Plan
They severally – retard – or further –
Unknown –

[742]

In this poem's strangely vacant opening, one hears the Stevensian "mind of winter," the listener who "nothing himself, beholds/Nothing that is not there and the nothing that is."[7] This voice prophesies as well that quality of provisional apprehension that haunts Stevens's most austere poems. Dickinson presents a stark scene of four trees standing isolate in an otherwise bare acre, invoking this vision to suggest the absence of assured meaning either in the trees' relation to other natural facts or to an ordering principle beyond themselves—some unnamed teleological force. There remains, however, a slight demurral from this absence in the "apparent" of the poem's third line. Asking the question Robert Frost will pose in "Design" when he observes the minute death-drama taking place on the white "heal-all," Dickinson sustains the possibility that there may be a design that governs over against her provisional denial.[8] The stanzas that follow elaborate this issue of motive or purpose beyond sheer physical presence. The sun "meets" (a word that suggests intent) the trees; yet, oddly, the effect of such a meeting is only to intensify the aura of isolation that demarcates the trees' existence. Distant light alone is this landscape's nearest neighbor—except God. Although the "but" that precedes "God" (stanza two, line four) would prepare the reader for a seemingly minor omission, an afterthought, it is here that the poem coyly confronts its central question, for the issue of the exclusion of God is an oversight of truly teleological significance. Despite this ironic maneuver, the poem resists any orthodox assertion of Divine omnipresence, proceeding instead to define other earthly relationships that are determined by chance and dependent upon the presence of an observer:

The Acre gives them – Place –
They – Him – Attention of Passer by –
Of Shadow, or of Squirrel, haply –
Or Boy –

"Shadow," "Squirrel," "Boy": the list moves from optical effect to sentient, hence potentially questioning, consciousness. In a movement that parallels the structure of the preceding stanza—in each case the final line introducing the crucial term with the offhandedness given an afterthought—the poem again evades as it draws attention to its own implications—this time, the impact of a human viewer's consciousness. Rather than resolve the underlying question of meaning, the problem of intelligence as well as the issue of belief, the closing stanza will not fully acknowledge the presence of a Divine or human observer who would imbue with meaning this bare landscape-vision, which thus remains equivocal and obscure.

Commenting more generally on the relationship between Dickinson and Stevens, Harold Bloom notes, "The connection with Stevens is that he and Dickinson, more than any other Americans, more than any other moderns, labor successfully to make the visible a little hard to see."[9] Here Dickinson creates this obliqueness of vision by questioning the reality of the observing eye as well as the presence of an hierarchical power that would invest meaning, the clarity of intent, into the otherwise desolate landscape. This poem eschews any such recuperative possibility that would ascribe a specific significance to the scene, choosing instead to bear witness to a complete ignorance of the scene's function or its meaning. By rejecting the relationships asserted in the poem, the final stanza poses the essentially ontological question: for what purpose do these trees exist? "What Plan/They severally – retard – or further – Unknown." The repeated "n" sounds separated by the long "o" of "unknown" re-sound the finality of the word's meaning and, simultaneously, the impossibility of ever achieving that meaning.

III

To live in such a world is to live, no matter how brilliantly, alone. Yet, if God will not reveal his meaning or the meaning of his world, there may yet be another faith to which Dickinson can turn, one based upon an alternative to the exclusive, rejecting patriarchal order she must herself renounce. This heterodox faith, or "other" way, may be founded upon the belief in the development of a tradition of women poets, distinct from that delineated by the male poetic tradition. In perhaps the most forthright and impassioned statement of this possible alternative faith, an order that would be founded upon the majesty of woman, Dickinson invokes the maternal forms of mountains as standardbearers of her especial truth. In contrast to those poems that sever the external manifestations of the world from an unknowable God's intent, here Dickinson maintains a connection between an alternative theodicy and the physical presence of natural forms. As one who felt herself inhabiting a world where order remains frustratingly provisional and God continuously hidden, how Dickinson must have yearned for the security of such imaginable, alternative relationships. In an imperative voice that, through its very assertiveness, conveys its desire to coerce geological forms into truth-telling mothers, Dickinson woos as she creates her distinct reality:

> Sweet Mountains – Ye tell Me no lie –
> Never deny Me – Never fly –
> Those same unvarying Eyes
> Turn on Me – When I fail – or feign,
> Or take the Royal names in vain –
> Their far – slow – Violet Gaze –
>
> My strong Madonnas – Cherish still –
> The Wayward Nun – beneath the Hill –
> Whose service – is to You –
> Her latest Worship – When the Day
> Fades from the Firmament away –
> To lift Her Brows on You –

[722]

Constancy, fidelity, and unconditional acceptance—those qualities which Dickinson found missing in orthodox Christianity, she now seeks among the monumental "Strong Madonnas." For such heresy, the taking of the "Royal names in vain" and her assuming the role of the "Wayward Nun," the "I" anticipates a reciprocal allegiance. This very waywardness ironically legitimizes the self's demand for such unwavering constancy on the part of the "sweet mountains," as heterodoxy is converted into belief in the alternative power of the maternal. As Sandra M. Gilbert and Susan Gubar state, "Surely these 'Strong Madonnas' are sisters of the mother Awe to whom, Dickinson told Higginson, she ran home as a child, and surely it was such mothers who enabled (and empowered) this poet to escape her Nobodaddy's requirements, if only in secret."[10] And yet, this alternative power receives only conditional allegiance; the imperative tone of the poem's opening: "Sweet Mountains – Ye tell Me no lie – / Never deny Me – Never fly –" assumes the voice of a command. The poem asks for the belief of the mountains in the "I" who usurps Christ's role but adopts a diametrically opposite position, beneath the hill as Christ was at its summit. This "wayward nun" is, moreover, at once savior and worshipper. In the first stanza, the "I" undergoes trials of faith as she plays the part of defiant actor. (Note the negative terms in which these trials are described: "fail," "Feign," "or take the Royal names in vain.") She performs in these ways, the second stanza recounts, for the sake of the strong "Madonnas" whom she addresses as "My," thus making her the daughter of the savior's mother—Christ's sister forming an alternative religion of the mother: "Whose service – is to You –," rather than of the son. To see the mountains as madonnas is not simply to see religion in natural forms, but so to transform religion as to transplant it in nature. If the mountains in this poem appear as strong madonnas, they are elsewhere subsumed into the more general vision of a hostile natural world that can offer no solace. Even more disruptively, the mountains may turn volcanic, representing no outward hope but a power at once destructive and potent that smoulders within the self. It is to "Vesuvius at home" that Dickinson grants her primary allegiance. All gods or goddesses beyond this mouldering self may receive intermittent recognition, but none earns the devotion Dickinson bestows upon her own power.

Such allegiance to one's strength, however, is not free from danger; rather, the stakes for poetic survival increase as trust in all external forms fades before the self-inflicting powers of the imagination. The tenuousness of all reality beyond the self, the difficulty of ascertaining any ontological certainty whatsoever—a radically modernist dilemma—finally makes her immune to the solace of religious solutions, no matter how subversive. Instead, when Dickinson writes of her experience, she characteristically sees it as an adventure, a journey through rugged, hostile terrain toward an end both untested and potentially fatal. For companionship, she takes along only her consciousness. Dickinson elsewhere describes the climax of this travail; the terror she faces when confronting "The Forest of the Dead" renders her paralyzed before her goal, which is her end as well:

> Retreat – was out of Hope –
> Behind – a Sealed Route –
> Eternity's White Flag – Before –
> And God – at every Gate –

[615]

The white flag of surrender and/or salvation may welcome the traveller or obscure the vision of God. But even prior to this moment of apocalyptic hesitation, the "routes" leading to it have been treacherous and fraught with danger. As a way of combatting the potential devastation of such risks, Dickinson vests her faith in the only internal power upon which she may rely, upon the power of the transformative Word. Renunciation becomes a viable strategy for poetic survival only to the extent that she can continue to articulate her rejection in the form of writing poems. If, in all other spheres, "Renunciation – is a piercing Virtue," language itself is not to be denied, but instead given renewed and redefined power through the force of her alienated imagination.

Once the poet grants that her word may supplant God's, however, she must be prepared to face the dangers of such redirected authority, hence those poems that witness the treacherous capacities of language, a language that may (with the very probity that lends the Word its force) cause it to shake the foundations of the self. How language can function in this way, as transcendent and transforming reality, is a difficult and problematic question. Dickinson both relies upon the process of articulation to serve for a weapon against her sense of isolation and exile and paradoxically dreads what this very act of verbalization may reveal concerning her hidden (what we would now call "unconscious") self. Such turning against the self, which produces a split identity, is a direct result of Dickinson's poetic ambitions. She fashions a poetics that functions as a counterlanguage eschewing communal identity, a poetics that depends upon, even as it attempts to transfigure the terms of, her exclusion.

I V

This concept of language as defense, as the only effective weapon in Dickinson's arsenal, develops into a strongly adversarial kind of poetics. A war rages in these poems, a war within the self for control over the potency of the word. Note the quasi-aggressive intimacy with which Dickinson describes such procedures:

> The Soul unto itself
> Is an imperial friend –
> Or the most agonizing Spy –
> An Enemy – could send –
>
> Secure against its own –
> No treason it can fear –
> Itself – its Sovreign – of itself
> The Soul should stand in Awe –

[683]

The repetition of "it's" serves to encode the doubling, the turning of self upon soul, the wrestling of intimate yet potentially antithetical identities. Out of such aggressive intimacy, there emerges awe, the same power Dickinson elsewhere identifies as the spur to her making poems. Even awe, however, contains within it its own paradoxical aspects: "I work to drive the awe away, Yet awe impels the work." What Dickinson asserts that she requires is the stimulus of defense, the sensation of warding off an external power that might destroy her. In response to such a threat, she reacts with a combination of fear and reverence that must be cast aside yet remains crucial to this process of composing poems. That awe is associated with the self's specific language-making function can be inferred from those poems that privilege the poetic act as they denigrate all authority that lies outside the single imagination.

In a hitherto largely neglected poem that directly addresses this conflict of world and word, a poem written during that great year of Dickinson's creative activity, 1862, she alludes to the process that will bestow joy upon the world, joy rising from the powers within the self. This regenerative process, however, leads inexorably to a chilling and personally devastating reversal. Particularly important is the role language assumes, functioning as the determinative power that creates a necessary distance between the self and the world as it staves off the world's destructive capacities. Dealing her "word of gold," Dickinson "dowers – all the World –." She transforms the world with her own resources. When she is robbed of her happiness, however, and finds in its stead only a barren existence, life becomes a "wilderness, which rolls back along (her) Golden lines," and, the poem implies, wipes them out. Language, with its transforming powers, extends over the landscape only to be vanquished by the emptiness of a world that reflects the poet's precipitating loss.

> It would never be Common – more – I said –
> Difference – had begun –
> Many a bitterness – had been –
> But that old sort – was done –
>
> Or – if it sometime – showed – as 'twill –
> Upon the Downiest – Morn –
> Such bliss – had I – for all the years –
> 'Twould give an Easier – pain –
>
> I'd so much joy – I told it – Red –
> Upon my simple Cheek –
> I felt it publish – in my Eye –
> 'Twas needless – any speak –
>
> I walked – as wings – my body bore –
> The feet – I former used –
> Unnecessary – now to me –
> As boots – would be – to Birds –
>
> I put my pleasure all abroad –
> I dealt a word of Gold

To every Creature – that I met –
And Dowered – all the World –

When – suddenly – my Riches shrank –
A Goblin – drank my Dew –
My Palaces – dropped tenantless –
Myself – was beggared – too –

I clutched at sounds –
I groped at shapes –
I touched the tops of Films –
I felt the Wilderness roll back
Along my Golden lines –

The Sackcloth – hangs upon the nail –
The Frock I used to wear –
But where my moment of Brocade –
My – Drop – of India?

[430]

The miraculous change Dickinson describes in the poem's opening four stanzas, the change she felt "publish – in [her] eye," extends to her infusing the world with her joy through language. In a series of deliberate gestures, she "puts" her pleasure all abroad, "deals" a word of Gold, and "dowers" all the World. In these successive phrases, the poem creates an active, purposive self, who draws on internal powers to fill the world with her "word of Gold," thus simultaneously conveying beauty and value to all around her. Once "beggared," in an alarming and abrupt reversal that recalls a fairy-tale narrative with its charmed inevitability, the "I" is suddenly bereft of riches, of dew. Wealth, formerly hers, has vanished, as has the "dew" that nurtured her; her palaces, now without occupants, "tenantless," drop, and she finds herself destitute. Clutching and groping in her desperation, she feels the return of the wilderness as it rolls back along *her* golden lines. These "lines" may signify both the inroads her former bounteous self has made on the world and the poetic lines formed by her words spun of gold—thus, the association between the powers of language and the sources of her capacity to transform her universe. Ironically, at the poem's close, the very lines that had earlier marked her extensive reach into the world now serve as tracks or "guide-lines" for the inescapable encroachment of the formerly banished wilderness. The specific linguistic activity she had performed in her bounteous days was an Adamic one: naming, apportioning, assigning a word to every creature she encountered: "I dealt a word of Gold/ To every Creature – that I met – /And Dowered – all the world." This Edenic condition, which derives its authority from the poet's own transformation, her excess of joy, recedes as sud-

denly as it came, erased by the nameless wilderness, a region devoid either
of human control or of organizing principle. With its clearly delineated
connection between linguistic power and continuous war waged between
the competing forces of self and world, this poem serves as a paradigmatic
expression of the conflict that marks Dickinson's understanding of her
relationship to everything outside herself. To see only two—the word
equal in power to its adversary, the world—is to envision a dangerously
austere, dialogic cosmos where internal energies either overcome the world
or are themselves devastated by it.

Even when Dickinson's poems attest to losing in such confrontations,
however, they nevertheless reveal the high ambition of the individual consciousness to transcend the inhibitory powers of rejection. By asserting
that one no longer wishes for or requires what one has been denied—by,
in other words, willfully embracing renunciation, Dickinson attempts to
conquer the forces that oppose the self. In the province of language, however, to do without another's voice, to deny all external sources of "inspiration," demands an intellectual self-sufficiency that may prove its own un-
doing, for the threat remains that devoid of others' language, the poetic
voice will be stifled by such defensive isolation. Dickinson writes of this
poetic double-bind, expressing a condition which may prove attainable in
the realm of the ideal rather than in any recognizable reality:

> To own the Art within the Soul
> The Soul to entertain
> With Silence as a Company
> And Festival maintain
>
> Is an unfurnished Circumstance
> Possession is to One
> As an Estate perpetual
> Or a reduceless Mine.
>
> [855]

The "Mine" that cannot be depleted would be the "mine" of the isolate
self. Dickinson's possessive pronoun converts the terms of her deprivation
into a potential resource whose hidden reserves will never fail because they
lie buried deep within. To protect the imagination against the barrenness
of circumstance, to guard herself against the deadening effects of a necessary isolation (the possibility that such an internal absence will produce
linguistic autism), Dickinson draws upon the transformative capacities of
the word. The word—her Word—thus may acquire the power to make
things new as she seeks the possibility of redefining the terms of existence
to coincide with the priorities of her individual consciousness. If language
can achieve such authority, as it does only intermittently in Dickinson's
poems, then it may indeed, as she asserts, challenge the preeminence of

God's holy Word. To re-make the world according to her own image—this is the ambition of Dickinson's boldest poems. That she must renounce this attempt only to take it up once again, that she testifies to her own failures, does not diminish, but rather reaffirms the extent of her ambitions. For Dickinson imbues her poetic enterprise with a vision of language operating as defense against the pressures of rejection and exile that define her world. Here is a definition of poetry that possesses, like Blake's visionary language, the capacity to mold the terms of existence within the fires of her own imagination. Such a vision of language originates in the perceived absence of external allies and the poet's compensatory devotion not to the conditions of the world, but, instead, to what Dickinson called the "Art within the Soul." If there is "ransom in a voice," if the bounty that will restore the world to the Self resides within, then to speak in words that challenge the world is the only way a poet can endow and so change that world to make it yield to her authority. Recognizing that "all is the price of all," Dickinson creates in her self-imposed, domestic exile, a poetics of high ambition, a poetics that foreshadows the experimental, fiercely defiant voices of modernist literary experimentation. Dickinson explores the latent ambiguities of language to construct a deeply paradoxical, if, at times, bafflingly equivocal voice. By insisting upon the articulation of her own version of experience, she develops rhetorical strategies that break with tradition as they depend increasingly upon indeterminacies, upon the disruption of linguistic structures that would otherwise provide recognizable, coherent meanings.

Out of this alienation, Dickinson shapes a language that challenges the Western literary tradition's shared assumptions about the very character of figurative language itself, for she disrupts the relationship between the signifier and the signified in two ways: first by trying to replace the signified with the signifier, to transcend the world through her word, and second by using signs so that their meaning itself is not simply ironic, but self-deconstructing. Words that can be read this way, however, do not reduce in meaning, but approach an indecipherability that seeks not merely to disrupt communal meaning but to move past language's image-making power to reach the word as insoluble, irreducible construct that defies any referent, or any combination of referents. To let the Word replace the World in both meaning and the irreducible "I am that I am" of immanence, this is Dickinson's double project and its tie to a modernist poetics that rejects normative definitions to strive for an alternative order privileged by art. If the pressures that led Dickinson to such experimentation were extreme, so the defensive poetics she employs threatens to slip at any moment into self-disintegration. Yet it is here, at the brink of poetic indecipherability, where the risks of language are greatest, that Dickinson achieves her full power. Finally, her feminist poetics emerges as an experimental project that approaches modernist theories of art, for Dickinson shapes a revisionary language that pursues the possibilities of internally generated meanings as it resists the confines of figuration, the potential clarities of signification. Thus, Dickinson pursues as well a sublime if potentially fatal course as she discovers within the very indeterminacy of language a radically modern linguistic home.

NOTES

1. Sharon Cameron describes the central tension of Dickinson's poems in these terms: "The conflict in the poems, put simply, seems to be between forces of sexuality and forces of death; the poems schematize experience for the explicit purpose of preventing the convergence of sexuality and death, of avoiding the acknowledgment that the two join each other in time, and that the self comes to its end at their meeting. A third voice, intervening in the dialectic, which takes its passion from the knowledge of sexuality and its vengeance from the knowledge of death, is often one of rage" (Sharon Cameron, *Lyric Time: Dickinson and the Limits of Genre*, [Baltimore and London: The Johns Hopkins University Press, 1979], p. 57). I would extend Cameron's observation to suggest that Dickinson not only seeks to prevent the convergence of sexuality and death, but that she continuously strives to mediate between a desire for union and the recognition that such union or fulfillment would inevitably result in the destruction of the poetic self.

2. Emily Dickinson, *The Poems of Emily Dickinson*, ed. Thomas H. Johnson, (Cambridge: Harvard University Press, 1955), poem 1651, vol. 3, p. 1129. All future quotations of Dickinson poems are identified by number in the text.

3. See Joanne Feit Diehl, "Dickinson And Bloom: An Antithetical Reading of Romanticism," *Texas Studies in Literature & Language* 23 no. 3 (September 1981).

4. See Dickinson, *The Letters of Emily Dickinson*, ed. Thomas H. Johnson and Theodora Ward (Cambridge: Harvard University Press, 1958), vol. 3, no. 743, p. 722.

5. Margaret Homans associates Dickinson's radical poetics with her understanding of her sexual identity. Homans comments, "It must not be forgotten that Dickinson's recognition of language's fictiveness, which has the effects charted above, came originally from her sense of femininity and of its place within the tradition that she then undoes. Once she has used her femininity as a force for disruption, she liberates herself from that too, because sexual determinism of any kind must be antithetical to her concerns." (*Women Writers and Poetic Identity: Dorothy Wordsworth, Emily Brontë, and Emily Dickinson* [Princeton, New Jersey: Princeton University Press, 1980], p. 212.)

6. Karl Keller, arguing from a different point of view in his recent book, *The Only Kangaroo among the Beauty : Emily Dickinson And America* (Baltimore and London: The Johns Hopkins University Press, 1979), traces the modernists' responses to Dickinson and contends that the strongest resemblance exists between her and Robert Frost, a relationship based largely on their shared concept of linguistic play (see Keller, pp. 294-326 *passim*).

7. Wallace Stevens, "The Snow Man," *The Collected Poems of Wallace Stevens* (New York: Alfred A. Knopf, 1968), p. 10, last two lines.

8. See Robert Frost's poem, "Design," where, in the second stanza, Frost asks three interpretative questions and then closes with a line of powerful equivocation.

9. Harold Bloom, *Wallace Stevens: The Poems of Our Climate* (Ithaca: Cornell University Press, 1977), p. 17.

10. Sandra M. Gilbert and Susan Gubar, *The Madwoman in the Attic: The Woman Writer and the Nineteenth-Century Literary Imagination* (New Haven and London: Yale University Press, 1979), p. 647.

INDEX TO POEMS CITED

179

ABOUT THE AUTHORS

JOANNE FEIT DIEHL is Associate Professor of English at the University of California at Davis. Her book, *Dickinson and the Romantic Imagination,* was published in 1981 by Princeton University Press. She is currently working in the fields of feminist theory, nineteenth-century American literature, and contemporary women poets.

JOANNE DOBSON is a doctoral candidate in English at the University of Massachusetts at Amherst. She has taught at the State University of New York at Albany and was assistant director of the International Emily Dickinson Symposium held in Amherst in 1980. She is presently writing a dissertation on Dickinson and the American women writers who were her contemporaries.

SANDRA GILBERT is Professor of English at the University of California at Davis. With Susan Gubar she has co-authored *The Madwoman in the Attic: The Woman Writer and the Nineteenth-Century Literary Imagination* (Yale, 1979), and co-edited *Shakespeare's Sisters: Feminist Essays on Women Poets* (Indiana, 1979). Her other books are *Acts of Attention: The Poems of D. H. Lawrence* (Cornell, 1973) and a collection of poems, *In the Fourth World* (Alabama, 1979). She has just completed a new collection of poems, *Emily's Bread,* forthcoming from Norton, and with Susan Gubar (and support from the Rockefeller and Guggenheim foundations) she is currently working on *No Man's Land: The Place of the Woman Writer in the Twentieth Century.*

SHERRI HALLGREN is a doctoral candidate in English at the University of California at Berkeley. Her short story, "The Weekend," won the University of California's Elizabeth Mills Crothers Prize for Literary Composition. She is writing a dissertation on fiction by women in the twentieth century.

MARGARET HOMANS is Associate Professor of English at Yale University. She is the author of *Women Writers and Poetic Identity: Dorothy Wordsworth, Emily Brontë, and Emily Dickinson* (Princeton, 1980) and articles on nineteenth-century fiction and poetry. She is currently at work on a feminist study of Romanticism and Victorian fiction.

SUZANNE JUHASZ is Associate Professor of English at the University of Colorado, Boulder. She is the author of *Naked and Fiery Forms: Modern American Poetry by Women, A New Tradition* (Harper and Row, 1976) and *Metaphor and the Poetry of Williams, Pound, and Stevens* (Bucknell, 1974). She has just finished *"The Undiscovered Continent": Emily Dickinson and the Space of the Mind,* with grant support from the American Association of University Women; it will be published by Indiana University Press.

KARL KELLER is Professor of English at San Diego State University. His books are *The Only Kangaroo Among the Beauty: Emily Dickinson and America* (Johns Hopkins, 1979), *The Example of Edward Taylor* (University of Massachusetts, 1975), and a textbook, *American Literature: Post 1945.* He has received fellowships from the Huntington Library, the National Endowment for the Humanities, and the American Council of Learned Societies. He is presently working on a study of Walt Whitman and a book on the Mormons.

CRISTANNE MILLER is Assistant Professor of English at Pomona College. She has published articles on Dickinson and Whitman and is writing a book on Dickinson.

ADALAIDE MORRIS is Associate Professor of English at the University of Iowa. She is the author of *Wallace Stevens: Imagination and Faith* (Princeton, 1974) and has co-edited, with Jane Cooper, Gwen Head, and Marcia Southwick, *Extended Outlooks: The Iowa Review Collection of Contemporary Women Writers,* (Macmillan, 1982). She has received a fellowship from the American Association of University Women for 1982-83 to finish her book on Rich, H. D., and Dickinson.

BARBARA ANTONINA CLARKE MOSSBERG is Associate Professor of English at the University of Oregon and author of *Emily Dickinson: When a Writer Is a Daughter* (Indiana University Press, 1982). A study of Sylvia Plath is under contract with Ungar Publications. She is presently writing a monograph on Genevieve Taggard for Western Writers Series, working on a new critical edition of Gertrude Stein's *Three Lives,* and with support from the National Endowment for the Humanities is working on *The Daughter Construct,* an interdisciplinary study of writers and visual artists whose work manifests the daughter sensibility.